ARCHITECTURE IS ALL OVER

EDITED BY
ESTHER CHOI
AND
MARRIKKA
TROTTER

Columbia Books on Architecture and the City

Introduction: The Crisis of the Crisis

Esther Choi
and
Marrikka Trotter

If we can begin a book meant to function as a projectile lobbed into an undetermined future, for the sake of that future, by taking stock of the present as it is already becoming the past, we might be able to state that architecture is indeed all over. A terminal callousness in the discipline was exposed, for instance, in the wake of Hurricane Katrina, amid the ill-concealed delight of a profession discovering that the phantasmagoric opportunities of the "third world" exist within the range of a domestic flight.

Demolition of Pruitt-Igoe housing complex, designed by Minoru Yamasaki, in St. Louis, Missouri on April 21, 1972

Or take our enthusiastic and largely unquestioning participation in fabricating the mirage of "sustainable development" with artificial islands on wetlands and air-conditioned towers in deserts while ignoring genuinely sustained global slums. More than a decade after terrorists' demolition of the World Trade Center in Manhattan, the bathos of the Freedom Tower's design and design process exposes the extent of architecture's imaginative exhaustion and its codependency on the most troubling, most ruthless aspects of a wounded yet still very much operational financial war machine. In the West—and this is, to state our limits right up front, a book about architecture from a largely Western perspective—some architects participate in art biennials; most interface with the increasingly complex technology that specifies the routines of architectural production more than any architect can pretend to specify them. What most architects actually do is attempt to align the modicum of novelty in every project with the increasingly stringent requirements of modern construction systems and rigorously predefined programs. Yet, students continue to submit to the privations of a design education promising a future that may no longer exist. The still-unfolding economic collapse of the late aughts has rendered the crisis within architectural patronage more apparent, but one has only to reread criticism written before 2008 to remember that the deeper crisis of any architectural strategy beyond that of tongue-in-cheek "customer service" stretches well back into the bad good old days.

A painting studio at the École nationale supérieure des Beaux-Arts after June 27, 1968

But perhaps this is precisely the point. When, in its entire modern development from the Renaissance to the present, has architecture *not* been in crisis? Certainly not in the 1980s, when the seemingly secure syntax of postmodernism thinned to self-referential hieroglyphics, nor in the 1970s, as is clear from Manfredo Tafuri's account of architecture's inability to critically engage with capitalism.[1] Architecture is always at the cusp of obsolescence; as a slow and weighty activity, it is contingent upon the ephemeralizing processes of capitalism. And architects have always constructed end games in response to this condition, ranging from Mies van der Rohe's emphasis on indefatigable programmatic flexibility to Archigram's "throwaway architecture."[2]

1
See Manfredo Tafuri, *Architecture and Utopia: Design and Capitalist Development* (Cambridge: MIT Press, 1976).

2
See Daniel M. Abramson, "Obsolescence: Notes towards a History," *Praxis: Journal of Writing and Building* 5 (2003): 110–111.

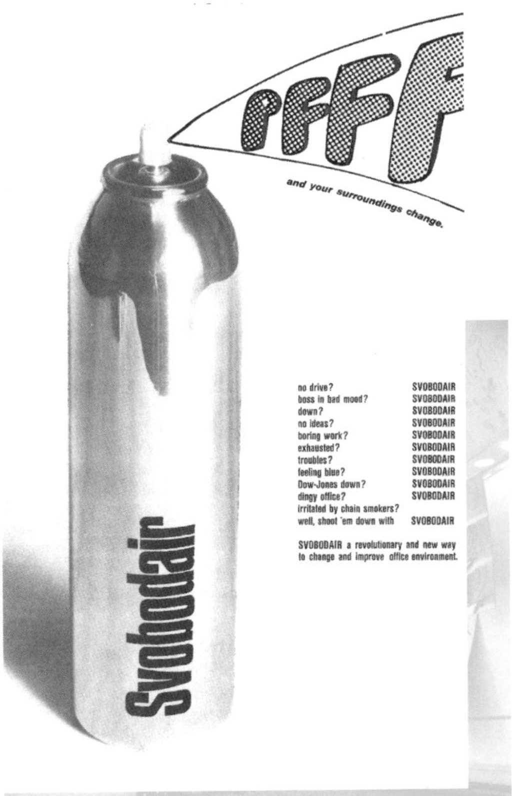

Hans Hollein, *Svobodair*, 1968, in "Alles Ist Architektur," *Bau: Schrift für Architektur und Städtebau* 23, no. 1/2 (1968): 20–21

Yet, at the same time, architecture is also continually annexing new territories: in other words, we can also understand architecture's being "all over" in the sense of Clement Greenberg's characterization of "decentralized" and "polyphonic" techniques of painting.[3] When Yves Klein declared his desire for an architecture of air in 1959, he imagined his immaterial architecture would comprise the basic elements of the earth and thus unite the subject with a cosmos unburdened by culture, economics and politics.[4] By extension, if architecture were bound to neither the traditional codes of building nor its materials, it could be everywhere and everything. Such was the maxim of Hans Hollein's "Alles Ist Architektur" manifesto (1968), which eschewed the didactic impediments of disciplinary

3 Clement Greenberg, "The Crisis of the Easel Picture" (1948), in *Art and Culture: Critical Essays* (Boston: Beacon Press, 1961), 155.

4 Yves Klein, "The Evolution of Art towards the Immaterial," in *Yves Klein: Air Architecture*, eds. Peter Noever and Francois Perrin (Ostfildern: Hatje Cantz, 2004), 44–45. See also Yves Klein with Werner Ruhnau, "Project of an Air Architecture," in *Yves Klein: Air Architecture*, 77.

conventions to propose that architecture could take the form of atomized sprays, furniture and ingested pharmaceuticals.[5] An important precedent for Hollein's undifferentiated architecture is the Independent Group, a collective of architects, artists and critics based in London in the 1950s, who shared a fascination with everyday visual culture and advocated for understanding architecture as an imagistic practice.[6] Near the end of the 1960s, Robert Venturi

Installation view of Parallel of Life and Art exhibition, Institute of Contemporary Art, London, 1953

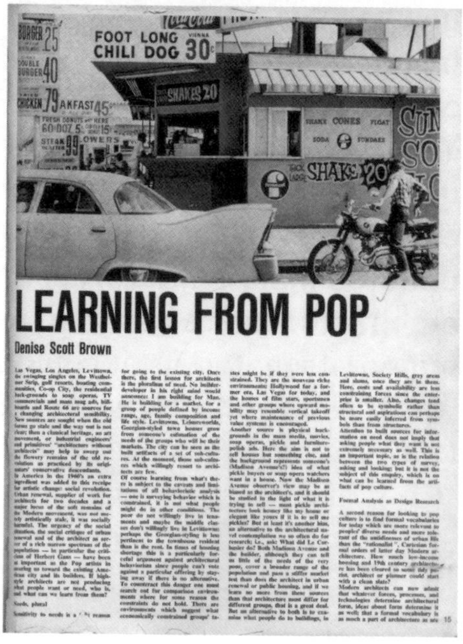

LEARNING FROM POP

Denise Scott Brown

Denise Scott Brown, "Learning from Pop," *Casabella* 359/360 (1971): 14–15

5 Hans Hollein, "Alles Ist Architektur," *Bau: Schrift für Architektur und Städtebau* 23, no. 1/2 (1968).

6 See Alex Kitnick, "Introduction," *October* 136 (Spring 2011): 3–6.

would proclaim that Main Street is "almost all right" and, with Denise Scott Brown and Steven Izenour, would celebrate the vernacular charm of the banal and the quotidian.[7]

Yet, the quotidian has an all-overishness of its own; it creates massive architectures that aggregate the realities of the world as we create it daily, out of habit. Our present-day interest in "informal settlements" parallels Bernard Rudofsky's catalogue of "architecture without architects" in the mid-1960s: the becoming-architectural of all kinds of materials, climates and cultures at the hands of all kinds of people, without the fustiness of professional "pedigree."[8] Today, Rudofsky's anthropological appropriation of such preprofessional or extradisciplinary artifacts in a moment of significant uncertainty within modernist architecture provides a possible precedent for contemporary trends. For instance, perhaps today's architectural enthusiasm for landform building and ecological urbanism is merely a touristic expedition. Likewise, it could be that our disciplinary appetite for the urban evinces an invasive intent to imbue architecture into all scales of life and thought. The problem with such campaigns is that architecture risks dilution to the point where expertise becomes amateur acquiescence. If everything can be architecture, or, conversely, if architecture can be everything, then architecture runs the risk of being nothing much—certainly nothing much more than a map of everything as it exists.[9]

Hence the critical point of this project: if architecture is always both all over *and* all over, then its constitutive dimensions include both extinction and emergence, both crisis and conquest, and both evanescence and ubiquity. When we see architecture as a series of crises—that is, as a series of inadequate and collapsing paradigms—we convince ourselves that we are dealing with emergency tactics and provisional measures instead of recognizing these procedures as the normal operations of architecture as such. Moreover,

7 Robert Venturi, *Complexity and Contradiction in Architecture* (New York: Museum of Modern Art, 1966), 102. See also Robert Venturi, Denise Scott Brown, and Steven Izenour, *Learning from Las Vegas* (Cambridge: MIT Press, 1972).

8 Bernard Rudofsky, *Architecture Without Architects: A Short Introduction to Non-Pedigreed Architecture* (New York: Museum of Modern Art, 1964).

9 See our first volume, *Architecture at the Edge of Everything Else*, eds. Esther Choi and Marrikka Trotter (Cambridge: 10 Work Books, Inc./MIT Press, 2010).

Bernard Rudofsky, *Architecture Without Architects: A Short Introduction to Non-Pedigreed Architecture* (New York: Museum of Modern Art, 1964)

architecture as an *endeavor*, rather than a condition, could use more rigorous attention. When we elevate architecture to the fictional status of an independently expanding domain, we absolve ourselves of responsibility for the maneuvers we accomplish under its rubric. After all, architecture is a creative act that is capable of generating possibilities that did not exist before. Yet, while the specific mechanisms of its creativity may vary over time, these practices do not emerge independent of human innovation. Accordingly, the contributions in this volume are organized as an unfolding spectrum of think pieces, conversations, graphic provocations and design proposals that speculatively engage a particular facet of architecture to project alternative modes of theory and praxis. Or, to animate two ignored and reviled aspects of this discipline, we might say the pieces in this book begin to collectively reimagine the ethical and entrepreneurial dimensions of architecture.

On ethics, it is perhaps helpful to think of the Aristotelian mandate that "methodology must match its subject matter."[10] Whereas architecture in crisis is content to borrow protocols from other disciplines, architecture that understands the crisis-making potential that it brings to the status quo could recognize that its practice demands certain considerations that its neighbors lack. For instance, an assessment of its material and contextual interdependence in certain conditions might occasionally mandate architectural abstention or demolition. Every piece in this book articulates a dimension

10
Stanford Encyclopedia of Philosophy, s.v. "Aristotle's Ethics," accessed April 9, 2012, http://plato.stanford.edu/entries/aristotle-ethics/.

of what such architectural ethics might be like. Similarly, perhaps we have too quickly jettisoned entrepreneurialism as an architectural concept even though it remains fundamentally tied up with disciplinary motives. Today, entrepreneurship is synonymous with marketability and capitalist exploits; but to be an entrepreneur is simply to discover the potential in risky opportunities, to undertake action with the pretense to innovate. We might remember that the modern distinction between discovery and invention did not exist prior to the eighteenth century; the finding of opportunity was the same as the creation of it.[11] The idea that one must simply either accept or reject what is, in order to even present the possibility of what is not, is a recent limitation on our thinking. Instead, architecture is by definition always inventing the very possibilities that it rediscovers later as constraints: it is the quintessence of entrepreneurship, and as such, it produces new terrain in need of new ethical models. Recognizing this fact allows us to move from the regime of emergencies to the fostering of emergence.

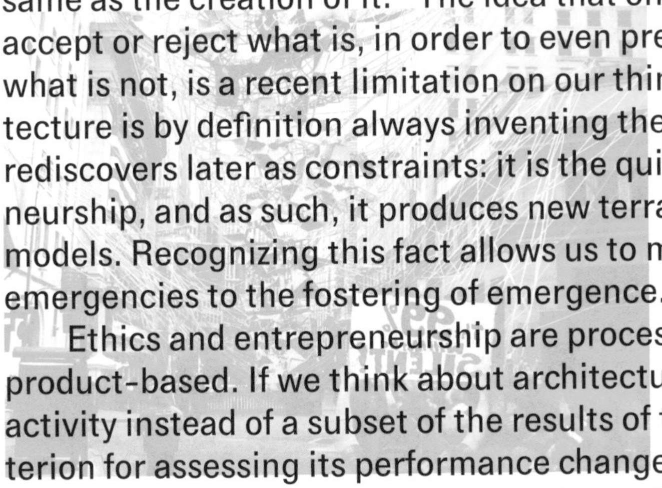

Ethics and entrepreneurship are process-based rather than product-based. If we think about architecture as an entrepreneurial activity instead of a subset of the results of this activity, our criterion for assessing its performance changes from the critique of its products to the conduct of its business. This conduct includes how architecture is taught, how it is designed, how it interfaces with commissioning systems, and how it is evaluated within the discipline. It requires us to ask new questions in response to the disciplinary pathologies revealed by contemporary symptoms. For instance, how can we conceive of an architectural response to natural disaster that avoids fetishizing the erasing power of catastrophes? What kind of architectural maneuvers would help us create a culture that truly sustains the nature we depend upon? How could architecture intervene to facilitate more robust self-organization in rapidly urbanizing areas? What potential for symbolic meaning remains for architecture after rhetoric? How do we educate students to critically evaluate existing systems and propose different disciplinary ethics? If we could design a new relationship between

11
Lorraine Daston, introduction to *The Coming into Being of Scientific Objects*, ed. Lorraine Daston (Chicago: University of Chicago Press, 2000), 4.

architecture and commissioning institutions, what would it look like? Can we imagine an architecture that is neither instrumentalized nor instrumentalizing?

A sustained examination of the challenges and contradictions inherent in the discipline's indeterminate identity offers an opportunity for crafting architecture as it could become. How might we formulate critical and interpretive vantages capable of reimagining the monstrous vectors we release into the world as possibilities rather than pathogens? This book attempts to address this question.

Ying Xiao and Shengchen Yang, *Occupy Skyscraper*, 2012

Unfinished State

Caitlin Berrigan

Unfinished State

Caitlin Berrigan

Stories from friends preceded my first visit to Lebanon in 2010, telling of streets with no names or forgotten names or names that are never used; buildings that look like lace, perforated by the passage of explosives; and apartment complexes bisected vertically by bombs, like open dollhouses on a carpet of rubble. I was expecting to see these spectacular modern ruins; to be perplexed by how they manage to stand, pillars in shreds, speechlessly testifying to violence and its resistance.

I also expected to see the hasty high-rises and primed commercial squares where whole neighborhoods have been built from scratch. Influxes of capital from around the Persian Gulf have purchased fountains and plazas identical to those that corporate developers erect in hotels and malls across the globe.

But I was not prepared to see the haunting of Lebanon's cities and coastline by a vast quantity of structures in an unfinished condition. Hollow buildings in colorless, poured concrete stand fixed in an interminable state of partial construction. Their unglazed window apertures and porous façades leave them exposed to weather. Construction tools and materials that might indicate some intention of progress are absent from the site. Often the buildings are foliated with weeds and trees, germinating aerial gardens in the penthouses of half-finished skyscrapers.

I photographed many of these suspended buildings along the coast from Sour to Beirut to Tripoli—a monastery, apartment blocks, mosques, decades-old skyscrapers and recent villas. Oscar Niemeyer's Rashid Karami International Fair in Tripoli is perhaps the best-known and longest-standing example of such unfinished projects. The complex of futuristic, poured concrete structures has remained a series of unused shells since the onset of the civil war in 1975. Rarely were there squatters in any location. One enormous skeleton of condominiums is perched on a cliff and frames an expansive seaside view above the city of Tripoli. A single woman lives there, watching a generator-powered TV in her house without walls.

These structures command a stark visual presence in the landscape—so ubiquitous, they are a phenomenon. Their etched figures speculate on unreliable flows of capital; confidence in the political system; the loose space-time of property, diasporas and territories. Inconspicuous forces and economies of protracted states of war produce these sustained, propositional spaces. Rather than ruin, they embody uncertainty in architecture—the social and kinetic potential of the built environment ossified in liminal forms.

Special thanks to Randa Mirza,
my partner in innocent crimes.

Rashid Karami International Fair, Tripoli

Rashid Karami International Fair, Tripoli

Tripoli, southern outskirts

Burj el Murr Tower, Hamra, Beirut

Near Saida

Saida, northern outskirts

James Building, Dawra, Beirut

SOME THOUGHTS ON THE PATHOLOGY OF ARCHITECTURE

K. MICHAEL HAYS

SOME THOUGHTS ON THE PATHOLOGY OF ARCHITECTURE

K. MICHAEL HAYS

The work of the contemporary historian or contemporary theorist should be a kind of symptomology—a diagnosis of architecture as a complex response to or manifestation of some underlying social and historical contradictions. I find it interesting that in both psychoanalysis and Marxism, which I take to be the two still-operative materialist traditions, the concept of symptom is central. The symptomologist of architecture must deal with the unrepresented and even unrepresentable material that is outside the field of consciousness as well as the artifact itself. A thick description of the latter is necessary but not adequate, for the architecture should unconceal things that would otherwise go unseen.

What I have in mind is less a symptom understood as an expression of the society's inner conflicts and more a recycling and recapitulation of architectural signifiers, *disciplinary* signifiers which are self-isolated and, as such, diverted from any pure expressiveness—in a diagnostic sense, say—and diverted from any pure indexicality. Consider the Baroque architect who must manage *architecturally* the trauma of the discovery of infinity, or the trauma of the realization that the earth and man are not at the center of the universe. The Baroque architect must identify with the symptoms of this trauma and build a dome that indirectly, anamorphically as it were, produces a sensation of infinite space; he must construct a façade that dislocates the humanist universal subject. The historian then writes the symptom outward from the dome and façade.

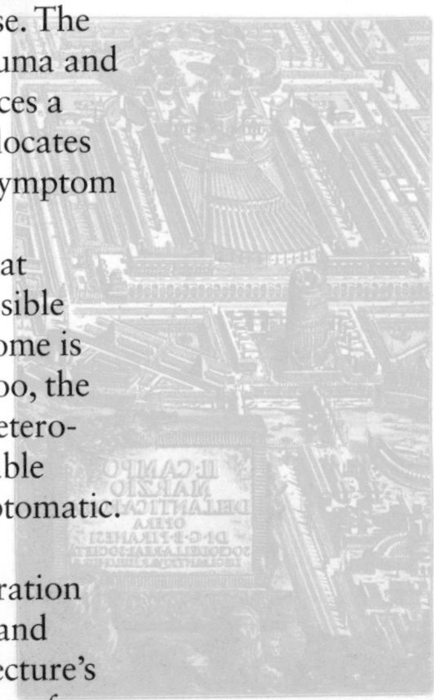

A materialist approach to the symptom refutes the idea that behind the formal system of architecture lies some easily accessible historical or social content—that, for example, the Baroque dome is a mere index to the Counter-Reformation. Though it is that, too, the dome is foremost a form that gathers up contradictions and heterogeneities that prevent us from ever completely settling on a stable content. In our work, it is architectural form that will be symptomatic. Historicity and the social will be found in form.

Now by form I mean more than just the designed configuration of the object itself. Architects assume a high degree of agency and autonomy in their practice, but there are constraints to architecture's possibilities at any given time. These constraints themselves have form and are structured. What Jacques Rancière called the "distribution of the sensible" is the social system of forms that determines what can present itself to sense experience. It is a delimitation of time and space, sense and nonsense. I find helpful, too, Louis Althusser's machinery of the *problématique*—a similar delimitation of what can be seen and understood, or not seen and therefore never coming to mind as a possibility. Social forms produce possibilities and constraints within which a material practice like architecture takes place, so we should be able to relate the forms of architecture's practice and its objects to the social formation, showing architecture to be, in Fredric Jameson's phrase, "a socially symbolic act."[1]

There is, however, a shortcoming in this tradition of theory as symptomology. It is not the detection of pathologies within a putatively normal development—as if there were ever a truly normal condition. It is rather that the pathology we end up detecting in architecture is, most often, the singular pathology of reification—a kind of epistemic leveling and bleaching that results from the systematic fragmentation, quantification and depletion of every realm of subjective experience. For example, both Palladio and Piranesi wrestle with the reification of the antique, not so much reviving ancient Roman architecture as using pieces and parts in architectural mashups like Palladio's villas and Piranesi's Campo Marzio. The Campo Marzio instantiates the materiality of architecture as an excess, an irruption of sensations. Piranesi's types are isolated signifiers that, while they have lost their relation to direct signification, are nevertheless treated materially; Piranesi revels in the materiality of the signifier. Palladio,

G. B. Piranesi, *Il Campo Marzio dell'antica Roma opera di G.B. Piranesi socio della real Società degli antiquari di Londra*, 1762

to me, also reveals the materiality of architectural language, but is more selective, more subtractive and perhaps, more relational insofar as the villas bring a new organization to the landscape and agrarian program. Both architects' efforts, though, can be understood as early responses to reification. For modern architects, of course, reification comes from capitalist development. And there is a clear trajectory of response from Piranesi's excess to Mies van der Rohe's abstraction to the blank repetitions of Aldo Rossi and Peter Eisenman, just to take the obvious examples. The symptomologists whom I most

1 Fredric Jameson, *The Political Unconscious: Narrative as a Socially Symbolic Act* (Ithaca, NY: Cornell University Press, 1982).

admire—Manfredo Tafuri, Jameson and T. J. Clark among them—all end up with reification as the ultimate pathology of modern cultural practices. Reification just is the pathology of modernism. To reinvigorate the project of critical historiography, we should search for other pathologies we have missed, especially since subjectivities have moved several stages past those on which reification theory is based.

My present thinking is that one sort of investigation that would move our project forward is the recognition of the loss of the symbolic authority of architecture's inaugural formations—the symbolic authority, for example, of antiquity, nature, technology or language itself. The authority given to earlier architectures by antiquity or nature is, in modernity, replaced by certain genealogically conceived conditions—epochal will, technological progress, human spirit—that produce analogous authority and augmentations like continuity and growth. But since these authorities are not natural but invented—replacements for an otherwise absent myth of origin—there is produced, immediately and necessarily, a transgressive, disruptive and exterior counterforce. This eccentric counterforce is responsible for characteristically modern avant-garde techniques of criticality, negation, resistance and the like.

But in our own time, the symbolic, disciplinary authority beyond representation, once regarded as the organizing force and inaugural source of architecture, along with its countervailing other, have been nullified by a mood of skepticism that ranges from pragmatism to cynicism to a dumb empiricism. Students and young architects don't seem to accept that they are part of a discourse or an intellectual continuity which stretches behind them and in front of them and which sets the conditions for practicing architecture, that there is an archive which must be disrupted. Without acknowledging the archive and its necessary transgression, then the decision to do architecture, to begin an architectural project, becomes a purely practical, rather than a theoretical, problem. Presentism and technicalization take over, and designers turn to more manageable issues of materials and fabrication rather than concern themselves with architecture as a mode of thought or a way of being in the world.

Let me very quickly try to list some symptoms of the demise of the instaurational authority of architecture, or symptoms of the difficult theoretical problem of beginning architecture. I detect four possible positions in contemporary architecture that I think are consequents of the eclipse of the authority of architecture's constitutive conditions.

First is the most prevalent and easiest one, which I will call simply a conservative or maintenance position. Out of a respect for existing institutions and standards of practice, most architects simply continue to practice as they always did, without ever raising the question of architecture as one of the founding discourses of how we *are*, of our being in the world.

2
Alejandro Zaera-Polo, "The Politics of the Envelope," *Log* 13–14 (Fall 2008): 193–207.

The second position is more interesting. I would call it opportunistic. It takes advantage of the demise of architecture's traditional symbolic authorities and asserts the discovery of a new, higher authority. The opportunistic position is likely to get a lot of attention because it claims at once a novelty and a new certainty. One example is Alejandro Zaera-Polo's declaration of the envelope as the newly discovered but also most primitive and fundamental element in the emergent design regime, and the disciplinary authority for architecture's political, technological and communicative performances.[2] What is missed, however, in such opportunistic reassertions of newly discovered authorities is, first, the necessary openness to excess and otherness—of something kept out of reach—that marks the human in its essence; and second, the exteriority of the disturbing counterforce. What results is a kind of cynicism. Recent shifts from representational to overly empiricist and performative models of architecture, including Zaera-Polo's, tend to cover over the definitive dimension of ornament and artificiality in architecture with quasi-functionalist performance criteria. To put it too simply, perhaps, these opportunists mistake the speech act for the system of language as a whole, and the immediate practice of architecture for the discipline and its history.

A third position sees that there are no longer discursive and collectively held rules of representation and therefore retreats back from the symbolic register, with its concern for shared codes and problematics, to a presymbolic condition of mood, atmosphere and affect. I'm thinking of some of the overly anxious objects we saw at the 2010 Venice Biennale, the fractal furniture of Aranda\Lasch; Lars Spuybroek's interactive, emotive, glowing D-tower; or the "heresies" and installations of François Roche. They seem to me prior to symbolization in Jacques Lacan's sense; they're rather precoded, prelinguistic, preanalytic. I don't mean to suggest they are regressive, only that these projects are released from symbolic coordination and legitimation.

Maybe not even an important position is what I would just call the glib position, which is also a kind of opposite of the first. This uses the knowledge that there is no symbolic authority to manipulate the situation, to bring in false parameters, to bring in fake issues. The example I think of, and I'm not sure if it's the best one, is Daniel Libeskind's Freedom Tower, which is 1,776 feet high—1776 because that's the year of U.S. independence. To me, that's just the most cynical kind of production of false meaning, as if there is nothing more serious or more profound to pursue.

Then, finally, there is the shift from the isolated, autonomous object to layered landscapes, ecologies with no definite boundaries, and different systems interacting and organizing, enduring in real time rather than anachrony. To borrow some symptomological terminology from Lacan, this has a certain self-organizing power that oscillates between *desire* and *drive*. Desire is bound up with the disturbance of the primordial oneness of the world; it seeks a pleasure that can never be present, an authority that is not one. The drive turns desire's failure, as it were, into satisfaction. The metonymy of desire is the transfer of the failure to find the lost object, or to fill the void—the transfer of that failure onto an endless arranging of partial objects, small-other objects, all of which are unsatisfactory; so we get fixated on the objects. Whereas the drive is satisfied with its endless circulation around its object without ever reaching its destination; it doesn't get anxious or fixated. Drive is the fixation.

The overturning of desire by drive is historical as much as it is philosophical. Piranesi's desire is motivated by an absent and irretrievable antiquity. But he ultimately detours toward an altogether new kind of architecture of the city by feeding on the dissatisfaction of his desire. That is his drive. The angst of Rossi and Eisenman, which is manifest as repetition and the search for difference, derives from unassuaged desire. I see "self-organizational" projects like OMA's Downsview Competition entry, which is characterized by quantitative multiplicity, continuous variation, open iteration, and mutation, as logical developments from Eisenman's project for Cannaregio, which comes close to a trace of pure system. Desire and drive are not always strictly opposites; rather, they are different parts of the same system and they often intermingle. Indeed, I would say they are dialectical.[3]

3 Discussions with Andrew Payne at the University of Toronto focused my understanding of the importance of the desire/drive relation.

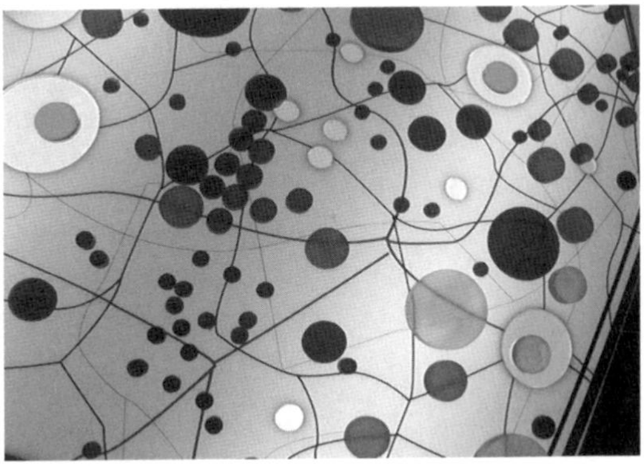

OMA, Bruce Mau Design Inc. and Inside Outside, with Oleson Worland Architects, Downsview Park, Toronto, Canada, 2000

There are recent works of architecture I can think of where the desire/drive dialectic exists. Preston Scott Cohen's Tel Aviv Museum of Art is one example. The central space, which Cohen calls "Lightfall," rips through the entire museum like some otherworldly force. It makes no symbolic claim to universal meaning but is rather a resistance to meaning, a friction against type and code. It is an excess, an exorbitance, we might say, of being over sense and, hence, organized by drive. At the same time, I would suggest that this useless excess, of which Cohen is a master, turns our relation to the architecture into one of desire insofar as it aims to demonstrate the impossibility of representation itself. Certain constitutive concepts of architecture—orthogonality, symmetry, seriality, the distinction between interior and exterior—are produced not as actual substance but rather through their being held just out of reach. This relation of desire preserves difference, preserves particularity, but at the same time posits something beyond, something otherwise inaccessible: I feel an affective charge because the architecture creates a sense that there is something more profound that is being withheld. Of course, this is an *illusion* of depth, but it is the essential illusion of architecture—this illusion of depth is architecture's desire. When architecture suspends that illusion, when it is just an elaborate gesture, then architecture is incapable of holding anything out of our reach. When it shows itself as complete and self-satisfied, I begin to lose interest.

In Cohen's museum there is no idealization of some transcendent origin of or authority for architecture. But neither is there mere performativity and immediacy. What I'm proposing is a need to rethink desire versus drive and transcendence versus the immanent experience. It is rather, if one can say this, that we have to think immanence without an opposite of transcendence or think the transcendent in the immanent. Perhaps we can think of a latent moment and movement of difference and otherness within the architecture itself, which never appears as such but serves to constantly disrupt and destabilize the architecture, so that we push forward, so that we have to constantly strive to "maintain" the architecture in the event of thinking and making.

This brings up the extreme artifice of architecture. Architecture as such is useless; it does nothing but construct a place of difference, frame a place that is *here* and not *there*. Architecture comes into being in order that we recognize that much of reality is outside our frame, beyond our understanding. Architecture's objects and images come into the world as substitutes or, better, markers for that which is blocked from representation. So, then, architecture is all over, everywhere, insofar as architecture is an inaugural phenomenon of our being in the world. Which is to say that architecture does not just host a specific event, it is a specific event of coming into being. But having achieved that status, it is all over, finished—a figuration of emptiness itself.

In a way, this dialectic of saturation *and* exhaustion maps the matrix of contemporary discourse. On the one hand is a position that emphasizes the discipline of architecture. Attending to the discipline entails dealing with the fact that architecture is fundamentally excessive; there is no practical reason for its existence. So here we are in the realm beyond need, the realm of desire. Starting with the discipline demands a lot of theory to decide how to begin to "do" architecture in a meaningful way. Opposed to this position is another that emphasizes design. Design tries to avoid ideology and artifice; it does not recognize the fundamental lack at the heart of the discipline, but rather tries to extend connectivity and incorporate different contexts. It thematizes architecture's projective efforts and its status as a system. Here we are in the domain of the drive. Across this dialectic, perpendicular to it as it were, is another. On the one side of this second dialectic is an insistence on methodological rigor and a rather strict adherence to "proper" philosophical developments and trajectories; an insistence, in other words, that treats architecture as the twin of philosophy. This position has its opposite in another that mediates philosophical concepts through historicizing operations. This position transcodes philosophical models into media-specific theories, not so much to get it right as to make it matter. I propose we think of these related positions as a kind of robust combinatory—a matrix. Across this matrix, between the aesthetic and the ontological, a debate can be played out about the directions architecture will take in the post-contemporary.

Subtractive Urbanism: The Morphology/ Ideology Homology

Matthew Allen
and
Cyrus Peñarroyo

In an extraordinarily drawn-out process of institutionalized self-criticism, architects have convinced themselves they have nothing to say about city form. The approach identified by Rem Koolhaas in the 1970s—ignore the city and retreat to the utopia of program[1]—has become the conditioned response of otherwise avant-garde architects. The city is no longer an object of speculative action; for fear of overstepping the bounds of expertise, architects have abandoned it to forces beyond our control. Left alone, the late-capitalist built environment—called "urbanism"—tends toward self-similar banality, with all pieces interchangeable and equally irrelevant to public life.[2] Architects since Koolhaas have overwhelmingly embraced the myth of urbanism and now content themselves with adding to the city more of what it already has.

Intervention at the level of the city is always political, but so too is abstention. The currently hegemonic regime of liberalism–urbanism–preservation, in which all is unique, all is systematized and all is protected, is as ideologically imbricated as the most overt examples of urban renewal. Easy acceptance of the platitudes of preservation and the architect's diminished role of adding local variety to otherwise untouchable urban fabric belies a fundamental lack of imagination and cedes all decisions regarding city form—decisions which must inevitably be made—to those who are able to disguise their ideology as bureaucratic necessity.[3]

This abdication of responsibility is the result of a category mistake. The role of the architect vis-à-vis cities is not that of builder, but public intellectual. The ideological terrain of urban morphology is at once visual, rhetorical and strategic. As experts in this delicate combination, architects ought to consider themselves the appointed articulators of a worldview—whichever they choose!—insofar as it can be manifest in the form of the city. The work of campaigning for a built reality adequate to social potentials can never be completed

1
See, for example, Rem Koolhaas and Elia Zenghelis (with the collaboration of Madelon Vriesendorp and Zoe Zenghelis), *Exodus, or the Voluntary Prisoners of Architecture*, *Casabella* 37, no. 378 (June 1973): 42–45, and Rem Koolhaas, *Delirious New York: A Retroactive Manifesto for Manhattan* (New York: Thames & Hudson, 1978).

2
See Pier Vittorio Aureli, *The Possibility of an Absolute Architecture* (Cambridge: MIT Press, 2011).

3
For the story of how the city came to be seen as a natural system to be ecologically managed, thereby expanding the power of technocrats, see Adam Curtis, "The Use and Abuse of Vegetational Concepts," episode 2 of *All Watched Over by Machines of Loving Grace* (London: BBC, 2011).

for a very simple reason: the motive force of every new morphological intervention diminishes through time. What begins as a projective monument to a new order almost immediately becomes an unwelcome reminder of its failure to be carried to completion. The fossilized remains of bygone sensibilities are therefore worse than irrelevant; they are in the way, taking up valuable space. It is every generation's obligation to rebuild the city in its own image, according to its own values.

Patterns of correspondence between morphology and ideology are never obvious—they always require comparative historical study. Manufactured urban catastrophes can be understood, with equal justice, as either radically progressive or cynically conservative. Yet, the consequences for social life of profound morphological changes to the city—for good or ill—are undeniable.

Every social system is created in part by a scripted routine of public appearance which requires its own specific space within the city. Take New York City, from which architects derive their contemporary ideal of urbanism. Its apolitical disposition is directly related to its morphology. In New York City, the overwhelming coincidence of public space with the circulation grid simultaneously equates life with commerce and neutralizes architecture's ability to serve as a counterpoint. Anything contained within a single block becomes nothing more than a private affair: sub-political. It is these self-contained worlds, circumscribed within architecture, that Koolhaas has always valorized. The problem is not that they do not produce subjectivities—they do, for small, self-selected groups—but rather that they abandon that part of the city *between* architecture that is able to produce political sensibilities at the scale of society.

Recapturing the political agency inherent in the form of the city as a domain of architecture must begin with understanding absence as an ordering principle. In the past, natural and man-made catastrophes—great fires, wars—did much of the destructive work required for urban transformation. These can no longer be counted on. Today, in a world already brimming with buildings, the primordial act of architecture is subtraction, carving the city from the inside.

Negative space determines the form of the city, not architecture. Because the city has been built to capacity and negative space cannot be *added* along with new architectural fabric, acting on the city today means *removing* architecture. Unprecedented information about the city along with the potential for coordinating mass involvement allow large-scale destruction to be approached with strategic clarity and confidence. But since political willpower is always short-lived, destruction must be approached with a dash of experimental freedom. Subtractive urbanism therefore treats building mass as an inert, characterless substance to be freely and expediently edited. It supersedes zoning and property rights and is agnostic to the worth of any particular piece of architecture.

In the past, such an approach has uniquely marked every politically significant city: the axial roads and piazzas of Sixtus V in Rome, the boulevards of Baron Haussmann in Paris, the freeways and parks of Robert Moses in New York, and, beyond the textbook cases, those caught up in experimental politics—the selective burning of Paris at the end of the Commune and the campaign to destroy the Four Olds in Maoist Beijing. It is from the conviction of these latter agents—who have most explicitly subjected urban morphology to ideology—that we, the constitutionally undecided, stand to learn the most. The following interventions, aimed at the heart of urbanism, New York City, isolate the morphological tactics used by these urban villains, with all their consequences for social life. Our task—the core of the architect's work—is to argue for the ideologically driven (and therefore socially relevant) deployment of form.

ISLANDS

The economic and social value of multiculturalism is nowhere more physically manifest than in the great cities of the world. The neutralizing block structure of New York is, however, an outdated holdover from a time that desired national unity above all else. Differences are limited to a city block, which is fine for individual fantasies but smaller than what is necessary for a self-sustaining community. The grid's homogeneity ensures that pockets of uniqueness are always in danger of colonization. In order to allow differences to thrive, I propose creating a series of canals or moats to separate areas of the city that aspire to uniqueness. Studies have shown that such physical separation creates enclave economies on the resulting islands, building cohesion and amplifying marketable idiosyncrasies. Boston's North and South Ends are classic examples. In a city such as New York, where Little Italy is always in danger of being annexed as a province of Chinatown, such intractable separation would certainly be welcome.

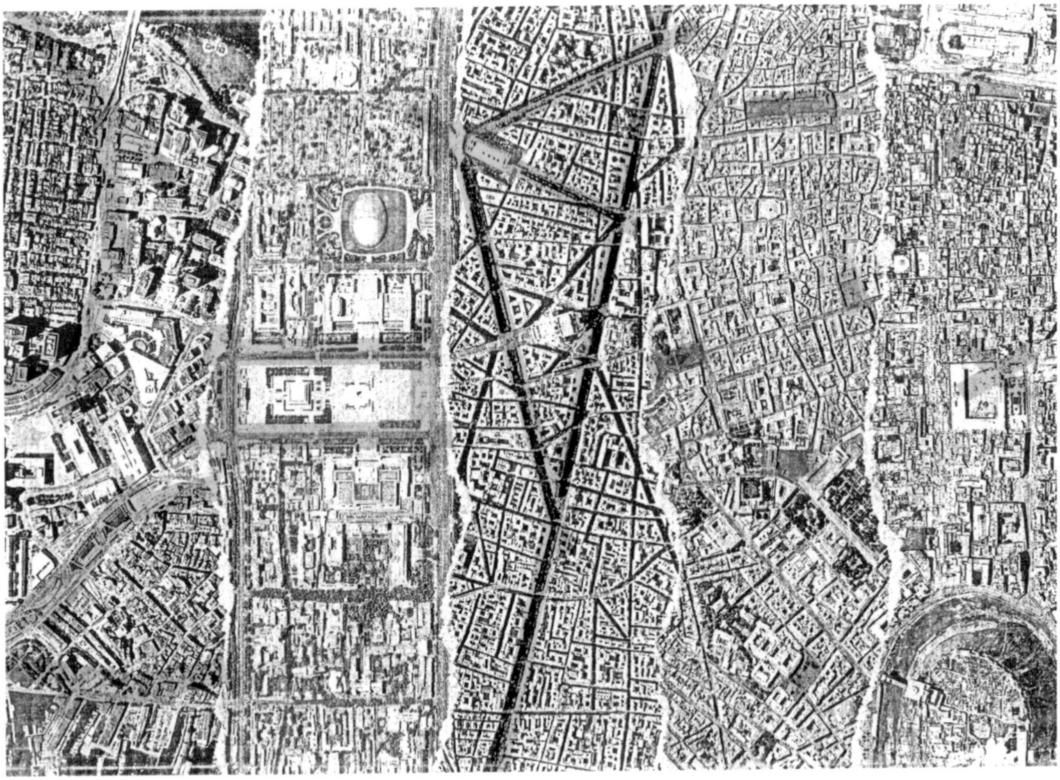

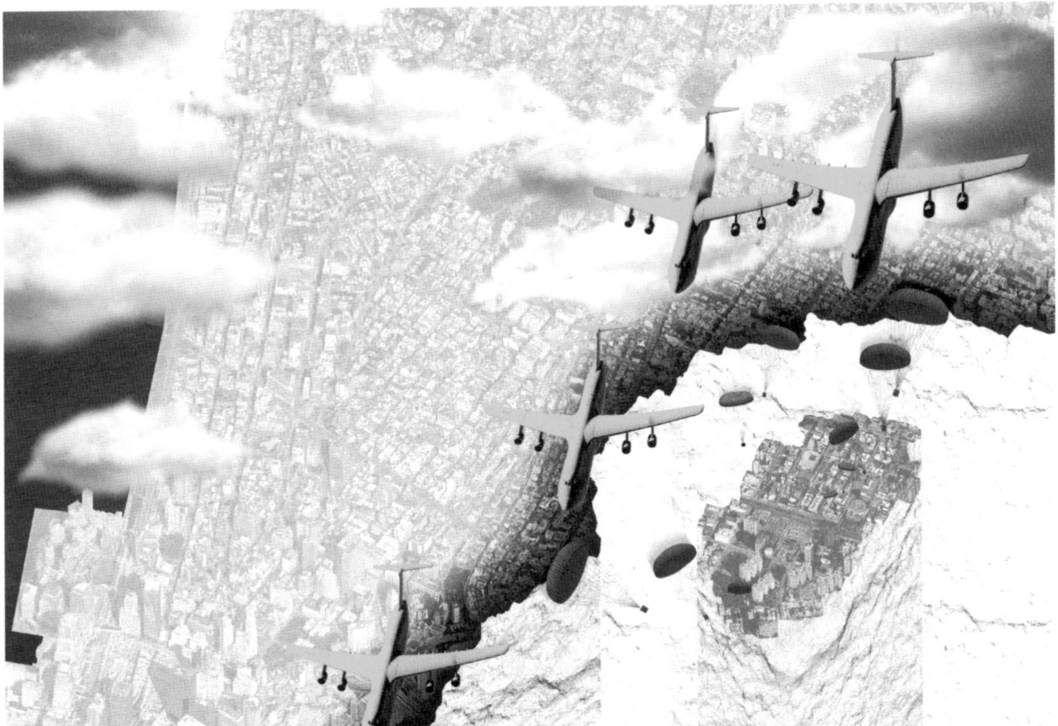

SQUARE

The history of mass society has demonstrated the value of the crowd as an embodiment of popular will. The crowd's attributes of unity and corporeal presence concretize the ordering concepts of a "nation" or "society"—groups which would otherwise be too diffuse to be comprehended as unified wholes. The physical signification of "everyone" at a particular time and place, ready to receive a pronouncement or to deliver an expression of protest, is uniquely able to underwrite or spur political action. Such a crowd requires a space adequate to hold it—a public square—usually located next to a seat of power. Perhaps the impotence of the United Nations is due to the absence of a square adjacent to its headquarters in New York; the omission of such a space both symbolizes the UN's lack of a constituency and disallows the mediating role of a crowd as a very real, bidirectional conduit between abstract institutional power and the global citizenry, itself an abstraction. The complete duality of a symbol of an institution (such as the UN Building) and its constituency (embodied by a crowd) is essential for functional governance, and if even this base level of efficacy must be sacrificed to repress signs of ill will, the institution is probably beyond help. Note: If the People's Republic of China found a square of 440,000 square meters adequate when it numbered 667 million people in 1959, a simple calculation shows that a square for the United Nations (representing the world, now with seven billion people) should be roughly ten times as large (4.6 million square meters).

AXES

As a formal device in the architectural repertoire, an axis is among the most despised. Though axes appear to incorporate symbolic focal points with symmetrical frontality, ensuring deadening stasis, they are, in fact, based on a dialectic of directionality and centrality, with centrality as the weaker of the pair. In the Deleuzian fashion, an axis establishes a "line of flight" that conceptually passes through any monument placed in its way. Far from establishing a center, a set of axes creates a distributed network, a Debordian psychogeography, linking a set of nodes nonhierarchically. As Michel Foucault would have insisted, axes do not establish power, but are devices for setting up power relations. Proof of the post-structuralist credentials of urban axes is their role within the political economy of Paris: though the definitive Parisian boulevards were carved by Haussmann as an apparatus to manage and control life in the mid-nineteenth century, they have made Paris the capital of the protest march. The "events of May '68" were, in large part, an interminable series of marches, often without destination, and there could have been no better rhetorical backdrop than the boulevards' bourgeois façades.

New York's grid allows the particular luxury of indecisiveness. To remedy this, I propose choosing a set of focal points and cutting axes to connect them. Axes would force us to manifest estimations of relative value, to locate centers where they may already be implied. A nodal understanding of the city could be superimposed upon its present field condition, creating new possibilities of willful itineraries on top of its current aimless equality.

URBAN ROOMS

The closest parallels in New York to the outdoor urban rooms found in so many cities around the world are its parks. But, stuffed as they are with trees and encircled by generous roads, they act more like oases set apart from the city than like the spatial interiors of the city itself. Creating exterior public rooms of appropriate scale should be among the simplest of planning moves, demanding the removal of only a few buildings each. A certain school of avant-garde architects have caught on to this tactic;[4] though couched in the rhetoric of form, the current vogue of creating archipelagos—islands of singular architecture—to counter the sea of indecisive urban sprawl could often be carried out just as well through the creation of well-defined and carefully bounded voids. The abstract form of exterior rooms—their dimensions in plan and the height of their enclosing walls—sets up the relevant parameters while remaining indifferent to the rest of what architecture has to offer.

As a start, I propose transplanting the forms of the iconic urban rooms of Rome—Piazza Navona, Piazza San Pietro, Campo di Fiori, etc.—onto the unremittingly regular fabric of the Upper East Side. Such empty pedestrian spaces would favor an almost premodern conviviality; though inevitably nostalgic and touristic, they would insert unexpected notes of spatial excess that would lend themselves to co-option across the spectrum, from communitarian performances to spectacles of commodification.

4
For example, see Pier Vittorio Aureli et al., *Brussels: A Manifesto Towards the Capital of Europe* (Rotterdam: NAi Publishers, 2007) and Alexander D'Hooghe, *The Liberal Monument* (Princeton: Princeton Architectural Press, 2010), both of which propose inserting networks of relatively unprogrammed, exteriorized spaces into cities as counterpoints to urban homogeneity.

FORCED OBSOLESCENCE

Though housed within and identified with some of the world's most loved buildings, cultural institutions are particularly prone to the irrelevance that comes with belonging to past worldviews. Residing within their comfortable shells, they are not only protected from inevitable change but also blind to their own inertness in the world at large. Think, for example, of the palatial Metropolitan Museum of Art building and its intimate relationship to the nineteenth-century master narrative of Art History; with such a perfect fit, it should come as no surprise that so much artistic and curatorial experimentation has taken place *outside* this museum and others like it. Artists and curators who try to expose the concealed nexus of power relations at play end up acting as if they belong to a heretical sect; those who believe in the institutional mission, always in the majority, can all too easily marginalize the radical elements. Far more effective would be to precipitate an internal crisis among the devout, thereby forcing unavoidable reconsideration. The best way to fight the slow entropic death of museums would be to proscribe them entirely, thereby requiring the rethinking of institutional goals and the means of achieving them. In this spirit, I propose razing the museums of Manhattan. The shock of their absence from the city—the sight, for instance, of a crater where the Museum of Modern Art once was—will be among museology's greatest assets: the faithful will be driven to carry on clandestinely with a new, creative vigor.

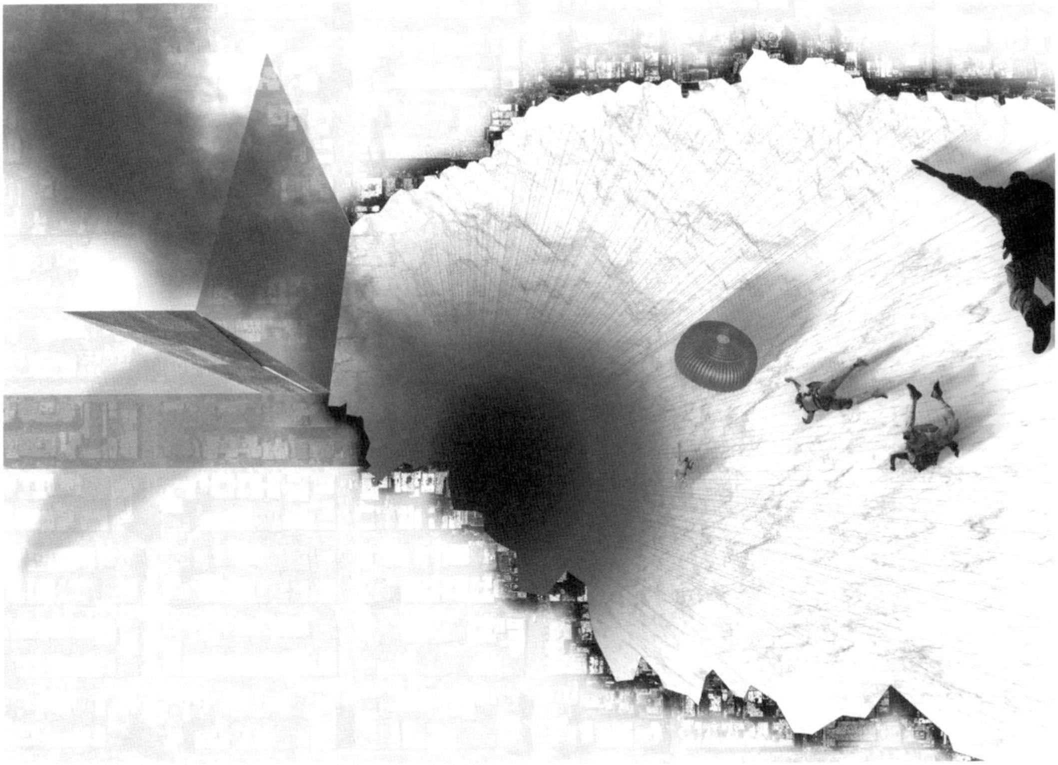

DESIGN AND KENOSIS; OR, THE ARCHITECT'S ABDICATION

KEITH BRESNAHAN

> I have an interest in professional activity, I want to build: to a frighteningly large extent that means basically accepting most of the time.
> —Rem Koolhaas[1]

> We all need someone to tell us what to do.
> —Ben van Berkel and Caroline Bos[2]

Throughout a range of practices variously labeled "pragmatist," "realist," "projective" or "post-critical," the past decade has witnessed the curious disappearance of a figure previously thought to be central to the scene of architecture: namely, the architect. Or, rather, we've seen the disappearance of a particular conception of the architect, the architect-as-master-designer, which held sway from the Renaissance through the late twentieth century. In place of this figure has emerged the architect as facilitator of external forces: a self-emptying mediator of given realities, pragmatically accommodating what *is*, rather than projecting what is not yet or what could be. The recent vicissitudes of the architect are worth considering for what they reveal about the continued role of the profession, and of *design*, within the expanded field of architecture today.

In their retreat from notions of autonomy, control, subjective agency and choice, many contemporary architects also ultimately abdicate responsibility for the final outcome. The design is projected onto other factors: statistical data derived from the intensive study of variables (of site, program, users, budget and so forth) and the parametric modeling programs applied to these; the input of multidisciplinary design teams and stakeholders in the project; "market forces"; and so on. All these factors coincide under the general rubric of "reality"—the key term in this recent development—as both the framework within which architects must work and the context toward which their projects are directed.

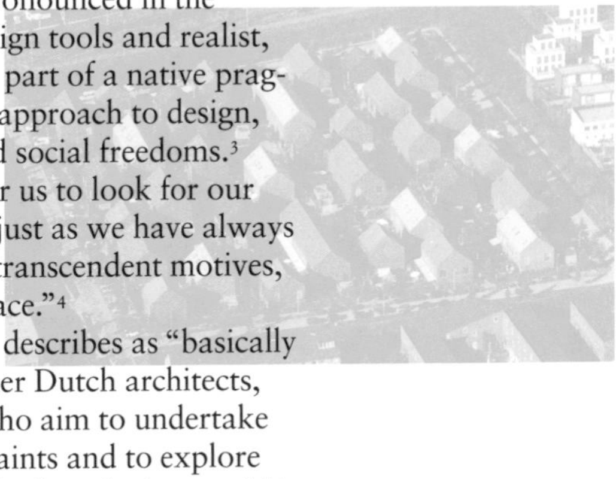

These tendencies have been perhaps most pronounced in the Netherlands, where the acceptance of digital design tools and realist, antitheoretical models of practice can be seen as part of a native pragmatic worldview reflected in the broader Dutch approach to design, problems of land and resource management, and social freedoms.[3] As one Dutch architect sums it up, "It is good for us to look for our motives on the level of usefulness and necessity, just as we have always done. ... Whenever we in the Netherlands have transcendent motives, the greatest possible design catastrophes take place."[4]

Thus, Rem Koolhaas's *realpolitik*—what he describes as "basically accepting most of the time" —is repeated by other Dutch architects, such as the Groningen firm De Zwarte Hond, who aim to undertake commissions *as is* with all accompanying constraints and to explore "what is within the bounds of possibility instead of producing a rabbit

1
Rem Koolhaas, in Alejandro Zaera-Polo, "Finding Freedoms: Conversations with Rem Koolhaas," *El Croquis* 53 (1992): 24.

2
Ben van Berkel and Caroline Bos, *UN Studio Design Models: Architecture Urbanism Infrastructure* (London: Thames and Hudson, 2006), 227.

3
I recall a Dutch acquaintance some years ago who summed up his country's "progressive" policies on drug use and sex work with the comment, "Ah yes, we like to legislate our margins." This remark strikes me as germane to understanding the role pragmatic realism plays in Dutch design, where even the most apparently "liberated" or "experimental" forms seem to be less about the subjective freedoms of the designer than about the *appearance* of play and freedom within strictly defined limits imposed from outside.

4
Dirk Sijmons, quoted in Marijke Beek and Ton Idsinga, "Op de schaal van het landschap dienen we de schoonheid het best door over haar te zwijgen," in *Over schoonheid: Architectuur, omgeving, landschap*, ed. M. N. Beek, T. Idsinga and A. Van der Woud (Zwolle, Netherlands: Waanders, 2000), 13; cited in Catja Edens, "Process," in *Dutch realist: De Zwarte Hond, Karelse Van der Meer Architecten*, ed. Jeroen de Willigen, Jurjen van der Meer, and Catja Edens (Rotterdam : NAi Publishers, 2005), 63.

from the hat as if magicians still existed."[5] Lucy Bullivant has outlined the parameters of a similar movement among young British architects who are "maneuvering in a commercially branded landscape and manipulating givens through microplanning in order to create a more open-ended public-private environment. ... They ask not what architecture represents but what it *does*."[6]

At one level, the pragmatist approach is an understandable response to the changing circumstances that have reshaped the nature of design and construction over the past few decades, not just in the Netherlands but throughout the global West. Pragmatist designers frequently cite the difficulties of practicing architecture in an age in which architectural projects—particularly those private-public partnerships so favored by neoliberal governments—are increasingly complex and overmanaged, with ever-tighter budgets and deadlines and a host of stakeholders that together restrict architects' already limited control to a small sphere in which "design" is understood as formal manipulation.

However, some of these same architects have chosen to see in this situation not so much an obstacle to practice, as the basis for a new and potentially positive reformulation of the architect's role. The principals of Rotterdam-based MVRDV, for example, suggest that if these networks of agencies, individuals and actions seem to wrest control of the project from the architect-as-author, they also create the opportunity for a new, operative mode of practice based in the analysis and modeling of these myriad constraints. Form, they argue, "is not only dependent on the subjectivity of a given author, but also on the handling of information about reality," understood as accumulated and computerized data about a site and its variables.[7] This view retains a partial, form-giving role for the architect while displacing other duties onto an externalized, partially automatic design process. As MVRDV puts it, "a part of the 'unexpressible' [sic] aspect of architecture has come down on the side of its statistical treatment."[8]

MVRDV, Hagen Island residential area, Ypenburg, Netherlands, 2003

This tendency is also manifest in the work of architects who employ conventional forms, prefabricated materials and standard processes while renouncing significant manipulation or intervention.

5 Jurjen van der Meer, "From the North" in *Dutch Realist*, 9.

6 Lucy Bullivant, "No More Tabula Rasa: Progressive Architectural Practices in England," in *The New Architectural Pragmatism*, ed. William S. Saunders (Minneapolis: University of Minnesota Press, 2007), 75–79. Similarly, Harm Tilman writes that recent "realist" tendencies in Dutch architecture have shifted emphasis "from representative to performative architecture. It is no longer what things mean that is important, but what they do and how they work." Harm Tilman, "From Regional Firm to Global Player," in *Dutch Realist*, 155–156.

7 Quoted in Jamie Salazar, ed., *MVRDV at VPRO* (Barcelona: Actar, 1998), 3.

8 Ibid.

Roemer Van Toorn has described the methods of Dutch architects Rapp+Rapp and Claus & Kaan, for example, as "work[ing] with received architectural language ... [and] deal[ing] in a craftsmanly and repetitive manner with windows, columns, doors, façade panels, and volumes ... [to pursue] a conventional architecture that inspires confidence and eschews controversy."[9] As Claus & Kaan have laconically asserted: "we use standard industrial materials, spans, and constructions: ordinary products and ordinary techniques."[10]

Claus & Kaan Architects, Block 24 housing complex, Ijburg, Netherlands, 2001–2005

This prosaic aspect of pragmatist practices strongly resonates with a concurrent development in Dutch graphic design, which the designer and critic Rob Giampietro has termed "Default Systems."[11] Like that of Claus & Kaan, this approach can be characterized by a straightforward acceptance of "ordinary products and ordinary techniques," such as the basic default settings—including fonts, templates, colors and so on—found in common design software. These settings automate certain aspects of the design process while ensuring a guise of homogeneous neutrality. The production of an *appearance* of anonymity and disinterestedness is seen as a visual correlative to the (partial) abdication of authorial intervention to the presets of ubiquitous technology. The Rotterdam-based collective Experimental Jetset, for example, has rejected the hyper-individualistic and labored works of earlier designers in favor of an avowed pursuit of banality.[12] Whereas a previous generation of Dutch graphic designers, like their architectural counterparts, evinced an enthusiasm for the new possibilities of endless manipulation afforded by computer software, Default Systems designers instead choose "minimal intervention,"[13] and in doing so, choose to curtail authorial control over the look of a project.

As with the new architectural pragmatism, the adoption of a Default Systems approach in graphic design has been linked to increasing demands by clients who ask for more work, quickly, and

9
Roemer Van Toorn, "No More Dreams? The Passion for Reality in Recent Dutch Architecture ... and Its Limitations," in *New Architectural Pragmatism*, 61–62.

10
Claus & Kaan, *Hunch* 6/7 (2003): 140; quoted in Van Toorn, "No More Dreams," 72 n20.

11
Rob Giampietro, "Default Systems in Graphic Design," *Emigre* 65 (New York: Princeton Architectural Press, 2003), 53–60. Available at http://blog.linedandunlined.com/post/404940995/default-systems-in-graphic-design.

12
Experimental Jetset asks their readers to "reconsider the notion of banal design, and imagine an object which is widely used, commonly accepted, but still has the ability to disturb. An object that has the potential to become part of society, but not to dissolve in it completely. ... The banalisation of graphic design? We should be so lucky." Experimental Jetset, "Lazy Sunday Afterthoughts," *Experimental Jetset* (November 2003), accessed July 28, 2011, http://www.experimentaljetset.nl/archive/lazy-sunday.html.

13
Giampietro, "Default Systems in Graphic Design."

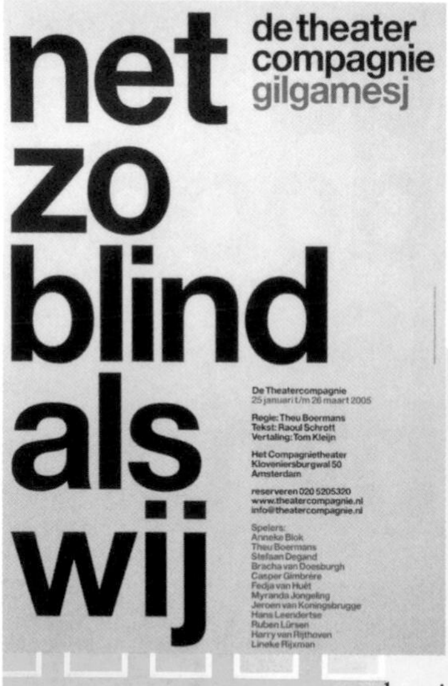

Experimental Jetset, Poster for production of *Gilgamesj*, De Theatercompagnie, Amsterdam, 2005

under tighter budgets. Any claims by these designers to have happily done away with their autonomy sound the hollow note of compensatory revisionism: although the designers face a real loss of agency in projects and are unable to mount a serious resistance, their powerlessness is reframed as a virtue. Seen otherwise, this allegedly neutral compliance with predetermined possibilities reinforces an image of the designer as, at best, a servant to pragmatic considerations, and at worst, disposable.

In the architectural context, MVRDV asserts that this restriction of the architect's agency "does not imply ... the absolute negation of the architect as author, but only a transformation of his status" to that of a mediator in processes of material and informational exchange.[14] Control has not been entirely relinquished, since the architect is still the one who selects from a seemingly never-ending stream of parametric possibilities generated by computer software, or who chooses from readymade templates and standardized building elements. Nonetheless, these architects and designers are largely abjuring a personal agency or responsibility for the resulting project, claiming that it bears little trace of individual, subjective taste.[15]

The architect's self-assumed loss of autonomy is particularly acute in the case of large projects, with complex programs and highly varied purposes that defy any single architectural gesture. Koolhaas has termed this tendency "bigness," which he describes as "the point at which architecture becomes both the most and the least architectural. The most because of the enormity of the object; the least because of its loss of autonomy. Architecture becomes an instrument of other forces, and becomes dependent."[16] If this loss of autonomy, this dependence, designates architecture at its *least architectural*, we might reasonably expect architects to seek to retain or regain whatever modicum

14
Salazar, *MVRDV at VPRO*, 10. What is lost in all this may be *design* itself, understood as encapsulating subjective input, control, creative intervention and, ultimately, responsibility for the final project. In a recent essay, Ben van Berkel and Caroline Bos of Amsterdam-based UN Studio give serious attention "to the question of *how to eliminate design from the practice of architecture*." Missing from their query is any sense that this elimination might be anything but positive. Van Berkel and Bos, *UN Studio Design Models*, 8.

15
As the designer and critic Michael Rock notes of the diagrammatic process of the Dutch Droog design collective, "Dutch design seems intent on erasing the sense that any designer imposed any subjectivity." Rock, quoted in Van Toorn, "No More Dreams," 59.

16
Rem Koolhaas and Bruce Mau, *S,M,L,XL*, ed. Jennifer Sigler (New York: Monacelli Press, 1995), 513 n9.

of independence, agency, and control they find possible, and thus to secure a continued relevance both for themselves and for architecture as such. What we find in recent texts and projects espousing a pragmatic-realist-projective view, however, is precisely the opposite: we see architects resignedly accepting or wildly embracing their loss of authority along with architecture's subjection to other forces, and seeking to accommodate these as the absolute precondition for architectural practice.

Today, this situation seems to be undergoing a further transformation. In light of the growing skepticism of what Koolhaas has termed "the regime of ¥€$"[17] of neoliberalization and global finance, many young architects are rejecting the pragmatist model of accommodation for another, perhaps equally naive, pragmatism in which the architect seeks to recoup a certain moral agency by provisionally seizing moments of autonomy at a micro-scale or in in-between spaces, wherever they might appear.[18] While intriguing and even heartening in its own right, this architecture of micropolitical possibility leaves the situation largely unchanged for the vast majority of architects who, like Koolhaas, maintain their desire to build in the context of shrinking tax revenues and new "austerity measures" and in spite of the growing role of technocratic managers in architectural projects. Rather than explore these "moralizing" practices, I propose that the architect's volitional *abdication* of agency, as outlined above, might offer an alternative strategy for reclaiming a sense of autonomy.

KENOSIS AND DESIGN

The paradigm of the self-effacing subject who relinquishes authorial mastery to become an agent of other forces and other wills finds a parallel in a longstanding tenet of Christian theology: the doctrine of *kenosis*, or the self-emptying of Christ. I suggest that this theological paradigm not only provides a potent heuristic for grasping the shifting status of the architect, but might also enable us to imagine a role for design that would escape both the too-easy complicity of pragmatism and the obdurate negativity of critical architecture.

The basis for kenotic theology (from the Greek κένωσις, "emptying") is the biblical passage Philippians 2:7–8, which says that Christ "made himself nothing," "of no reputation" and "emptied himself," taking the characteristics of a servant.[19] Essentially, in becoming incarnate in Christ, God emptied himself *of himself* in order to fully participate in human existence. Theological debates on this passage over the past two millennia have focused on the nature of this emptying and its implications for the Trinity—including whether God abdicated *all* of his divinity for the duration of the Incarnation or whether Christ was emptied only of certain divine attributes; or even whether he retained all of these, but merely concealed them from other men.[20] For the Christian, this divine kenosis finds a counterpart

17
Rem Koolhaas, "The Regime of ¥€$," in *Anything*, ed. Cynthia Davidson (New York: Anyone Corporation; Cambridge: MIT Press, 2000), 180–188.

18
One might look, for example, to the small-scale radical urbanist projects cropping up in Detroit, a ground zero for experiments in the future shape of the postindustrial landscape.

19
Phil. 2:7–8. Versions quoted: North American Standard Bible; King James Version; New International Version.

20
For a discussion of these viewpoints, see Oliver D. Crisp, "Divine Kenosis," in *Divinity and Humanity: The Incarnation Reconsidered* (Cambridge: Cambridge University Press, 2007), 118–153. Crisp writes that most serious Christian theologians today rightly reject an account of kenosis that has Christ *completely* abdicating his divinity during the incarnation. Crisp's own interpretation favors a "kryptic" understanding of the incarnation, in which Christ did not abdicate any of his divine powers but merely hid them from others in his presence.

in *ekkenosis*, or the riddance of individual will and interests in order to become entirely receptive to God's will and to be filled with divine grace.

Both kenosis and ekkenosis parallel the architectural phenomenon I have been describing. The architect-as-God abdicates his powers so as to enter more fully into contingent reality, and foregoes individual agency to become the transparent instrument of a larger force and purpose. The death of the architect as a total and autonomous designer capable of intervening in any or all aspects of the material world and stamping it with his subjective mark is a starting point for both the "critical" paradigm of postmodern architecture and the projective model explicitly opposed to it.[21] For both, the positive figure of a benevolent designer directly shaping society in accord with an a priori utopian vision is a moribund and dangerous fantasy—for critical architects, because utopian possibility (where it exists) can be described only negatively through moments of resistance or difficulty inserted into a reality which must always be kept at a distance; and for projective architects, because reality as it exists is more productive than any utopia, and the architect must acknowledge that he or she was always merely a facilitator rather than an originator of other forces to begin with.

In the kenotic tradition, God's partial abdication of his divinity in the incarnation was a sign of his love for humanity: Christ enters with greatly reduced powers into the "real" world of human beings in the most crucial instance of divine *syncatabasis*, or God's "lowering" himself beneath his own transcendence to intervene in the world of men. While most such instances in the biblical narratives are momentary and partial, the example of kenosis is of another order.[22] The abdication of divine powers (omniscience, omnipotence and so forth) in Christ—even to the point of death[23]—presents the central paradigm of the economy of sacrifice and submission that has dominated Western religious and philosophical thought for much of the past two millennia.

But there is an important difference between this theological doctrine and contemporary architectural self-abnegation: what architects and designers today are emptying themselves out *for* and allowing themselves to be wholly directed *by* is not the will of God for the love of man, but rather "reality."[24] And in keeping with the antitranscendent character of the postmodern, this "reality" is not an eternal perfectibility or timeless ground but simply whatever is *given*—including standard material and technological elements, neoliberal development frameworks, and the flows and interests of global capital.

If a resurrection and full restoration of the God-designer with all his powers seems both unlikely and undesirable, what hope remains for design? Drawing on the Italian philosopher Gianni Vattimo, who

21
For a brief outline of the origins and historical vicissitudes of this figure, see Mark Wigley, "Whatever Happened to Total Design?," *Harvard Design Magazine*, no. 5 (summer 1998): 18–25. Today, this question would have to be reformulated as, "Whatever happened to *design*?"

22
Some have argued that God's creative acts in making the world and human beings—as the divine "architect"—also constitute an emptying or pouring-out of himself in the sense of a painter creating a picture (the example is C. S. Lewis's, in *Mere Christianity*), and yet he nonetheless remains wholly himself and distinct from his works. See C. S. Lewis, *Mere Christianity* (1943; repr. New York: Simon & Schuster, 1996), 44.

23
I speak here not merely of Christ's death on the cross, but also the proposal by particular theologians and philosophers, such as Thomas J. J. Altizer and Gianni Vattimo, that the incarnation signals the *death* of God as a transcendent being.

24
Leo Tolstoy, in his religious memoir *A Confession*, perfectly sums up this attitude (substituting our "reality" for his "progress"): "The faith of the majority of educated people of our day was expressed by the word 'progress.' It then appeared to me that this word meant something. I did not as yet understand that, being tormented (like every vital man) by the question how it is best for me to live, in my answer, 'Live in conformity with progress,' I was like a man in a boat who when carried along by wind and waves should reply to what for him is the chief and only question, 'Whither to steer,' by saying, 'We are being carried somewhere.'" Leo Tolstoy, *A Confession* (1882), trans. Aylmer Maude (Oxford: Oxford University Press, 1958), 12. Thanks to Marrikka Trotter for this reference.

Lucas Cranach, *Christ Washing the Feet of His Disciples*, 1521

has done more than any other contemporary thinker to restore the philosophical significance of kenosis, we might see in this loss the possibility for a new ethics and responsibility of practice. The concept of kenosis is key to Vattimo's notion of "weak thought" (*il pensiero debole*),[25] which proposes a potential philosophy after the nihilist and postmodern destructions of transcendence and metaphysics—a process Vattimo sees as having its origin in the kenotic incarnation of Christ, and its gradual erosion of the ontological centrality of God the Father.

"Weak thought" would draw on the possibilities opened up by the retreat of master narratives and transcendent beings (God the Father, the Architect-God, etc.) to propose a kenotic ethics that would use the subject's detachment from both dreams of mastery and pure subjection to a higher power, to pursue ethical activity in favor of further weakening all hierarchical structures.[26] In Vattimo's formulation, kenotic ethics holds the potential for moral action beyond both theism and atheism, as an "orientating principle that enables [hermeneutics] to realize its own original inclination for ethics whilst neither restoring metaphysics nor surrendering to the futility of a relativistic philosophy of culture."[27]

This would be a weak ethics at the same time as it would be a weak thought, whose power would consist in the pursuit of immanent goals in a world in which nothing is given in advance and nothing can be taken at face value: not even (or especially) reality. The nihilism of kenotic ethics—and of kenotic design—would instead necessitate a dialectical relationship to reality, as the framework within which we must function but whose status we must always put into question. Such a relationship would entail neither longing for lost autonomy in some putative "outside" of the system nor a happy embrace of the status quo.

25
For Vattimo, the theologian Frits de Lange writes, there is "a causal relationship between the Christian narrative of kenosis and philosophical nihilism. ... The consequence of the gospel is nihilism." Frits de Lange, "Gianni Vattimo, Reading 'The Signs of Time,'" in *Letting Go: Rethinking Kenosis*, ed. Onno Zijlstra (Bern: Peter Lang, 2002), 25–68.

26
The radical potential given to kenosis in Vattimo's work has precedents in G. W. F. Hegel's *Phenomenology of Spirit* and in the "Death of God" theological movement of the 1960s and after. See particularly the work of Thomas J. J. Altizer, such as *The Gospel of Christian Atheism* (Philadelphia: Westminster Press, 1966) and *The Self-Embodiment of God* (New York: Harper & Row, 1977).

27
Gianni Vattimo, *The Transparent Society* [1989], trans. David Webb (Baltimore: Johns Hopkins University Press, 1992), 119. On Vattimo's theories of weak thought and kenosis, see Gianni Vattimo, *The End of Modernity: Nihilism and Hermeneutics in Post-modern Culture* [1985], trans. John R. Snyder (Cambridge: Polity Press, 1991), and *Belief* [1996], trans. Luca D'Isanto and David Webb (Stanford: Stanford University Press, 1999).

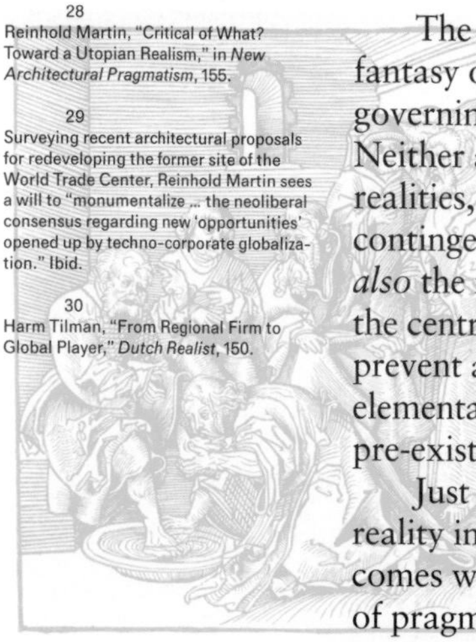

The end of architecture's God delusion—the substitution of its fantasy of control for a pragmatic engagement with messy realities governing design, construction and use—is not in itself a bad thing. Neither are projective practices and parametric analyses of these realities, which may return architecture to a greater sensitivity to the contingencies of site, program and users. But what is needed today is *also* the return to architecture of an ethical orientation—embedded in the centrality of design and the responsibility this entails—that would prevent architects from making what Reinhold Martin calls "the elementary mistake of assuming that reality is entirely real—that is, pre-existent, fixed, and therefore exempt from critical reimagination.[28]

Just as the architect-as-God was a fantasy that attained a certain reality insofar as it was embedded in practices whose concrete outcomes were taken as affirmations of it, so the contemporary "reality" of pragmatist design is a fiction whose "realness" is propped up by projects and processes whose instrumentality is based in a circular logic. In other words, since these projects and processes have been developed to accommodate a certain vision of reality, we should not be surprised when they function in accordance with this vision. But the troubling result of this self-reinforcing system is that alternatives become increasingly difficult to imagine. If certain tactics work because they are tailored to what *is*, it is not difficult to see how their affirmation of the status quo also becomes a reification of this status quo, as simply the way things must be—and, thus, will be.[29]

And it is here that the approach I have outlined above might intervene in the sphere of contemporary practice: those architects and designers who are today abdicating a fantasy of mastery in favor of submersion in the banal givens of software presets, standard elements and the minute particulars of site and budget may be opening up a space of possibility for thinking otherwise, from within the "realities" of contemporary practice itself. Like the incarnate Christ's acceptance of certain aspects of his historical reality ("Give to Caesar what is Caesar's...") while remaining radically apart from these—refusing them any true significance—the kenotic designer's apparent complicity with the givens of neoliberal governance and corporate interests would at the same time maintain a tenuous resistance to these, by way of an ironic distance opened in the act of conscious abnegation. This would certainly be a "weak power," constantly risking mere complicity and lacking a promise of salvation via positive solutions. But this weak power, and its weak potential for a recuperation of the architect's autonomy, would seem necessary today given the alternative of reducing the architect to a mere functionary approving choices already taken elsewhere by others. As Harm Tilman suggests, if this latter tendency continues, "architects will at a certain moment no longer be able to fulfill any other tasks."[30] At which point, it really will be all over.

28
Reinhold Martin, "Critical of What? Toward a Utopian Realism," in *New Architectural Pragmatism*, 155.

29
Surveying recent architectural proposals for redeveloping the former site of the World Trade Center, Reinhold Martin sees a will to "monumentalize ... the neoliberal consensus regarding new 'opportunities' opened up by techno-corporate globalization." Ibid.

30
Harm Tilman, "From Regional Firm to Global Player," *Dutch Realist*, 150.

ERASURE URBANISM

PATTY HEYDA

Incorporated in 1948, Kinloch was the first all-African American community to become a municipality in the state of Missouri. Located just outside the St. Louis city line, the town soon became known for its strong schools and churches, which anchored a robust public life while sustaining local businesses and institutions in a successful "loop" of mutually supported development, urban space and residential stability.[1] Yet, despite these internal successes, Kinloch was undervalued at the regional scale, and depicted in the St. Louis County media as a problematic suburb. The reasons for Kinloch's poverty are complex, but they result in part from deeply ingrained inequalities stemming from racial tensions that remain significant in St. Louis today. In 2010, Kinloch was ranked the poorest of the ninety-one municipalities composing St. Louis County.[2]

1
John Wright, Sr., *Kinloch: Missouri's First Black City* (Charleston: Arcadia Publishing, 2000), 8.

2
Keegan Hamilton, "A Video Tour of Kinloch, The Saddest City in St. Louis County," *The Riverfront Times*, March 23, 2010, http://blogs.riverfronttimes.com/dailyrft/2010/03/a_video_tour_of_kinloch_the_sa.php.

Kinloch, Carrollton and Lambert–St. Louis Airport in St. Louis County, Missouri

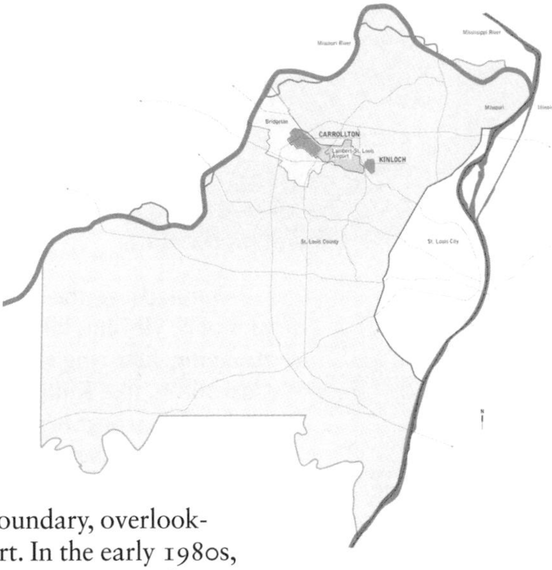

A highway delineates Kinloch's western boundary, overlooking the Lambert–St. Louis International Airport. In the early 1980s, the airport extended its main runways in an attempt to propel Trans-World Airline's (TWA) expansion and establish St. Louis as an international hub for regional economic growth. As part of the process, the Federal Aviation Administration (FAA) adjusted the acceptable noise-decibel level for the areas surrounding the airport and instituted a noise-abatement plan. Under the pretext of meeting these new FAA noise mandates, local elites devised two types of abatement measures: a home-insulation improvement program, which was offered to most properties in municipalities surrounding Kinloch, and a buyout plan disproportionately targeting Kinloch residents.[3] The airport authority acquired the land through a take-over process that lasted well into the 1990s, claiming over two-thirds of the small municipality and ultimately leading to the demolition of over 75

3
Two maps found on the Lambert–St. Louis International Airport website's Noise Mitigation and Land Management Section, *Acoustical Area (2005)* and *Eligible Sound Mitigation Areas (1999)*, show the identified baseline noise-mitigation areas qualifying for sound-insulation upgrades to homes falling within the appropriate decibel-level zones. Both maps depict Kinloch without any qualifying properties for this type of baseline mitigation despite the fact that *other* qualifying areas fall within the same noise contours as Kinloch's central and eastern quadrants. Instead, Kinloch properties become "eligible" for the residential buyout option under the noise-mitigation plan. These maps were initially accessed September 2009; since that time, some of the maps have been removed from the website. Lambert–St. Louis International Airport, http://www.lambert-stlouis.com/flystl/about-lambert/noise-land/, accessed September 2010.

4
Ishmael Ahmad, "Kinloch Sues St. Louis to Halt Home Buyouts near Lambert; Redevelopment Deal Was Broken, Community Says," *The St. Louis American*, March 9–15, 2000, http://www.awj-law.com/news.php?article=2.

5
Hamilton, "A Video Tour of Kinloch." Additional population data is from *U.S. Census Reports* from 1990, 2000, and 2010, and from the Missouri Census Data Center, *Missouri Population 1900–1990*, http://mcdc.missouri.edu/trends/historical.shtml. See also 2010 US Census Fact Sheet: http://factfinder2.census.gov/faces/tableservices/jsf/pages/productview.xhtml?src=bkmk.

percent of Kinloch's homes. This dramatic depopulation collapsed the city's already thin tax base, further straining municipal services at a critical moment of need. Crime and neglect thrived in the vacated spaces, reshaping the lives of those who defiantly chose to remain in the disappearing city. Kinloch residents spoke out in the media and filed lawsuits, with one attorney describing the process as a "massive federally financed land grab which had the effect to ruin a black community."[4] Kinloch's population, once more than 10,000 residents, plummeted to around 4,500 in the early 1980s, to less than 3,000 in 1990, and 449 by 2000. In 2010, the number was around 200, as Kinloch's residents are still slowly departing.[5]

Aerial view of Kinloch, Missouri, c. 2010

6
United States Department of Transportation–Federal Aviation Administration, *Environmental Impact Statement: Record of Decision; Lambert–St. Louis International Airport; City of St. Louis, St. Louis County, Missouri* (September 30, 1998): 22.

7
"Best Of Awards," *Riverfront Times*, September 24, 2003, http://www.riverfronttimes.com/bestof/2003/award/best-boondoggle-31425/.

Similarly, to the airport's west, only infrastructural traces remain of a once vibrant, largely white neighborhood called Carrollton. An aging, first-ring suburban community founded in the 1960s, Carrollton, like Kinloch, was affected by economic speculation that promoted airport expansion as a means of achieving regional growth. In Carrollton, the scheme involved the planning of a new runway that would cover half the community, with an associated new noise-mitigation zone mandating the buyout and demolition of the other half. Local residents, backed by the mayor of the wider municipality of Bridgeton, resisted with organized citizen-groups and by filing a major lawsuit against the Federal Aviation Authority. Nonetheless, Carrollton was completely eradicated. Between 2000 and 2009, 2,000 homes, seventy-five businesses, six schools and several churches were demolished.[6]

Meanwhile, during the course of runway construction, the events of September 11, 2001, resulted in an unexpected reduction in flights to and from St. Louis. As a result, the airport lost its hub status with TWA—now American Airlines—and planes were downsized to smaller, quieter models. In the end, the runway project coincided with decreases in plane landings, rendering the noise-level boundary changes irrelevant. In 2003, a local newspaper voted the runway project St. Louis's "Best Boondoggle."[7]

The demolition of 12679 Grandin, the last of the 2,000 homes demolished in Carrollton, 2009. Photograph by Jami Desy Schoenewies

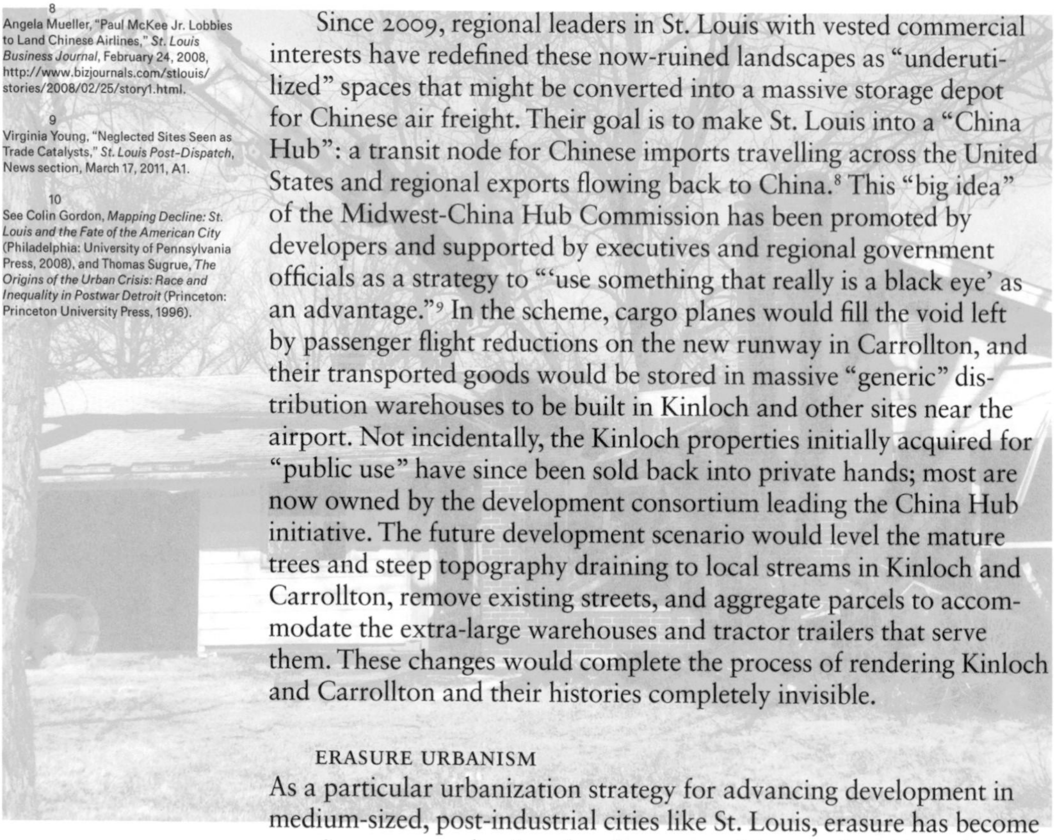

8
Angela Mueller, "Paul McKee Jr. Lobbies to Land Chinese Airlines," *St. Louis Business Journal*, February 24, 2008, http://www.bizjournals.com/stlouis/stories/2008/02/25/story1.html.

9
Virginia Young, "Neglected Sites Seen as Trade Catalysts," *St. Louis Post-Dispatch*, News section, March 17, 2011, A1.

10
See Colin Gordon, *Mapping Decline: St. Louis and the Fate of the American City* (Philadelphia: University of Pennsylvania Press, 2008), and Thomas Sugrue, *The Origins of the Urban Crisis: Race and Inequality in Postwar Detroit* (Princeton: Princeton University Press, 1996).

Since 2009, regional leaders in St. Louis with vested commercial interests have redefined these now-ruined landscapes as "underutilized" spaces that might be converted into a massive storage depot for Chinese air freight. Their goal is to make St. Louis into a "China Hub": a transit node for Chinese imports travelling across the United States and regional exports flowing back to China.[8] This "big idea" of the Midwest-China Hub Commission has been promoted by developers and supported by executives and regional government officials as a strategy to "'use something that really is a black eye' as an advantage."[9] In the scheme, cargo planes would fill the void left by passenger flight reductions on the new runway in Carrollton, and their transported goods would be stored in massive "generic" distribution warehouses to be built in Kinloch and other sites near the airport. Not incidentally, the Kinloch properties initially acquired for "public use" have since been sold back into private hands; most are now owned by the development consortium leading the China Hub initiative. The future development scenario would level the mature trees and steep topography draining to local streams in Kinloch and Carrollton, remove existing streets, and aggregate parcels to accommodate the extra-large warehouses and tractor trailers that serve them. These changes would complete the process of rendering Kinloch and Carrollton and their histories completely invisible.

ERASURE URBANISM

As a particular urbanization strategy for advancing development in medium-sized, post-industrial cities like St. Louis, erasure has become a mainstream mechanism that disrupts architectural notions of site as a physical space and draws our attention to site as a processual locus of law and power. As post-industrial city regions seek to insert themselves into global trade, resource and capital circuits, such practices wipe out weak communities and local histories to clear space for prospective accumulation of capital in a region. The geographies of erasure urbanism are thus visible and nonvisible, spatial and aspatial, generic and unique, extraordinary and systemic.

Erasure in this context should be distinguished from other processes of urbanization that inevitably involve forms of clearing. Urbanization must embrace clearing as a component of transformation, but ideally, it does so by maintaining attention to contexts, cultural-ecological histories and citizenship rights. Erasure urbanism operates in a much narrower way, with hyper-efficient articulations of transformation as a vehicle for profit alone.

The examples of Kinloch and Carrollton demonstrate that the dismantling of communities relies on identifying and targeting weaker constituents in discrete territories through policy maneuvers that are initiated *long before* physical clearing occurs.[10] St. Louis has witnessed these maneuvers before, in political decisions underlying the massive urban renewal efforts that paved the way for projects like Pruitt-Igoe during the 1950s, as well as in the policies that assured its failure twenty short years later.[11] In Kinloch and Carrollton, destabilizing mechanisms were honed in legal and political practices at state and regional levels that accumulated during routine processes of governance and bureaucracy over many years.[12]

Designers often lament the absence of site-specific aesthetics in development scenarios like those projected for Kinloch and Carrollton by focusing on their "generic," formally standardized warehouses and leveled landscapes. However, it is equally important to realize how instruments leading to the erasure of these communities operated in particularly site-specific ways prior to the construction process. Personal relationships, local negotiations, legislative lobbying and the media were navigated by business leaders to secure the appropriate legal, political, financial and public endorsements across local, regional and state arenas. Contrary to easy assumptions, then, site-specificity exists in the changes sanctioned for such communities; it is simply located in a set of procedural operations rather than in formal outcomes alone. These operations are not dramatic acts of violence but banal events that are taken for granted and even deemed "good" in the public discourse of those who are not immediately affected. In the aftermath of the Holocaust, Hannah Arendt theorized that injustice at a variety of scales and severities is incubated by the very "banality of evil," as functionaries carry out their everyday practices.[13] More recently, development sociologist Shelley Feldman and her colleagues have drawn on Arendt's work to remind us that such mundane activities as the production of planning tools, codes, acts, laws, policies and congressional appropriations have the power to either reinforce or erode the rights, stability and security of daily life.[14]

11
See *The Pruitt-Igoe Myth*, documentary film, directed by Chad Freidrichs; produced by Paul Fehler, Jaime Freidrichs, Brian Woodman (First Run Features, 2011).

12
An inventory of the Missouri State Senate and House Bills from 1995 to 2011 reveals numerous legislative measures that incentivize external corporate development activity while reducing the power of local municipalities. Missouri House of Representatives Bills database, www.house.mo.gov, accessed October 2010.

13
Hannah Arendt, *Eichmann in Jerusalem: A Report on the Banality of Evil* (1963; repr., New York: Penguin, 1994), 287.

14
Shelley Feldman, Charles Geisler, and Gayatri Menon, eds., *Accumulating Insecurity* (Athens: University of Georgia Press, 2011), 2. I draw on the editors' descriptions of destabilizing mechanisms of the everyday, like economic policy, which undermine personal freedoms over long periods of time but could be equally destructive as destabilizing events, like the violence of war and threats to national security. Another useful illustration of the scales of assault exists in St. Louis. After an area southwest of the airport was devastated by a tornado on April 22, 2011, the media described how the storm "shattered homes, lives," and yet far more residents have been affected by the forces of development for "regional growth." Paul Hampel and Mark Schlinkmann, "Sudden Storm Shattered Homes, Lives," *St. Louis Post-Dispatch*, Local section, April 23, 2011, http://www.stltoday.com/news/local/metro/article_266793e0-821e-5437-bbcc-232c64be82b2.html. Displaced residents from Carrollton shared sentiments similar to those of the tornado victims; see Jami Desy Schoenewies, *56 Houses Left: Destroying Homes since '92* (blog), http://56housesleft.wordpress.com/.

Sign painted on a Kinloch car wash business contests local tax increment financing (TIF) incentives as unfair, 2010

For Kinloch and Carrollton, these prosaic mechanisms generated fatal local insecurities while reproducing environments suited for externalized capital accumulation. For example in Kinloch, the airport's noise-mitigation plan was rhetorically packaged as an aid to residents and imposed regardless of the fact that they had always lived with the noise of incoming and departing planes. It was hardly accidental that these measures eventually allowed changes in the land-use designation from residential to industrial, rendering Kinloch available for larger scales of outside development. While the mitigation plan's land acquisition program was "voluntary," by the time it was instituted, few had options but to sell, due to Kinloch's longer-standing suffering from inequities in social support and revenue distribution in the county and region.[15] When basic cable services were installed in neighboring areas during the 1990s, for instance, they were not installed in Kinloch, leading remaining residents to speculate that regional authorities were already planning their community's future destruction.[16] Recently, Kinloch's only polling location was moved outside of the jurisdiction, compromising residents' abilities to access and practice their rights to vote.[17]

Carrollton residents, who were also accustomed to the noise of the planes, received letters between the early 2000s and 2006, notifying them that their property would be purchased using powers of eminent domain. Prior to the start of demolition shortly thereafter, many may not have been aware that local leaders had passed legislation effectively paving the way for these actions. For example, one 1999 bill proposed and passed in the Missouri House of Representatives suspended constitutionally protected zoning rights, exempting the airport authority from adhering to local land-use laws in cases of property acquisitions for airport expansion.[18] The mandated purchases that followed in Carrollton happened haphazardly, following no set pattern of demolition. Residents whose land had not yet been purchased because of various delays and funding issues lived as "hostages" on deserted blocks for months, unable to sell their property on the private market and waiting for the government buyouts.[19] Such destabilizing incidents are subtle, yet insidious; collectively, they reduce a person's ability to be informed of and participate in government and democratic processes. Erasure is embedded in these banal events that can de-legitimate place without due process.[20]

DESIGN'S EMERGENCE

In countless cities like St. Louis, built landscapes are rapidly leveled in schemes to attract what Keller Easterling has termed the logistically efficient "spatial products" of speculative capital.[21] The erasure machine seemingly churns with or without designers' engagement, yet the very nature of the client-designer relationship tethers the livelihoods of architects and urban designers to private capital investment. Rem Koolhaas famously admitted this when he remarked that architects hold a contemptuous yet covetous "hypocritical relationship with power."[22] This fact raises questions about architecture's self-referential concerns for visibility in connection with the "making invisible" of entire communities. Is such a focus ethically untenable? Perhaps it is

15
In the 1950s, when Carrollton was growing into a modern, fully equipped suburb, Kinloch remained without sewers, sidewalks or street lights until the latter half of the 1960s. In fact, Kinloch was *founded* by way of systemic exclusions. Prior to 1948, Kinloch was part of a larger territory. Over time, as its African American population grew, and as local leaders came into positions of power, they gained voices on the district school board. In 1948, Kinloch was backed into incorporation out of isolation because its white neighbors legally broke away to create a separate jurisdiction and, with it, a separate school board. See Wright, *Kinloch*, 105, 110.

16
As told to Alana Fields by an anonymous resident in an unpublished interview, March 2010.

17
Norm Parrish, "Kinloch Protests Polling Site in Berkeley," *St. Louis Post-Dispatch*, Metro section, March 2, 2006, B1.

18
Missouri State House Bill 971 St. Louis Airport Expansion (Shelton) was voted *do pass* on April 21, 1999. The bill allows a suspension of zoning rules as protected in the Missouri Constitution. The bill summary states, "This bill allows the City of St. Louis to construct, reconstruct, or expand an airport or landing field on property owned by the City of St. Louis notwithstanding any land use plan or applicable zoning of any county, city, or special charter city." A review of other Missouri Senate and House of Representatives bill proposals and hearings between the period 1995–2010 reveals multiple legislative actions tied to the noise-abatement programs and economic incentive zones created to spur airport development. Missouri House of Representatives Bills database. www.house.mo.gov; accessed October 2010.

19
As told to the author by former resident and *56 Houses Left* blog author Jami Desy Schoenewies in an unpublished interview, August 1, 2011.

20
A draft scheme from 2010 entitled "Proposed Land Use Measures" identified additional large tracts of land surrounding the airport for future land-use changes termed "recommended corrective measures." Other legislation has ensured that special incentive areas, including a Tax Increment Financing Zone, a Business Enterprise Zone, and a Foreign Trade Zone, will protect and spur private development investments around the airport. For erasure's legitimization, the mere potential for privatized capital accumulation is necessarily valued higher than existing spaces serving communities or the environment. In this way, these territorial enclaves are justified, even though they intentionally and undemocratically exempt private businesses from the tax rules that most residents are obliged to follow. Lambert–St. Louis International Airport website, Noise Mitigation and Land Management section, http://www.flystl.com/AboutLambert/NoiseLandManagement.aspx, accessed September 2010.

21
Keller Easterling, *Enduring Innocence* (Cambridge: MIT Press, 2005), 2.

22
Rem Koolhaas and Bruce Mau, *S,M,L,XL*, ed. Jennifer Sigler (New York: Monacelli Press, 1995), 967.

time to reevaluate how designers might operate *amid* the processes of global capital and stratagems of law in order to better discover, advocate and reinforce the self-organizing potentials in every community.

The geographies of erasure urbanism are often predicated on a limited conceptualization of development that suggests intolerance for diverse scales and uses, since these are seen as potential elements of resistance and conflict. Investors prefer clean slates devoid of the risk and complications that can drive unplanned costs up; in this model, established neighborhoods are unpredictable variables. To prevent capital risks, erasure becomes an ordering mechanism whereby the "chaos" of public life is rebranded through clearing, replaced by new and sometimes imaginary "orders" of predictability and protections that promise dependable revenue streams for a select few. When the revenue fails to materialize, or even if it does, the imperfect and conflicting former order of habitation has been replaced by debased land values and barren tracts or generic ubiquity.

Scales, economies, interests and modes of use that are deemed incompatible with this view of growth are eliminated rather than approached through critical and creative thinking about how urban alterities might be articulated and addressed. If we embrace the views of sociologist Manuel Castells, who suggests that conflict is a necessary component in the shaping of cities and urban meaning, then the kinds of friction we expect between an existing neighborhood and a new development might be anticipated and embraced. When spaces are inflected with competing agendas and pressures so great that they are threatened with complete erasure, designers might draw on Colin Rowe and Fred Koetter's notion of urban collage,[23] for example, or the more recent urban editing techniques proposed by Jacqueline Tatom. Tatom reminds us to draw from what is, instead of assuming what should be, so that design might "focus on *what might be*, given a progressive agenda of change."[24] If resistances are conceptualized as constitutive and productive motivators of urbanization rather than as obstacles to progress, design might facilitate and enable productive forms of agonistic exchange.[25] By identifying and integrating potential resistances, design can reframe development's engagement with local life, leading to richer projects serving an expanded constituency—the resident public—in addition to a corporation's own bottom line.

23
Colin Rowe and Fred Koetter's Collage City was a strategy for countering the modernist era's isolated spaces devoid of human scale and texture. In this context, collage becomes an instrument for sampling from multiple existing urban conditions in order to achieve richer, more integrated urban environments. Colin Rowe and Fred Koetter, *Collage City* (Cambridge: MIT Press, 1978), 65–83.

24
Jacqueline Tatom, "Programs for a Metropolitan Urbanism," in *Making the Metropolitan Landscape*, eds. Jacqueline Tatom and Jen Stauber (London: Routledge, 2009), 195.

25
Manuel Castells, "The Process of Urban Social Change," in *Designing Cities*, ed. Alexander Cuthbert (Oxford: Blackwell, 2003), 23–25.

AGENCY

At the turn of the last century, Ebenezer Howard challenged the perceived dichotomy between town living and country living, noting that while each condition was a "magnet" with specific benefits, neither choice was ideal. Illustrated in his well-known "Three Magnets" diagram, his solution to the binary paradigm was a hybrid town-country magnet, which proposed a tertiary typology of settlement. Rather than focusing on aesthetic mandates, his Garden City proposals articulated

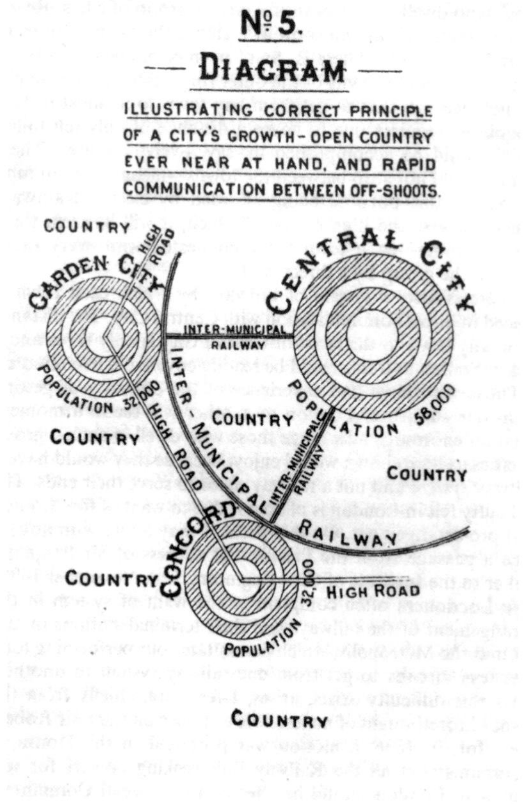

Ebenezer Howard, *Garden Cities of To-Morrow*, c. 1902

principles of spatial relationships. In particular, his model relied on literal programmatic adjacencies that juxtaposed "conflicting" land uses while guaranteeing open space between the garden cities and the central city.[26]

Using Howard's framework as a base, I propose an updated scenario, where Howard's original "city center," "garden city/suburb" and the connecting "main road" infrastructure are complicated by capitalism's invisible infrastructural overlays—the logistics of freight, air space, campaign financing dollars, subsidies, political deals and related legislative trajectories—that superscribe a place and that Miwon Kwon has termed its respective "locational identity."[27] When made visible, these previously immaterial infrastructures become a new dimension of a site and present new opportunities for architectural action within the explicit and underlying processes transforming places like Kinloch and Carrollton.

In an echo of Howard's question, "Where will the people go?," today's magnets are recast to ask, "Where will the revenue go?" Does it flow outward through mechanisms of erasure, or does it meet the needs of local life at costs to regional "growth"? In the spirit of Howard's blended model, how might revenues flow toward both?

26 Ebenezer Howard, *Garden Cities of To-morrow* (London: S. Sonnenschein & Co., 1902).

27 Miwon Kwon, "One Place after Another: Notes on Site Specificity," *October* 80 (Spring 1997): 85–110.

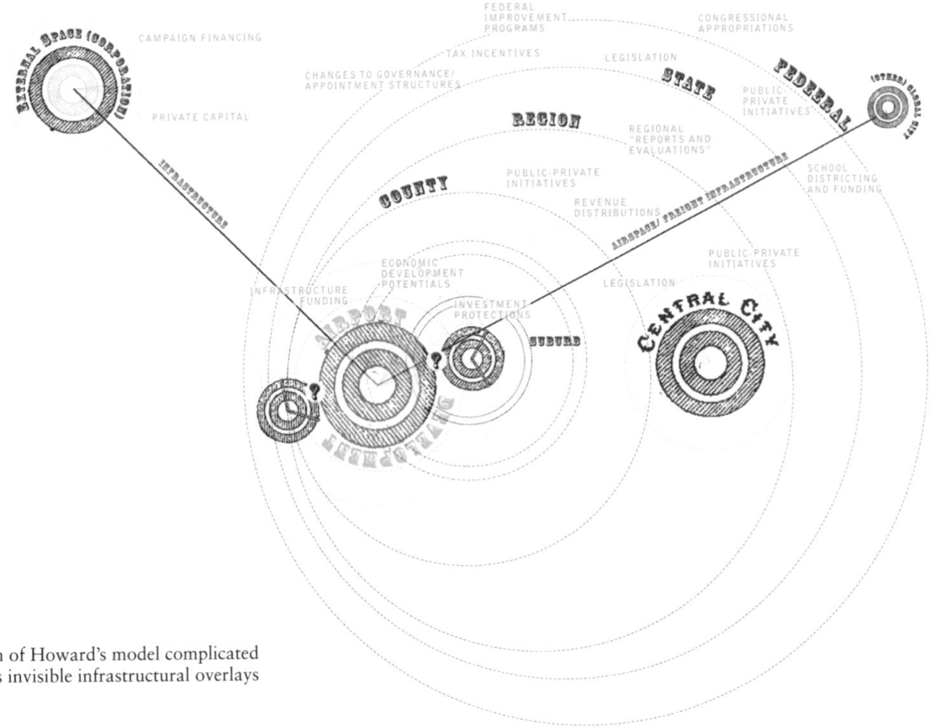

An application of Howard's model complicated by capitalism's invisible infrastructural overlays

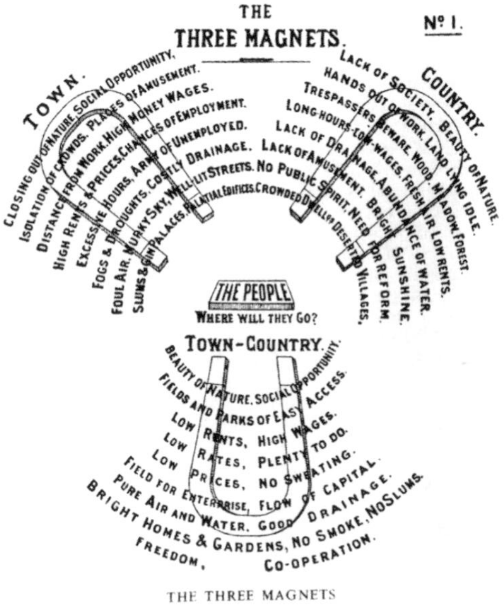

Ebenezer Howard, *The Three Magnets*, c. 1898

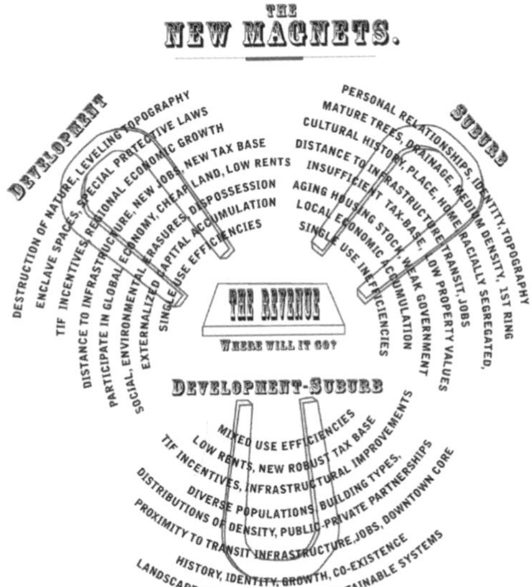

Patty Heyda, *The New Magnets*, c. 2011

Contemporary designers might then envision alternatives to erasure's absolutes by advancing an amalgamated infrastructural typology that merges economic improvement with the specific characteristics that define a local place. As an expanded articulation of Howard's "hybridization," this contemporary model proposes new possibilities for recombining developments and suburbs across multiple scales and territories, both visible *and* invisible. Functioning first and foremost as an operational proposition, the twenty-first-century development-suburb paradigm could open multiple routes for navigating capital's dominant procedures by infusing design into legislative or economically incentivized protocols. Such creatively reimagined protocols could then bolster existing communities or re-democratize dispossessed land. How might Kinloch be repositioned under land ordinances that upheld true notions of "public" in policies of ownership and control? What if legal directives were infused with locally specific spatial, aesthetic or performance criteria? Could tax policies be scalable to leverage longer-term regional goals with more precise and transparent aid at local levels—beyond rhetorical claims of "bringing jobs"? What are the possibilities for governance and policy making where residents, rich *and* poor, have an equal voice?

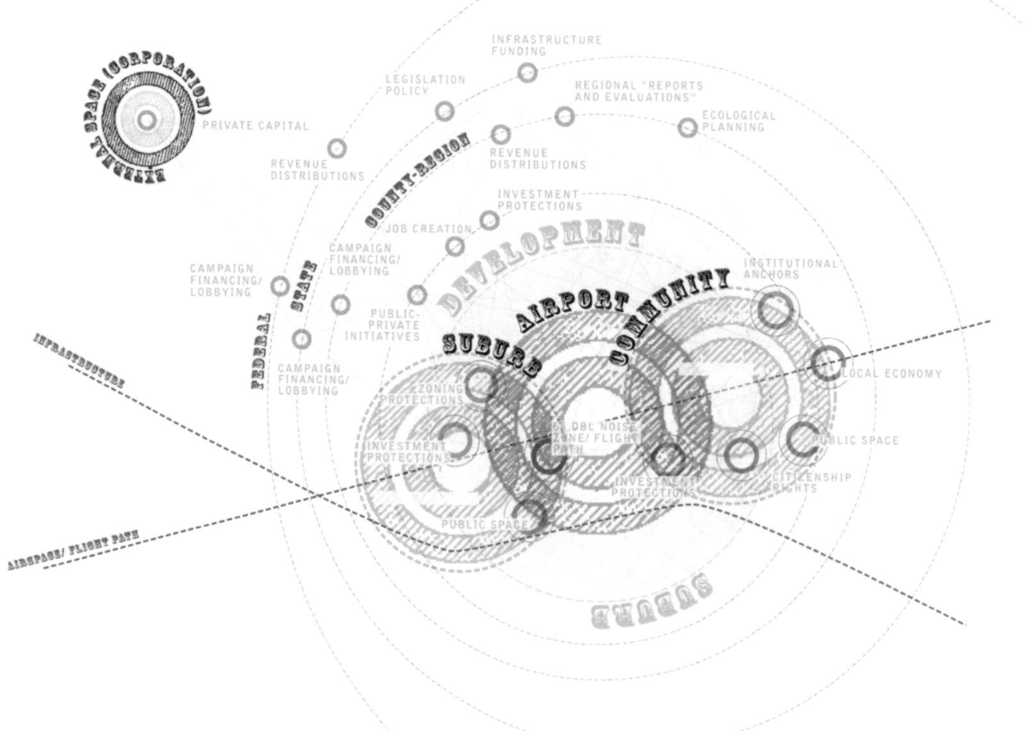

Hybrid Development-Suburb

28
Schoenewies, *56 Houses Left*

The updated development-suburb hybrid is an organizational diagram for locating relationships and spaces where designers might productively complicate the public-private project. The model articulates sites like those around St. Louis's airport as places of complex territorial contestation marked by the dynamics of multinational development corporations and city-regions vying for capital. This designation directs and opens new territories of design action. My call for design's different participation in processes of suburban urbanization aims to counterbalance capitalism's fetishization of efficiency with other strategies that ultimately reinforce democracy and redefine typical notions of eminent domain and public space. The hybrid model seeks to reposition the designer in contexts of erasure urbanism *before* physical clearing, such that design functions as advocacy in fields formerly marginal to the discipline: the legislative, logistical or political domains where erasure begins. A proactive, citizen-oriented public process for architecture and urban design emerges whereby designers might work more productively—and earlier in systems of development—on behalf of the public realm.

In this reclaimed view of urbanization, we might also ascertain a different kind of value in erased landscapes like those of Kinloch and Carrollton, despite the compromises of meaning and place that have been inflicted upon them. Retooled and reconstituted modalities of place have, in fact, emerged in the wake of erasure, even if these remain marginally visible and fragmentary. Jami Desy Schoenewies, a former Carrollton resident, created a blog titled *56 Houses Left* to document the destruction of the last fifty-six of the two thousand homes to be cleared in the runway expansion project.[28] With Carrollton's entirety gone, the website has become a virtual reemplacement of the lost community and a valued space of social interaction for other displaced residents. Likewise, the churches of Kinloch, perched in the midst of overgrown vacant fields, have attracted relocated residents to return to Kinloch for Sunday services. These traditional neighborhood "anchors" still serve as catalysts for social and cultural exchange, despite their disconnection from residential space. They remain potential loci for the further repositioning of these spaces in a new, hybrid model of development.

A church still stands in Kinloch, 2010

29
Howard wrote, "How shall it grow? How shall it provide for the needs of others who will be attracted by its numerous advantages? Shall it build on the zone of agricultural land which is around it, and thus for ever [sic] destroy its right to be called a 'Garden City'? Surely not. This disastrous result would indeed take place if the land around town were, as the land around our present cities, owned by private individuals anxious to make a profit out of it. For then, as the town filled up, the agricultural land would become 'ripe' for building purposes, and the beauty and healthfulness of the town would be quickly destroyed. But the land around Garden City is, fortunately, not in the hands of private individuals: it is in the hands of the people: and it is to be administered, not in the supposed interests of the few, but in the real interests of the whole community." Howard, *Garden Cities of To-morrow*, 19.

Ebenezer Howard predicted the loss of public space as a casualty of privatized growth. In his Garden City proposal, he suggested that his new city-suburb model might flourish without the loss of valued public space by upholding an administrative process dedicated to maintaining the interests of the community.[29] Howard's prediction has played out in municipalities like Kinloch and Carrollton in more complex ways than he might have ever imagined. Nonetheless, his emphasis on the preservation of a democratic mandate as a necessary protection of place is a critical reminder to us all. Urban design and architecture must not only counter "bad aesthetics" but also challenge its own complicity in urban dispossession. In short, design must reimagine how it may prevent the erosion of our collective political, aesthetic and affective rights to inhabit and feel secure in a place. This kind of creative process will rely on our own recognition that architecture may not always produce visible products, but might instead seek to reframe and redesign the dominant political narrative that maintains erasure as a sanctioned mode of contemporary urbanization. Making visible the making of invisibility is the first step toward this goal.

The Nebulous and the Infinitesimal

A CONVERSATION BETWEEN D. GRAHAM BURNETT AND DAVID GISSEN

D. GRAHAM BURNETT In the 1927 edition of *Paterson*, William Carlos Williams delivered himself of that great admonition to the metaphysically inclined: "No ideas but in things." His warning weighs on our theoretical aspirations. And so, for this conversation, David and I have decided that we will try to move under, or perhaps out from under, the spell of this materialist mantra. We are going to get to ideas, *if* we get to ideas, *only* from things. The format? Tag team. I'll go first, and talk about a thing that seems germane or otherwise moved my spirit in connection with our assigned topic, "the nebulous and the infinitesimal," and then at some point, I will "tag" David and he will do the same. After a few of these iterations, we'll see where we come out. I certainly won't try here to set up any theoretical grounding for such a performance, since that would seem rather to foreclose on the whole idea. But suffice it to say that there is a theory sniffing around down there somewhere, and we'll see if we flush it out in the next forty minutes.

I begin with the magic of plumbing, and thereby draw your attention to what I will argue is the architectural instantiation of concern for the infinitesimal at its most numinous and uncanny. Every Catholic church, both now and basically since the fourth century A.D., contains within it a very peculiar apparatus which is called the piscina, or sometimes the sacrarium. It's a small sink, now generally located in the vesting rooms where the priest and the altar boys prepare themselves for Mass. It looks like an ordinary sink except that it is covered with a lid and is usually kept under lock and key. The piscina was developed as a feature of the architecture of the Christian church in almost direct connection to the formalization of the doctrine of the "real presence" in the Eucharist.

One of the basic problems of thought is the relationship between immanence and transcendence. Catholicism concentrates this conundrum in the doctrine of transubstantiation, which sets out to explain how what appears to be an unleavened wheat wafer could, in fact, be the "real presence" of Christ. The *real* presence—so that the words "this is my body," said at the consecration, are, in one line of Christian doctrinal development, understood not metaphorically but literally. Though what it means to be "literal" in this context, when the properties of that wafer remain constant—that is, when the sensory information you might derive from that object seems to indicate that it remains an unleavened wafer—has been a main driver of some of the most sophisticated philosophical work to be done in the last two thousand years. Without reprising the full history and legacy of the Fourth Lateran Council (which is, anyway, beyond my ability), we can simply note here that for Catholics this doctrine is a core orthodoxy of the faith and not a free topic of dispute. It is also, despite the recondite character of the technical theology, a gateway to some perfectly concrete and terrifying problems of the infinitesimal.

So, if I've just said the Mass and I've consecrated the Eucharist, I've touched the Eucharist. I presumably have, on my fingers, some very small particles of the Eucharist—and those particles are, in fact, particles of God, in a nonmetaphorical way. This fact raised, from very early on, cataclysmic problems of disposal. How do I wash under those conditions? How would I wash anything that came into contact with such a holy thing?

The sacrarium is the solution. It is a sink, which, from its earliest introduction in churches (probably as a *détournement* on a traditional baptismal font), was directly piped into sacred ground. Its conduit leads down to a kind of sepulchral space deemed suitable to the disposition of divine residue. There are some that were piped out to the sacred ground of the graveyard and there vented. As time proceeded, there were more of them built, in a sense, *over* a sepulcher—a final drywell that was under the foundations of a church.

What can and can't go into a piscina, and under what circumstances, is, again, a nice theological question. But I want to leave you, for starters, with the piscina as an object, and ask you to reflect on it in its peculiar historicity: across most of the Middle Ages—in fact, from the fall of Rome to the rise of modern systems of sewage—indoor plumbing was effectively unknown in Western Europe as a means of sanitary evacuation. So I put to you a counterintuitive observation: plumbing was preserved across roughly 1,700 years of Western history, not as a mechanism of cloacal disposal but rather as a mechanism of sacred preservation. Tag.

David Gissen So, trying to focus on *things*, and continuing to talk about drainage, I'd like to discuss a thing that speaks to a lack of drainage—puddles. I suppose I'm cheating because I'm talking about a thing—a puddle—but I'm going to provide a few examples of this thing and its role within the history of architecture. While I was putting together the book *Subnature*,[1] I kept thinking about how to talk about these types of things that are infinitesimal and nebulous—how to write about things like puddles or dust. It's not easy.

When you think of images about drainage, particularly in the history of modern architecture and cities, you often think of images that speak to an optimization of the city's flows. For example, the famous sections of Pierre Patte, or the underground, dimly lit photos of the sewers built by Baron Haussmann, both of which influenced Le Corbusier so much. But in addition to images that emphasize conduits and flows, we also see a series of images that position stagnancies—the lack of drainage—as theory. These puddles—which is basically what they are—emerge as interesting sites of stillness, and they literally conjure up additional images within their stagnant surfaces. There are two images that were made at roughly the same time, that I think present some new, less instrumental, ways to think about drainage, and that suggest how the image of drainage—literally, the water that's released off buildings—might somehow figure within the discourse of architectural history. Here, we have two images: the first, made in 1964 by Michael Carapetian, is of the Economist Plaza; the second image, of the Bauhaus, was made roughly at the same time by Leonardo Benevolo, an Italian architectural historian.

1
David Gissen, *Subnature: Architecture's Other Environments* (New York: Princeton Architectural Press, 2009).

Alison and Peter Smithson, Economist Building, London, UK, 1965. "The Man on the Economist Plaza." Photograph by Michael Carapetian, c. 1964

Walter Gropius, Bauhaus, 1925–26. Photograph by Leonardo Benevolo, c.1970

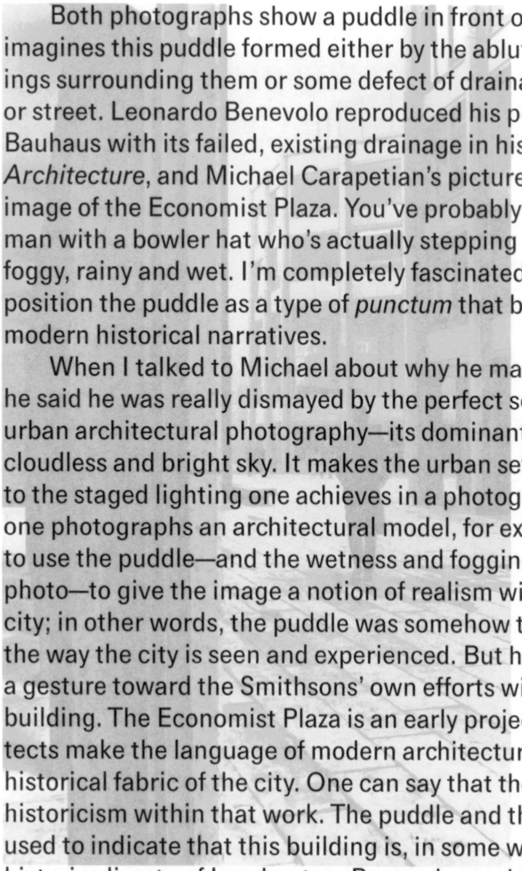

Both photographs show a puddle in front of these buildings. One imagines this puddle formed either by the ablutions of the buildings surrounding them or some defect of drainage within the plaza or street. Leonardo Benevolo reproduced his photograph of the Bauhaus with its failed, existing drainage in his *History of Modern Architecture*, and Michael Carapetian's picture became *the* dominant image of the Economist Plaza. You've probably seen it: There's a man with a bowler hat who's actually stepping into a puddle and it's foggy, rainy and wet. I'm completely fascinated by these images that position the puddle as a type of *punctum* that breaks through various modern historical narratives.

When I talked to Michael about why he made that photograph, he said he was really dismayed by the perfect settings one sees within urban architectural photography—its dominant image of the fixed, cloudless and bright sky. It makes the urban setting of a building akin to the staged lighting one achieves in a photographer's studio—where one photographs an architectural model, for example. He wanted to use the puddle—and the wetness and fogginess that pervade his photo—to give the image a notion of realism within the context of the city; in other words, the puddle was somehow the *real* in relation to the way the city is seen and experienced. But he also wanted to make a gesture toward the Smithsons' own efforts within that particular building. The Economist Plaza is an early project in which the architects make the language of modern architecture an extension of the historical fabric of the city. One can say that there's a prefigured historicism within that work. The puddle and the foggy sky were also used to indicate that this building is, in some way, relating to the historic climate of London too. Benevolo used the puddle to recast historically significant buildings as occupying our time—not as sacred objects in a book or as one of many modern and completely mediated structures (in the ways described by Beatriz Colomina, for example). The puddle enabled him to depict the building as being simultaneously within and outside the platforms of architectural mediation. It's still within media, because it appears in a photograph in a book; but it offers a fleeting glimpse of something somewhere—besides the pages of a history book—without offering up a sentimental image of locale and place specificity. So in both ways, a puddle is one of many possible unsentimental indexes of site and realism within architectural history and in its photographic depictions. Tag.

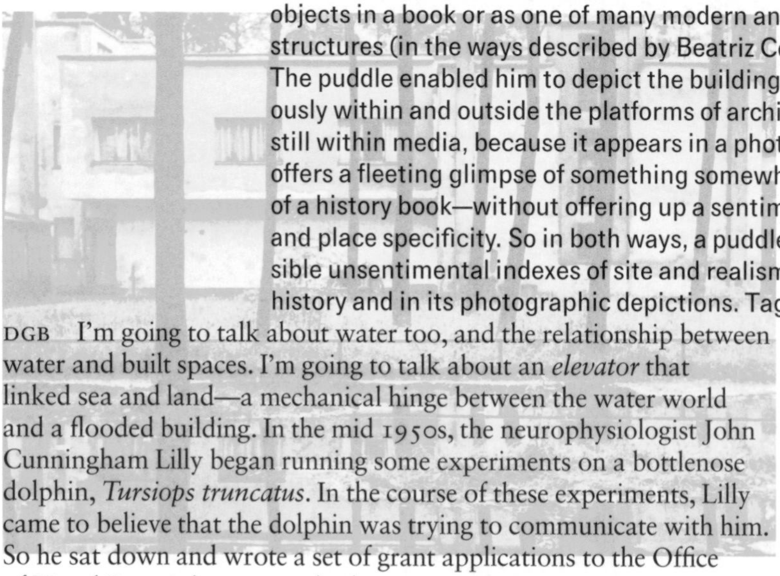

DGB I'm going to talk about water too, and the relationship between water and built spaces. I'm going to talk about an *elevator* that linked sea and land—a mechanical hinge between the water world and a flooded building. In the mid 1950s, the neurophysiologist John Cunningham Lilly began running some experiments on a bottlenose dolphin, *Tursiops truncatus*. In the course of these experiments, Lilly came to believe that the dolphin was trying to communicate with him. So he sat down and wrote a set of grant applications to the Office of Naval Research, NASA and other government agencies to support a dolphin research program. He put the dolphin forward as a very promising model organism for thinking through how we would "break through" to a nonhuman species—i.e., extraterrestrials.

It might be surprising to us now, but this flew, and he raised enough money to build a dedicated laboratory in the U.S. Virgin Islands, which he called the Communications Research Institute (CRI). Across the period from 1961 to 1965, he undertook, in this space and on government contracts, a set of experiments with cetaceans, testing their communicative abilities and concurrently examining their capacity for echolocation, sound fixing and ranging, and other things that interested the Navy.

Meanwhile, Lilly was tuning in, turning on and dropping out in a Learyesque way. He had first made use of LSD in connection with experiments in veterans' hospitals to increase the sensitive responsiveness of patients undergoing psychotherapy, and he came to believe that LSD was a very powerful psychotropic agent for enhancing communicative possibilities between subjects. It was also good for breaking recalcitrant (read "enemy") agents; the CIA experimented with the drug in that capacity in those years. Lilly thus came to believe that it might also be good for making a researcher commensurate with his experimental subject. To that end he combined LSD with another bit of Cold War technoscience that was about to make the same transit across from the military industrial complex to the swampy territory of the counterculture: the isolation tank, the use of which Lilly had pioneered at the National Institute of Mental Health (NIMH). One of the main questions of this period, as far as the Cold War sciences were concerned, was "What would happen to a subject absent from any sensory input for a long period of time?" Lilly worked on this problem as part of a larger project to break into, or, indeed, possibly just to break, an enemy agent (and/or an alternate intelligence). But the weird thing was he came to find that in those spaces he felt really *good* and really *strange*. Especially listening to stereo headphones. He began to figure this must be something like the *Umwelt* of the dolphin, our aquatic familiar. So Lilly hung in the isolation tank at CRI, wired up to the dolphin tank, and he *tripped*.

In the incandescent endgame of this story, Lilly wanted to meet the dolphins in their own world. So he arranged for his laboratory to be cantilevered over the dolphin pools, and he flooded his working space to make it dolphin-friendly. A slinglike elevator dipped down into the holding pond, and lifted the dolphins into the lab space, where they could flop along in the shallows of a shared dolphin-human domesticity. The plan was to have the elevator operated by the dolphins themselves, but this never worked out. The Navy got wind of the weirdness and pulled the plug.

The dolphin elevator: I think of it as a kind of stent, holding open that occluded and nebulous passage that links nature and culture, science and fantasy, human and animal, inner space and outer space, mind and madness.

Yes, Lilly was a consultant on the movie *Flipper*. Tag.

DG We'll continue to talk about architectural technology, and my thing will be the Ford Foundation atrium garden, which is something that interests me quite a bit. The Ford Foundation building was designed by Roche-Dinkeloo Architects in the late 1960s. Have you been to this room in New York City? It's a semi-public atrium space filled with plants and greenery. Kevin Roche and John Dinkeloo proposed this atrium space in their initial design and asked the landscape architect Dan Kiley to design it. No one had grown a landscape quite like this inside an office building before. This was during the rise of the climate-cooled "HVACed" building (heating, ventilation, air-conditioning). This type of climate engineering was built into virtually every office building in New York City, and standardized through protocols like "the comfort zone"—that is, the idea that every worker in the office will have a 70 degree and 50 percent humidity environment. Kiley was brought into this context and said, "Let's grow a forest within the space. But since the comfort zone in this building is fundamentally about providing a comfortable, functioning environment for a human being, how do I think of the comfort zone as a context or an environment for plant life?" To understand what this could be and how it might work, Kiley turned to a Dutch colonial botanist named Fritz Went, who studied plant life in a space he called a phytotron, a facility in which he examined the growth of plants and made idealized atmospheres of urban and nonurban contexts; for example, he studied the ideal temperature, humidity and artificial sunlight conditions for tomatoes. Went believed that if you standardized the environment for a plant, you could standardize the plant! Kiley was very influenced by Went's exceedingly mechanical vision of biology, but where Went began with the plant, Kiley essentially reversed the process. Given an environment—the office building's comfort zone—Kiley's task was to assess the possibilities for life within it. Kiley reasoned that the 70 degree and 50 percent humidity environment was like the Virginia Shenandoah landscape. He assumed that the same kind of plants would grow in the atrium. As a result, a lot of the initial species of plants he introduced, such as maples and oaks, were from the Shenandoah Valley area.

Well, the trees died. Not only did they suffer from the bits of pollution that made their way into the HVAC system (no HVAC system can be completely rid of pollution), but they experienced enormous climate stress. While Kiley discovered that interior, architectural environments can be interpreted as a representation of some place—a fascinating observation of the comfort zone—he incorrectly identified the comfort zone's representational analog. What the landscape technicians who maintained the plants ultimately realized was that the temperature and ventilation conditions in the building were essentially tropical. So, they removed all the American woodland trees and replaced them with tropical trees that were grown and cut to look like the original species. When you visit the Ford Foundation today, almost all the species (ficus, etc.) look like the plants of the

Shenandoah Valley. It's a very WASPy organization, so they weren't going to give up on Virginia as their ultimate reference.

I think Kiley's innovation was to understand this air around us, in this room right now, as a representation—which also suggests that the air in this room is a thing. A much more important theorist of environment—Reyner Banham—regarded HVAC as either an assemblage of instrumental gadgets or as a counter-environment situated within and through technology. In the Ford Foundation garden, we see technology and the environment itself as having a representational and, frankly, monumental, character. What I find inspiring is that the environment within architecture, *made* by architecture, can have a monumental quality that is exhilarating in some ways, and makes us think about the environment very differently from the ways that we generally do: it becomes a form versus a mechanism or a flow. Tag.

DGB Should we do two more? Two more?

DG Okay, yeah.

DGB In 1958, Vannevar Bush, who was, at that point, probably the most powerful scientist in the world (having played a leading role in the Manhattan Project, and having been central to the reorganization of the American science and engineering community during the Second World War), turned his attention to a most improbable device. This was a person who had, at his command, the entire resources of science and technology as they were then practiced in the United States. And he set his mind on the *microtome*. A microtome is just what its etymology would suggest: a *thin-cutter*. It's the basic tool of a pathological anatomy lab: a salami slicer on a tiny, tiny scale.

Let's say you want to look at things that aren't transparent naturally, using *transmitted* light—in other words, you don't want to try to shine light on them and have that light reflect back up the microscope's tube, but rather want to be able to put light directly below the stage of the microscope and illuminate them *filmically*, which is much more efficient, especially when you start to have compound microscopes with higher magnification. To do this, you have to be able to cut a slice of that solid material thin enough to make it susceptible to the transmission of light in the visible range. So, until you have a microtome that allows you to make a microscopically thin shaving of an opaque material, you are limited in the level of magnification you can achieve in looking at a surface.

But this thing has been around for a long time by the 1950s. It isn't rocket science. Why does Vannevar Bush care? He has a very wacky new idea for a radically novel kind of microtome, which he realizes in prototype, though it never enters large-scale manufacture. So, imagine, if you will, the shutter of a movie camera transformed into something like a blade. And then imagine, cartoonishly, pressing an object, salami slicer–like, against that whirring blade. Imagine each of the shavings that comes off, as that blade whirrs, being immediately applied and fixed to a piece of 35mm film running through the device.

What you could do, then, is take a tidbit—say, the heart of a mouse—embed it in paraffin, set it on the stage of the microtome, and press a button. What would ribbon out is a strip of 35mm film, each frame of which is a sectional thickness of that mouse heart, each no thicker than a single cell.

So, what you have here, I would argue, is something like the reification of our desire to experience a world liberated from matter—Bush's "automatic" microtome had the power to convert all solid things into a receding dance of diaphanous veils. The ostensible advantages of the device were that it enabled you to print off a set of these images for demonstration purposes using the same technologies that you'd use for copying a film—so you could transfer directly from the real to the photorealistic via simple projection. It also allowed you (in principle) to do histological stains using the same techniques used for the development and fixing of emulsions in filmic processes. But, given that the device met no actual need in the period and was eventually abandoned, I think it's more interesting to understand it as a very peculiar robotic reification of a perennial visual fantasy: the flight of the eye through solid things. Tag.

DG So we're supposed to be somewhat manifesto-like, right?

DGB Go.

DG You talk about linear trajectory of the eye. The next thing I'm going to talk about is related to this. The vector: it's that thing that instructors of environmental architecture tell you that you have to draw to make a building green or sustainable, but it's also that thing that you draw to depict any flow in and through a building. In an environmentalist context, it shows the air moving in and out of buildings. We can trace vectors to seventeenth-century drawings of mechanical objects and their operations. It eventually enters into fluid dynamics. Today, it has become the visual, representative language of the infinitesimal and the nebulous in architecture, right? It becomes the representation of air; it becomes the representation of water; landscape urbanists use it to represent schools of fish. We often represent these things and others as flowing or moving, using the language of vectors. And yet, I want to give a manifesto, in three minutes, against the vector, because I think that the vector ultimately reduces everything to pulse. And while I'm sympathetic to the vision of the world and the city as flow, it is not how I understand myself to experience it. I imagine the environment, again, always as some kind of representative or monumental feature.

When I look at a photograph of the smoke over Pittsburgh from the early twentieth century as an image of air, I don't think the vector has anything to tell us relative to that image. I think we look at that, we understand that there's something about the sky over our heads, and we occupy a very different sky when we stand in Pittsburgh today. The air of the past takes on a monumental, representational character. It's the air of another time. To draw air as vector—or any other "flow"—is to deny that representational possibility of our environment. Within architecture, we don't have a visual representative language to think about our environment under the historical terms within which we think about the environment every day. When people talk, today, about reducing carbon emissions to their levels of thirty years ago, it's really a historical argument. If we reproduce the sky over our head, like it was thirty years ago, somehow there will be salvation, right? If we recreate streams, or recreate brownfields, into something that's green and verdant, we'll return the earth itself into some preindustrial, premodern form. The vector cannot articulate that historical mentality that lies within our contemporary discussion about environment, nature and change. And so, I would love to see an architecture that deals with the environment, with nature, that can drop the vector, whatever that might look like. Tag.

DGB I want one more just because of the "sky over our head" line. What I hope is going to happen is that maybe in the closing movements of the conversation now, we might turn a little bit to self-consciousness about what it is to move from objects to the relationship between sense and signification.

So, you've got your Platonist readings of the basic pathology of the relationship. You've got your hopeful Aristotelian adequation of these registers. And, of course, you have Christian apologetic accounts that spool out across two millennia in both the Platonic and the Aristotelian modes. Some of these tell you that the relationship between the thing I touch or see and the idea that I form of it is akin to the miracle of the incarnation (something like the original "transubstantiation"). In my view, that's a very exciting, Bonaventurian reading of the way matter and spirit could be entailed to each other. Admittedly, for those without an appetite for such things, it's a pure mystification—even madness. On the other hand, you have stranger but, in some ways, more easily rehabilitated accounts that come, in part, out of the anti-iconoclast writings of the early Middle Ages. I'm thinking of Saint Theodore of Studium, for instance, who suggests that what happens in that relationship between the sense of the thing and the making of ideas isn't a mystical transmutation of essence, but a kind of "economy" of participation—a redistribution or circulation of a shared element.

This latter sort of argument is what undergirds those theories that tried to protect and defend the power of icons. It's not, according to this view, that the icon is a fraudulent picture of God (and therefore must be destroyed, since it's simply a bait for our illusion). It's, rather, that God has, in Christ, a kind of circumscribable form, and that the icon participates in that space that can be circumscribed. As a result, a genuine icon circulates within the larger economy of the Divine Being. If we know how to bring ourselves to the icon properly, we can, in fact, participate in the Divinity and there is a kind of exchange between us: a trade, if you like. We are in the "trading zone" of spirit and matter. This story, which is, in its proper philosophical constructions, alien and perhaps rebarbative, nevertheless might be salvageable, in that it seems to promise a way to reimagine the relationship between thought and matter. In these strange ideas we detect a mighty aspiration: an extravagant, even desperate, desire to overcome the terrible dialectic between ideas and things. To go back to William Carlos Williams: "No ideas but in things." But what would that look like? What would it be to have ideas in things? We don't think things, right?

I can't resist offering one more real, concrete story that is something more than a metaphor for how the "clouds over our head" (the space of ideas) and the way before us (with its impedimentary objects) could be set into a mutually reflecting and, at the same time, enabling relation.

I need a date again: 1822. The year that saw the publication of William Scoresby's two-volume *Natural History of the Arctic Regions*. Scoresby was a whaler who spent his life chasing down bowhead whales near Spitsbergen in the first decades of the nineteenth century. He was also a philosophically inclined person who didn't think of himself merely as a grubber in whale oil. To prove his elevated capabilities, and to reflect his admission to the Royal Society, he composed a vast repository of philosophical knowledge about the Arctic, which was one of the main texts upon which Melville drew while writing *Moby-Dick*. Scoresby presented, in a section on navigating pack ice, a fantastic account of how the whalers of Hull learned to find their way as the freezing sea began to close over at the tail end of the season. He described a particular kind of atmospheric condition, which was by no means universal, but was like a kind of salvific grace when it was obtained. Imagine: you're in the crow's nest of a whale boat; you're trying to find your way out through the Greenland straits before the winter ice packs you in tight enough that you may end up having to walk out (if you're lucky). And the question is, how should you navigate through what is a shifting maze of block ice ahead of you? You can only get up so high; maybe you can see a dozen miles from the crow's nest to the horizon. How do you see beyond the horizon line? In the atmospheric condition that Scoresby could not explain, but which he had himself experienced (and which Melville, too, talks about as "looming"), the reflected light under the cloudy sky could actually throw up onto the underside of the clouds a nebulous and difficult-to-read, but nevertheless legible, *reverse image of the patterns of pack ice beyond the horizon.*

DG A representation.

DGB Right. So you're looking up, and what you're seeing is, if you know how to read it, a pattern of what's below, what's *ahead*. And that was how they found their way out, when the meteorological graces permitted. It's a version of "looking up to see down" that seems promising, at least metaphorically, as we to try to think through this business of thoughts and things. Do we immolate objects into the sweet smoke of their meanings? And if not, how do we keep them present as the sacrificial fires of signification are lit? Part of the game here, in this conversation, was to erect an ekphrastic cabinet of curiosities. Should we get wood, put it on the altar? Say what we *mean*?

DG What interests me about that is that one of the ways that architects in the last ten years, in particular, have transmitted their interpretations, their aesthetic sense of objects and things, has been through history. History has played a very vital role within our profession. It's one of the sites in which we can witness a kind of vanguard thinking about architecture. So, now that we have all this truly enormous historical knowledge, what do we do with it? We've been warned, those of us who have been trained in this discipline, that we should not instrumentalize our history, which is to say, simply, that you shouldn't make buildings by approaching historical assessments as scripts for future works. Nonetheless, this historical mentality is everywhere, in terms of the writing in architecture, right now. One of the things I'd like to suggest is that our largely historical mentality, within which we see, may begin to reinform the object itself. But in informing objects, I'm not imagining an instrumental relation between object and text. Rather, I want to imagine an object that takes on a historical character—but in a way quite different than, let's say, a nineteenth-century historicist building. Here I'm going to bring up some specific examples: if you look at the work of Philippe Rahm, a Swiss architect who reconstructs historical atmospheres from the past, or the work of Jorge Otero-Pailos, who preserves the dust that history has left on buildings, history is becoming the content of architecture. But this is not an explicitly populist postmodernism. We're seeing a historical reflection, on the object, pushed back onto the surface of the object; it's "history without historicism." So it's a reflection of a historical mentality, but it's not one in which you say, "That's a classical building." The interpretation and the thing exist *within* each other, similar to how you described it, but history is very important.

DGB "History without historicism." That's a very elegant formulation of the historicity of a cabinet of curiosities, right? It is only historicism that can "redeem" the merely historical aggregation of past particulars, and it does so by affording that dreaded (if also irresistible) *theoretical basis*. As theories go, it's pretty flat-footed, but it is big and powerful and flat-footed. Historicism can thump just about any solid proposition, *mano a mano*. That is the Nietzschean point: there are no definitions, only genealogies. Are you really willing to live in that world? It should feel a little odd. The only out, as far as Nietzsche was concerned, was art. And, indeed, perhaps this "history without historicism" play that you say is happening in architecture parallels a certain kind of pseudo-anti-historical "play" that's happening in contemporary art right now, where the archive becomes a medium for artistic works, or creative types navigate and generate historical records, and historically oriented "research practices" are characteristic of certain forms of artistic life. All well and good, except I do think at a certain point, the old-school critical thinkers are going to put to us the question: Isn't this just so much miscellanea? Isn't this ostensible *omnivorousness* just the recrudescence of a simple kind of bourgeois, self-stroking with *mucho* do-dads? Do-dads that are kind of, "*Oh! How, um, curious! [cue frisson] How … interesting!*"

DG It has a pretentiousness.

DGB Well, it might be even worse than pretentious, which is, at least, a kind of style. We might be looking at something closer to the dreaded *death-by-a-thousand-medium-sized-dry-goods*, you know? And right there we're back again at the basic problem, which is *particulars*. Things. Dumb things. They don't say anything. You just aggregate a bunch of freaking *things*, and then what?

DG Obviously, the word "bourgeois" is extremely loaded, right? Because it talks about not only pretense, but frivolity, and a certain kind of audience, of a particular class. But, just to pick up on that point specifically, you can also see the examples I brought up as part of a working-class history. You can see it as neo-Marxist. If I'm going to preserve the dust of a factory in a city, I'm acknowledging the indices of a certain form of labor that no longer exists in the city. Today, when I watched workers washing the Bank of Montreal building, they're creating an *image* of a building that reproduces the post-industrial sky under which it sits: the sky that no longer has smoke. They're making that building a reflection of the sky overhead. And I think developing a curatorial or preservation-oriented approach toward pollution, of all things, is far from bourgeois. In fact, I would say that it definitely brings imprints of a history that is gone in every American city, which is both an industrial and a working-class history, back in and through an architectural image or form of representation. So I think we need to look more closely at the material at hand, and see how these imprints potentially enforce our memory of certain forms of economy and labor that don't appear as meaningful aspects of a city's history. Personally, I think that's very far from a kind of middle-class city. It's only upper middle class in the sense that we recognize that this doesn't exist anymore in any kind of productive, economic fashion.

DGB OK, so, politics. We get to politics. But only in *things*. So, tag me, I want one more *thing*. [Tag]

I want *dots*. 1946. Rome. The semi-fascist Italian philosopher of art Cesare Brandi is the founding director of the Istituto Centrale per il Restauro (the Institute for Restoration), which had been created under Mussolini to help restore the grandeur that was Roman *imperium*, back at a moment when that was much on Mussolini's mind. "Restoration," however, had a very different feel after the war, since it meant trying to put back together the shattered artistic heritage of Italy. It is in this context that Brandi develops, and eventually publishes, his "theory of restoration." Brandi's theory is one of the really weird and wonderful folds in the fabric of modernism, and it is an effort to place the relationship between the present and the past (at least in architecture and the arts) on a firm philosophical footing. He was basically a Hegelian, out of the pessimistic, Neapolitan, Benedetto Croce school. As such, he believed that restoration has been painfully split between two camps.

"Empirical" restorers had a kind of *sprezzatura*, or clairvoyant gift, for imagining what ought to happen in that big, missing section in a damaged fifteenth-century painting. Let's say you have a lacuna, and it needs to be filled in. An "empirical" restorer would say, "I know what that should have looked like," and he paints it in. For Brandi, this is pure forgery.

On the other hand, you have the new "scientific" restorers, who are basically archaeologists. All they want to do is stabilize the damaged object, and put it back on the shelf. Say it's a broken pot: you don't try to remake the pot; you take the shards you've got, stick them out there, and say, "Look. There was once a pot, and this is what we have left."

Neither of these methods is right, according to Brandi. Why? Because the empirical restorers fail to understand the sacrosanct qualities of the original work; they corrupt it by mingling themselves with its historicities, and thereby violate its essential originality—which lies in the precise physical form taken by the sacrosanct *idea* of the original artist. All we have of the idea is the material instantiation of the fragments that remain. We can't mess with that. But the "scientific" restorers are even worse, because they don't understand what an art object is; that is, they think they're restoring an *object*, but they forget the *idea*. They just attend to whatever remains of the thing, but in doing so they fail to remember that these bits secrete an Idea—with a capital I; the Hegelian Idea—that demands attention. You can't just leave the painting stabilized in its damaged condition, because we can't actually see *the painting* if you just give us the canvas with this big hole in it.

Antonello Da Messina, *Ecce Homo o Cristo alla Colonna*, 1473, oil on panel, 48.5 × 38 cm. Piacenza, Collegio Alberoni (during and after restoration)

So, here's his unbelievably crazy and magnificent solution to this problem. It's all about the infinitesimal and the nebulous—remember those? Our themes for this conversation.

The solution is dots. Brandi developed a strategy for restoration, for "in-painting," that involved pure hues, unmixed pigment, and single strokes (nearly invisible, *pixilated* strokes), through which the restorer repainted the missing region, using only the kind of post-Seurat, high-modernist technique of optical blending to create mixed hues (and painterly forms). Why would you go through such a crazy process? Because what Brandi wanted to do was choreograph your experience of the work of art as an "idea" (super-historical, transcendent), and your experience of the work of art as an "object" (material, historical artifact), by f*orcing the in-painted image to dissolve, at a distance, into the painting.*

So, imagine, I'm standing ten feet from the painting, and the pixilated region looks exactly like the left shoulder of the Madonna. But once I come close, it resolves back into its pixilated form. At a distance, I grasp at the idea of the original work. Up close, I immediately discern the historical object of the original work. Back and forth. Past and present. Back and forth. Image and canvas. Back and forth. Idea and thing.

So, here is Williams's problem—"No ideas but in things"—moved from the monitory register of the *axiom* onto a plane defined by the axes of time and space. Thought or Matter? Spirit or Flesh? Forget it. Any fixed answer is going to be the product of *standing still*. But that won't do. You've got to *move*, baby. And *keep moving*.

DG Like in a *tag team*.

DGB Exactly! Like in a *conversation* ...

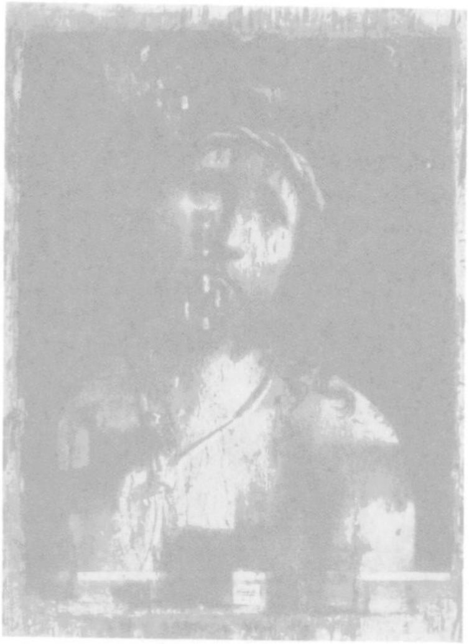

Reimagining Shrinking Villages

Marta Guerra-Pastrián
and
Pablo Pérez-Ramos

In absolute terms, the human population on the planet is growing. In relative terms, this global growth is often experienced locally as regional population loss, as previously tenable lifestyles and livelihoods are rendered archaic by a more interconnected socioeconomic culture. Moreover, regions do not simply grow or shrink: in most cases, they are rather polarizing, as some well-defined points attract people from broader areas that in turn cede their residents.

While additive philosophies that can be applied to growth and development exist in abundance, there are few conceptual frameworks for subtraction beyond moribund teleologies of decay and abandonment. Not even the paradoxical argument of so-called sustainable development applies: "development" has become synonymous with "growth," yet any process that considers growth the only strategy for improvement cannot be sustainable. Today the image of growth is so firmly anchored that any shrinkage can only be interpreted as a loss rather than an opportunity.

Architecture has also been operating within the assumption of limitless growth over the last two centuries. However, as Philipp Oswalt and Tim Rieniets have noted, after a projected zenith in 2100, processes of growth and shrinkage will reach a balance, and decline will become as common as it was before industrialization began.[1] If the premises of the discipline are still rooted in growth patterns that will progressively become less and less applicable, architecture as such risks its relevance.

1
Philipp Oswalt and Tim Rieniets, introduction to *Atlas of Shrinking Cities*, ed. Philipp Oswalt and Tim Rieniets (Ostfildern: Hatje Cantz, 2006), 6.

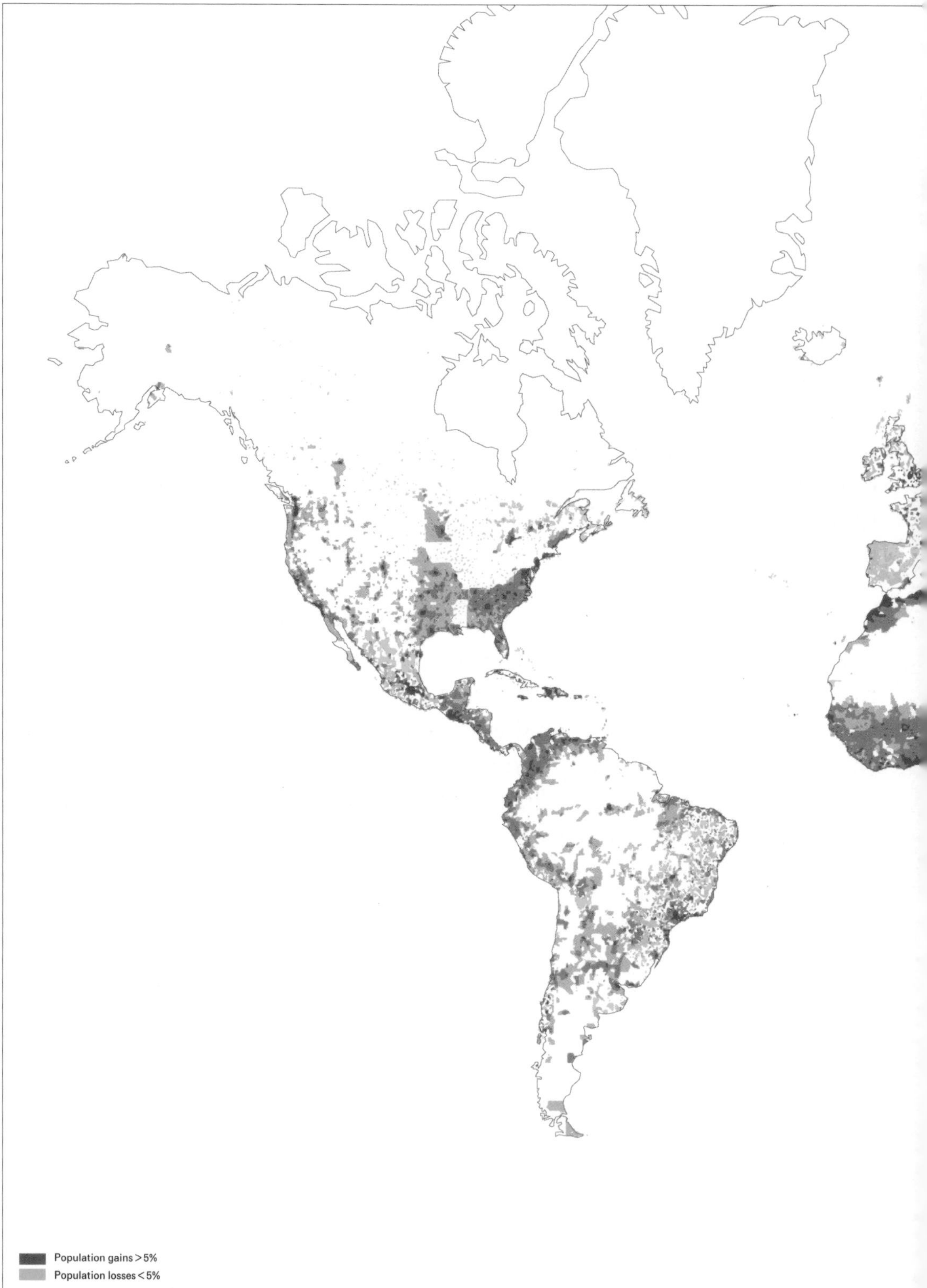

World's pattern of shrinkage and growth, population development 2005-2015.
Source: Center for International Earth Science Information Network (CIESIN), Columbia University, 2008.

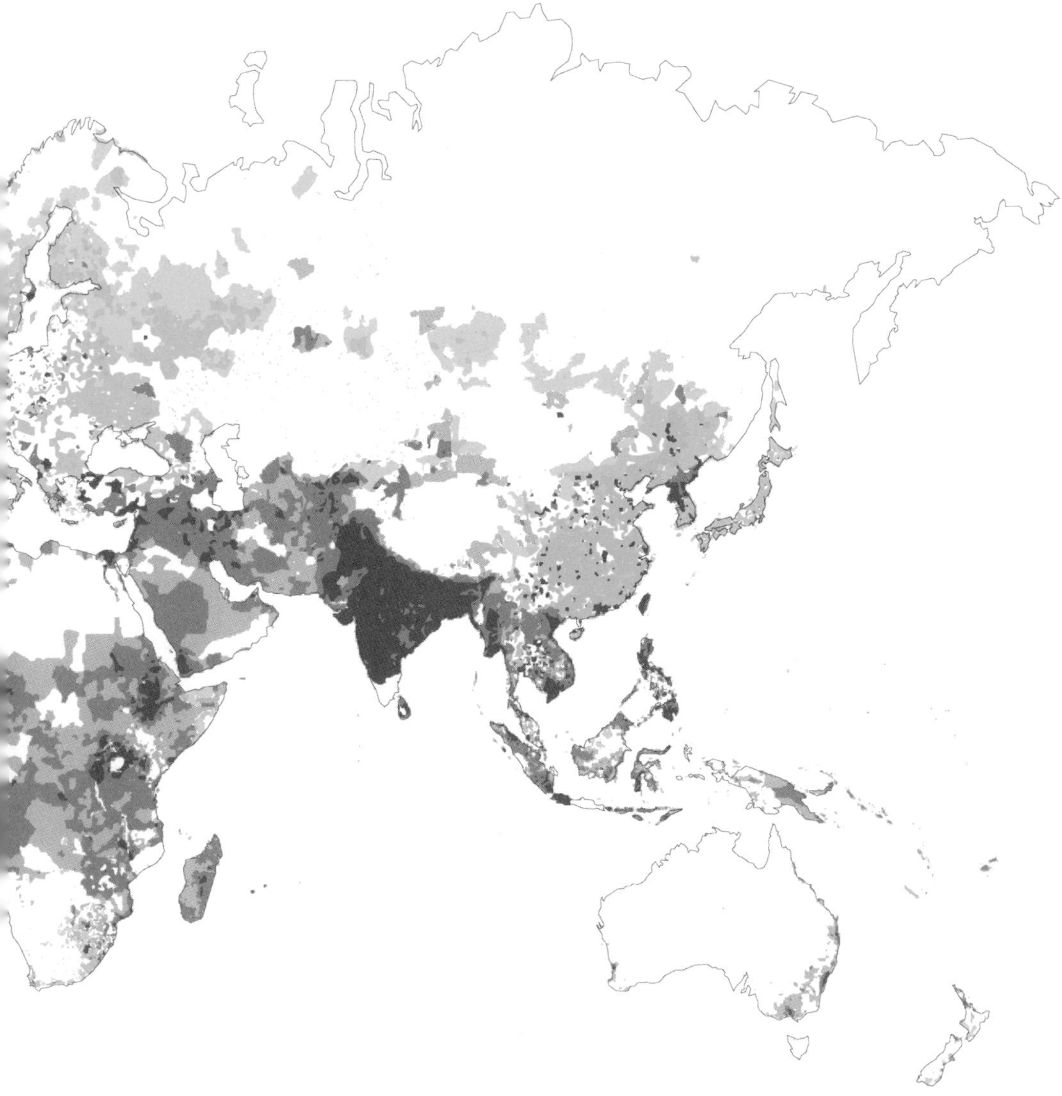

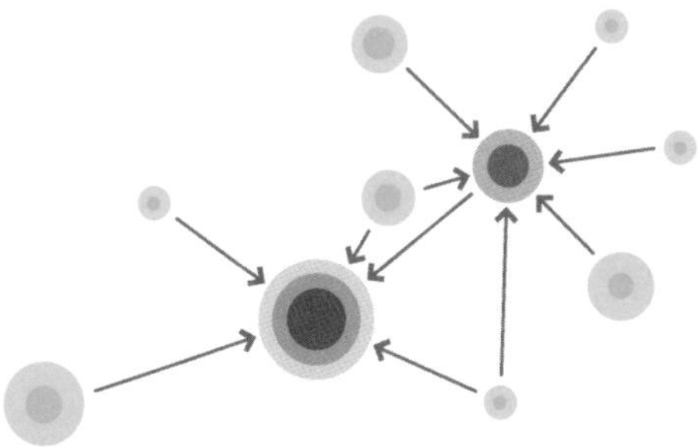

Polarization dynamics

In Spain, 2,600 villages across 8,100 municipalities had already been abandoned as of 2010, despite policies that have focused on retaining the rural population.[2] The policies have been ineffectual because they are rooted in economic and social studies developed under the general rubric of "growth," and they dismiss the essential and intimate psychogeographic bind existing in rural societies.

Rural flight in Spain has occurred steadily since the industrialization projects of the 1960s under the regime of Francisco Franco. The average age in rural areas such as Valle de Valverde, in the northwest, is 69 years, as opposed to 40.9 years in the country overall. Recent policies of territorial consolidation have merely accelerated the abandonment of arable land.

In the context of this unavoidable future, we propose that Spain's shrinking rural population can be treated as a field for a different kind of architectural performance.

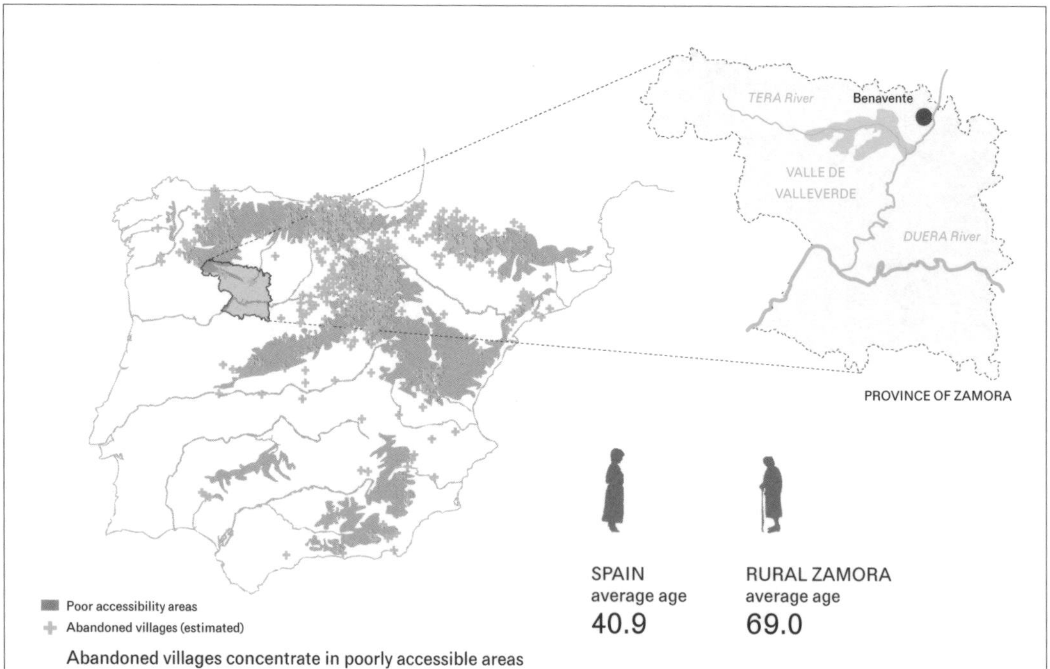

Abandoned villages concentrate in poorly accessible areas

2
Information compiled from Instituto Nacional de Estadística, accessed June 2010, http://www.ine.es, and from *Pueblos Abandonados*, accessed March 2009, www.pueblosabandonados.es.

VALLE DE VALVERDE: A CASE STUDY

Located in the province of Zamora, Valle de Valverde is organized along the Tera River and situated close to an important regional center. The valley's villages were never formally laid out; they cobbled themselves together in fits and starts after they were founded during the Christian reconquest of 722 to 1492. Each village covers an area of approximately 24 square kilometers, and its boundary nodes roughly correspond to the crossings of ancient paths.

Self-sufficient settlements like Valverde's villages evolved around agricultural production. Today, villages closer to fertile areas are able to maintain their productive status, while those in higher, less accessible, and more arid lands struggle to survive. Some infrastructural and agricultural elements appear repeatedly in the landscape and have progressively helped to shape built and social patterns.

Historically, three different productive landscapes can be identified across the Valle de Valverde:

The *dehesas* are the wooded pasturelands usually located on higher rises between villages with limited agricultural value due to poor soil and a higher exposure to wind and rain. *Dehesas* usually belong to the municipality, though residents may forage non-timber forest crops.

The croplands are areas around and between villages that have traditionally been shaped for large agricultural production. These landscapes are for the most part located in lowlands, sometimes associated with a watercourse, and are easily accessible from villages.

The orchards are located adjacent to and sometimes within the built edge of the villages. They are small plots, usually tended by women, which produce seasonal fresh food for self-consumption and trade with neighboring villages.

VALLE DE VALVERDE: A CASE STUDY

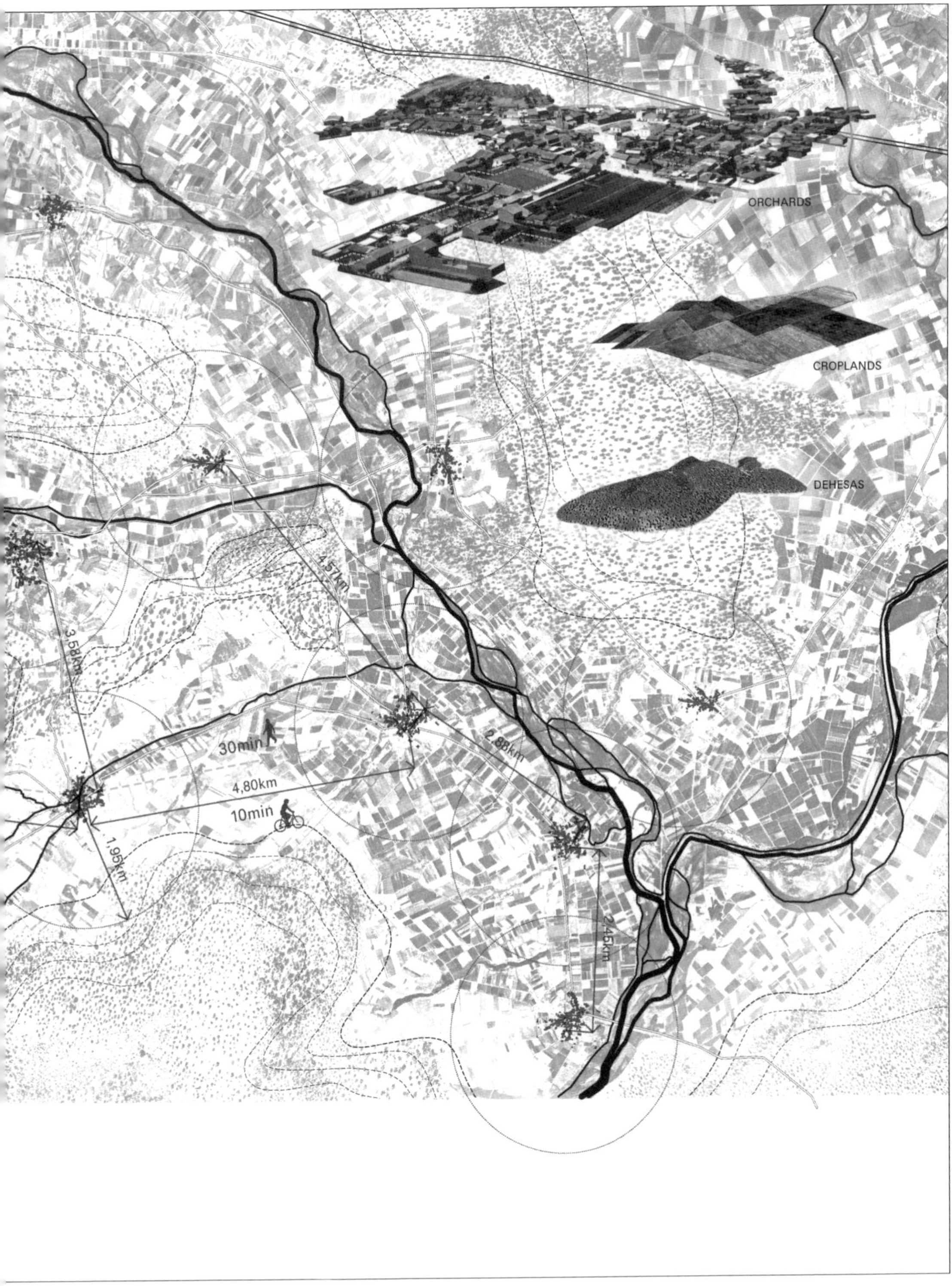
ORCHARDS
CROPLANDS
DEHESAS
4,57km
3,58km
30min
2,88km
4,80km
10min
1,95km
2,45km

VALLE DE VALVERDE'S EVOLUTION, 1950 TO TODAY TO 2025

During the postwar period of the 1940s and '50s, landscape cultivation was based on a model of self-sufficiency: large families provided plenty of labor, supported by livestock and independently excavated wells. Subsequent legacies and inheritance traditions divided these large properties into smaller parcels with each generation, successively impoverishing established families.

Over the 1960s and '70s, this atomization combined with processes of late modernization to produce a general rural flight into the emergent service-cities. The concurrent industrialization of both agricultural production and regional infrastructure favored the model of farm cooperatives. This change was also promoted by new consolidation policies, implemented from 1952 to 1982, that aimed to merge and redistribute agricultural holdings to increase production.

At the beginning of the twenty-first century, the rural population continues to dwindle and age, prompting the abandonment of farms and villages and accelerating soil erosion and other effects of lessening land maintenance. However, these phenomena also give rise to new opportunities for those who decide to stay and rent adjacent fields, fostering small-scale land ownership possibilities. In this context, depopulation and scalar shifts can become important components in reimagining Spain's agricultural landscapes.

In the future, a second wave of property consolidation could regroup the croplands into larger and more productive plots. Smaller properties and orchards closer to the villages or within their limits could remain for leisure gardening and community interaction.

Villages could keep their morphology, but spaces of production could be dissociated from dwellings. New patterns of land ownership could be introduced to eschew the failed model of large, self-sufficient agricultural families. Collective private ownership could exploit the land, attracting a seasonal and rotating workforce, while abandoned and undesirable plots could be purchased and reforested by the government. Other vacant plots could be more affordably valued and thus easily purchased or rented by enterprises which are less dependent on soil quality and more able to propose agrarian alternatives, such as greenhouse growing or aquaponics systems.

In addition to these land-use changes, we propose that a portion of Spain's national and European rural development funds[3] could be annually invested into the introduction of towers for this pilot project, a new infrastructural system that would initially provide certain services and eventually help to render the evolution of the landscape legible.

At the outset, these towers might host hubs for farmers' markets and remote irrigation controls that would break the spatial bind between owners and land: one could live in a larger town, for instance, and still irrigate one's crops at a remove. No longer limited to roads or water paths, infrastructure could extend to virtual network connectivity: Wi-Fi hubs located on the towers would alleviate isolation, allowing rural communities to access urban services and providing the possibility for rural residents to connect to remote jobs in the city.

3
The Common Agricultural Policy (CAP) is the current system of European Union agricultural subsidies and programs. Since 2000, there has been a Rural Development Policy, which aims to stimulate the economic, social and environmental development in the countryside. Its budget, 11 percent of the total EU budget, is today allocated along three main areas: improvement of the competitiveness of the farm and forestry sector, improvement of the environment and the countryside through support for land management, and improvement of the quality of life in rural areas, encouraging diversification of economic activity.

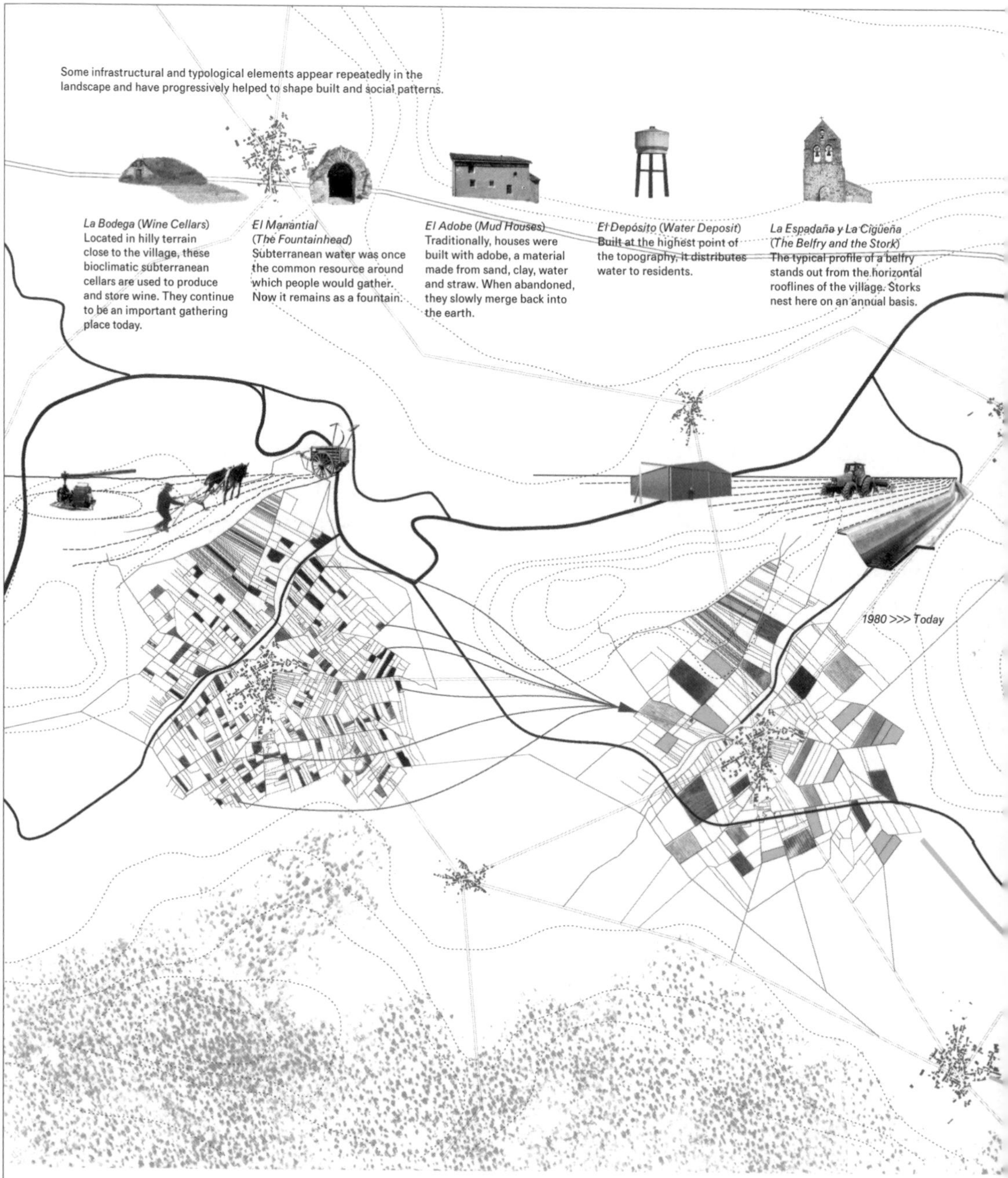

Some infrastructural and typological elements appear repeatedly in the landscape and have progressively helped to shape built and social patterns.
La Bodega (Wine Cellars) Located in hilly terrain close to the village, these bioclimatic subterranean cellars are used to produce and store wine. They continue to be an important gathering place today.
El Manantial (The Fountainhead) Subterranean water was once the common resource around which people would gather. Now it remains as a fountain.
El Adobe (Mud Houses) Traditionally, houses were built with adobe, a material made from sand, clay, water and straw. When abandoned, they slowly merge back into the earth.
El Depósito (Water Deposit) Built at the highest point of the topography, it distributes water to residents.
La Espadaña y La Cigüeña (The Belfry and the Stork) The typical profile of a belfry stands out from the horizontal rooflines of the village. Storks nest here on an annual basis.
1980 >>> Today

VALLE DE VALVERDE'S EVOLUTION
1950–TODAY–2025

€
THE PILOT TOWERS
A portion of Spain's national and European rural development funds could be annually invested into the introduction of pilot towers, a new infrastructural system that would initially provide certain services and eventually may help to render the evolution of landscape over time legible.
2015

VALLE DE VALVERDE 2050

Rural development programs may try to bring new populations to the countryside, but they make communities dependent on subsidies. Towers could ultimately help to accelerate what we might think of as a new form of "natural selection," forcing an even more unequal evolutionary future for different villages across the territory.

Over time, some communities may manage to reinvest government subsidies by gradually adding expanded capabilities to the towers such as satellite infrastructure, windmill power generation, electric car recharging stations, and so forth, fostering population and technological growth around them. The towers could become landmarks in a rural landscape that is being redefined in the information era.

On the other hand, weaker communities may not have the same advantages: villages that have not invested in using and improving their infrastructure may continue to disappear. The towers may even accelerate the abandonment of such terrain as these villages confront their inability to coalesce around new opportunities. In the wake of this depopulation, abandoned villages could provide space for new *dehesas*, areas of reforestation and ecological reserves.

In the face of population decline, the towers' geographically privileged network could allow them to evolve into alternate forms of ecological infrastructure: they could become mechanisms for registering climate change and surveying the landscape. Towers could also serve as seed and water storage units, refuges, and animal observation towers, fostering scientific research and resource conservation while contributing to the creation of a visual identity in the landscape.

VALLE DE VALVERDE 2050

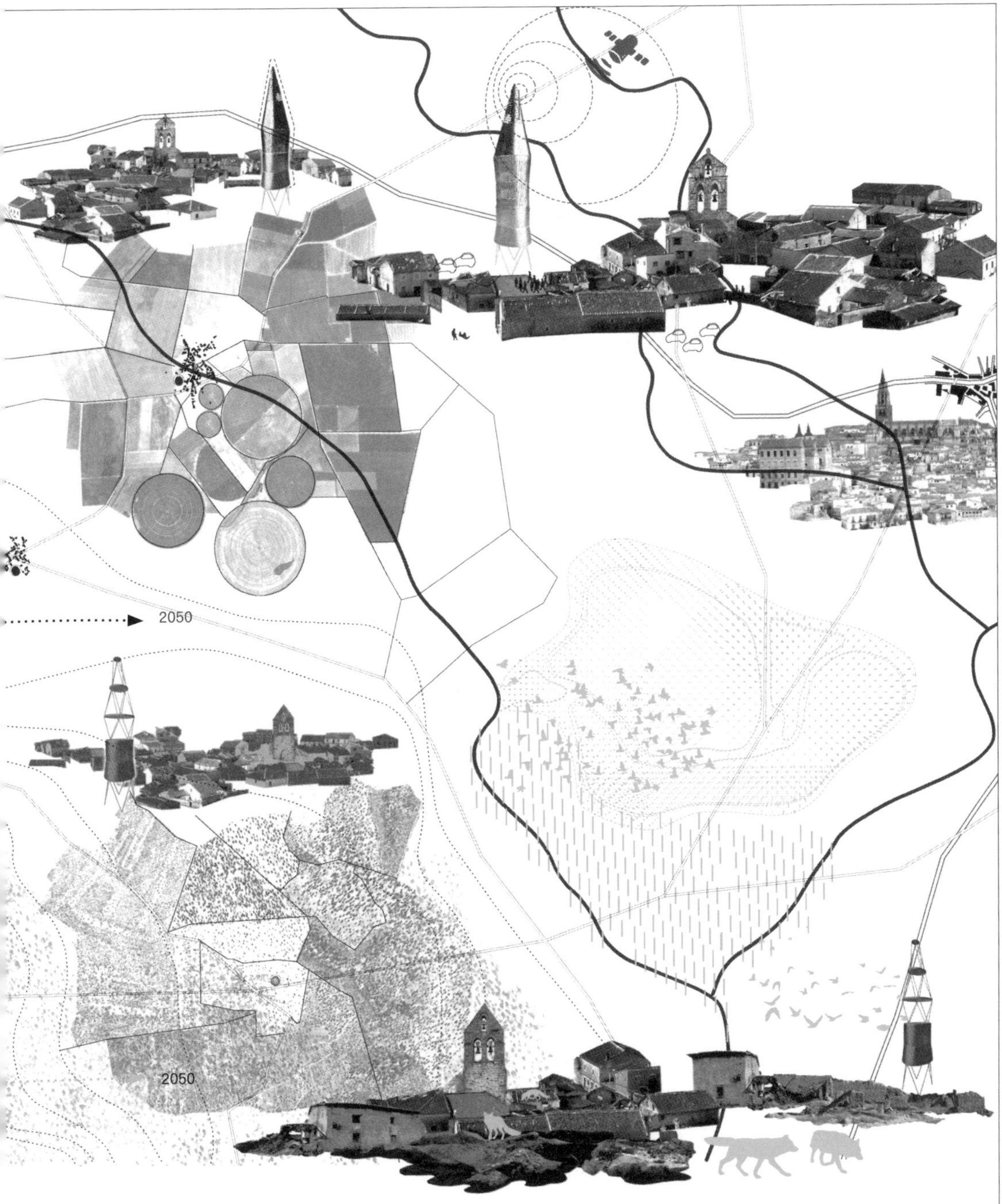
2050
2050

VALLE DE VALVERDE 2100

Division and individualism threaten shrinking villages, which could benefit from stronger social connections.

An infrastructural long-term investment in high-speed trains may serve as a trigger for regional population redistribution. Re-Link 2055, a holistic plan for restructuring rural Spanish territory, could be implemented in parallel with the existing and underutilized high-speed railway network and its future expansion. The plan could ask villages to describe their agendas and advocate for the changes that would be most material to their goals. Ideas from citizens, architects, planners and associations could be solicited to foster a national conversation about the programmatic transitions taking place in exhausted agricultural regions. Instead of focusing on the survival of existing rural systems, this effort could focus on new and hybrid programs.

A pan-municipal funding structure, distributed by the national Re-Link 2055 program, would allow platforms for farmers' markets, local wineries, rural tourism, summer camp associations, solar energy fields, reforestation areas and wildlife reserves in various municipalities to emerge as an amalgamated region.

A long-term investment in technology may trigger new social networks, which would enable villages to circulate information on prices, market areas, new ventures and pan-municipal programs. Virtual platforms for selling produce and livestock would reduce operational costs and overhead, allowing freelance professionals to work from rural environments.

Patterned "skins" for the towers could act as regional markers for the Re-Link 2055 plan. These changeable surfaces could communicate the unique programmatic agendas of each village to passersby and other settlements from a distance.

Towers in depopulated villages swallowed by reforestation and wildlife repopulation would take on new uses. Existing as cabins, seed storage units, or bird-watching towers in large expanses of *dehesas*, they would belong to a new ecological cycle.

Adapting to a variety of needs, the towers could be continually repurposed to facilitate programmatic strategies for the landscapes of Valverde, even after their human usefulness has altered beyond recognition.

REIMAGINING VALLE DE VALVERDE

Shrinkage creates spatial opportunities. From a homogeneously treated territorial panorama, it is possible to envision a meaningfully polarized country where villages and towns are no longer fighting the inevitable but rather embracing the new. By accepting shrinkage as part of our thinking process, we can imagine human-depopulated areas where diverse communities of flora and fauna have established themselves together with compact villages that have moved past a total dependence on agriculture for their survival. Different scales of intervention can respect the intimate attachment of inhabitants to their land while projecting a long-term planning strategy.

Whether shrinking villages remain inhabited or are abandoned, they offer potential to support both the programmatic performance and cultural value of emergent ecologies and future social orders.

VALLE DE VALVERDE 2100

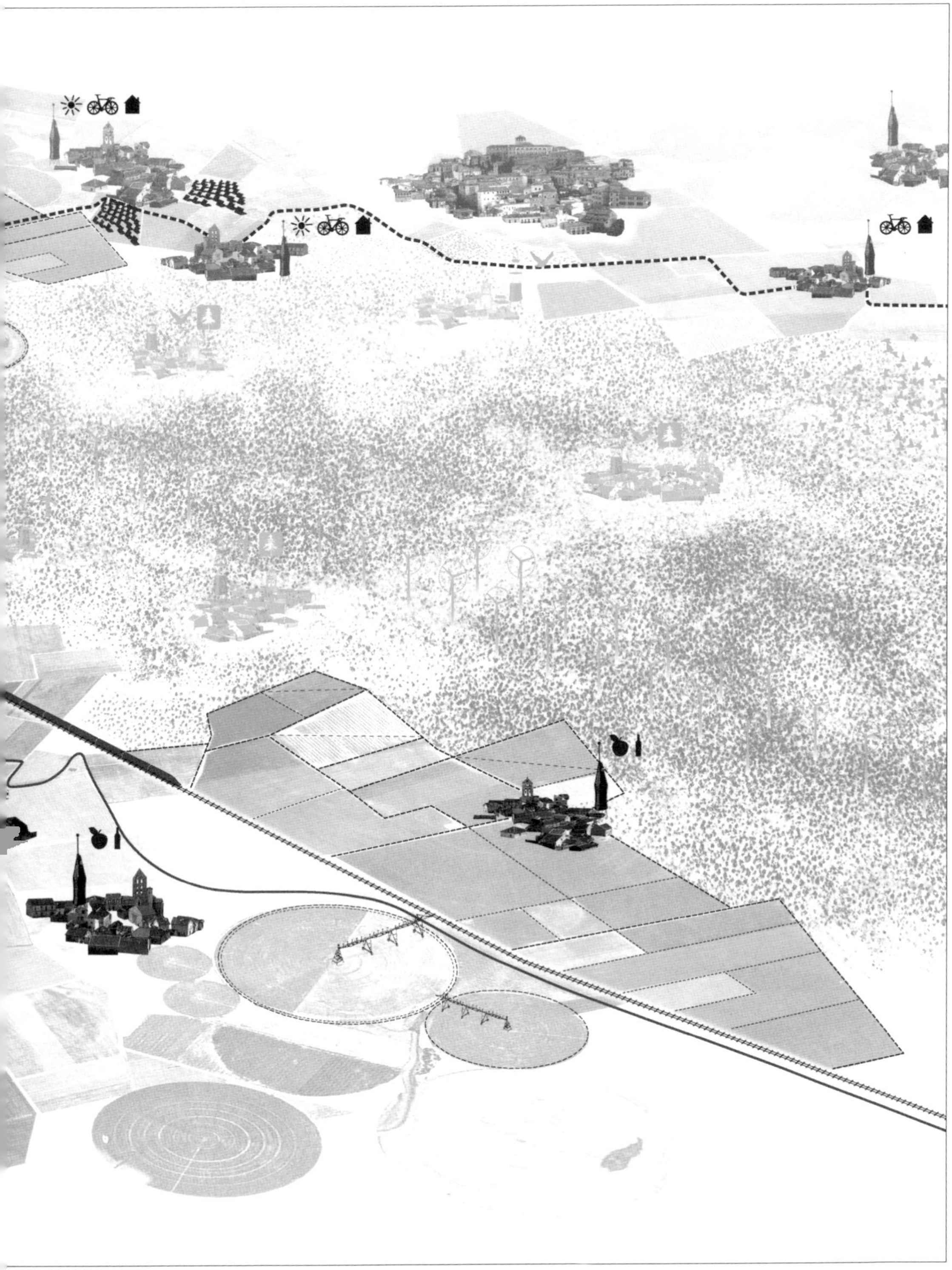

VALLE DE VALVERDE 2100

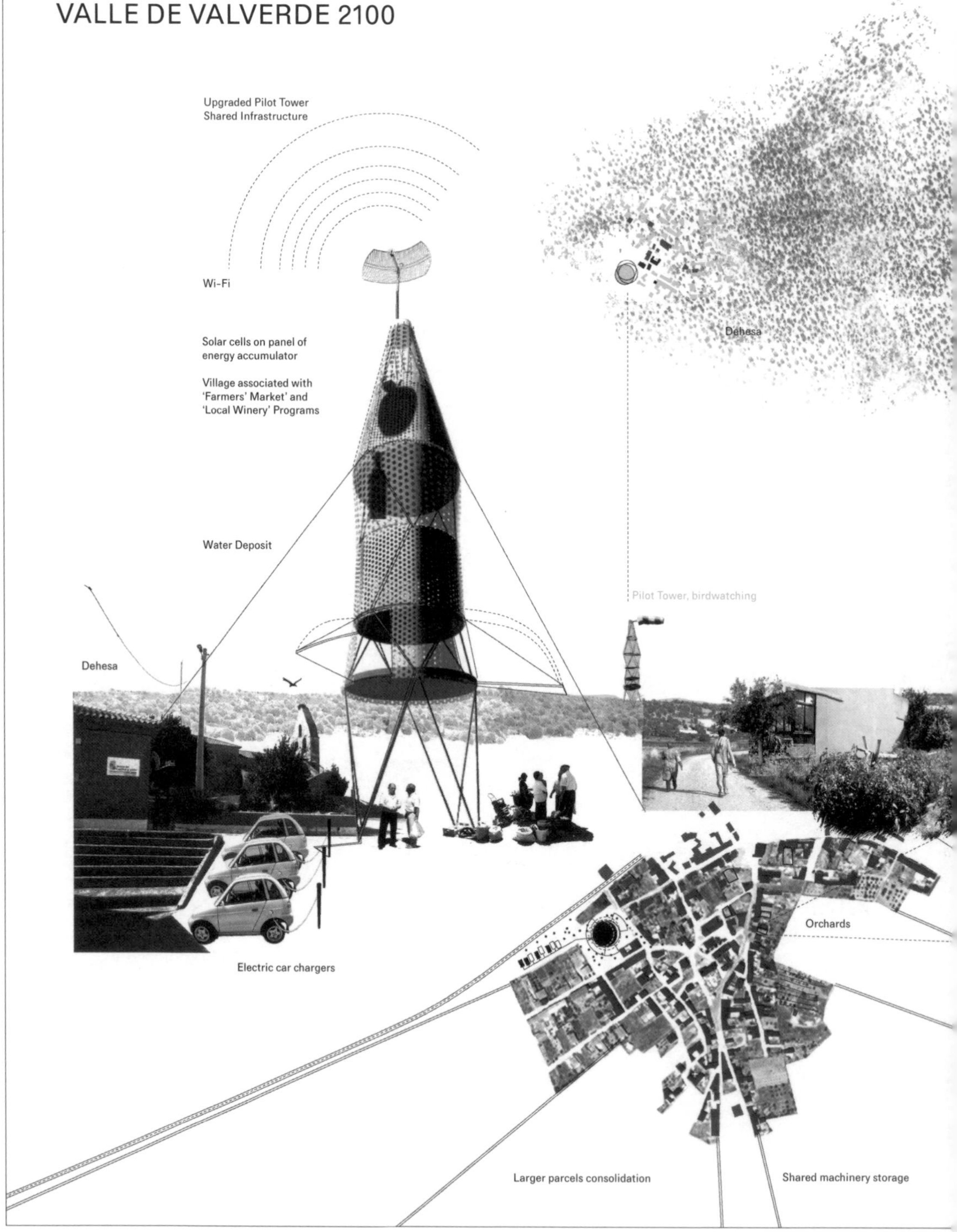
Upgraded Pilot Tower
Shared Infrastructure
Wi-Fi
Solar cells on panel of energy accumulator
Village associated with 'Farmers' Market' and 'Local Winery' Programs
Water Deposit
Dehesa
Dehesa
Pilot Tower, birdwatching
Electric car chargers
Orchards
Larger parcels consolidation
Shared machinery storage

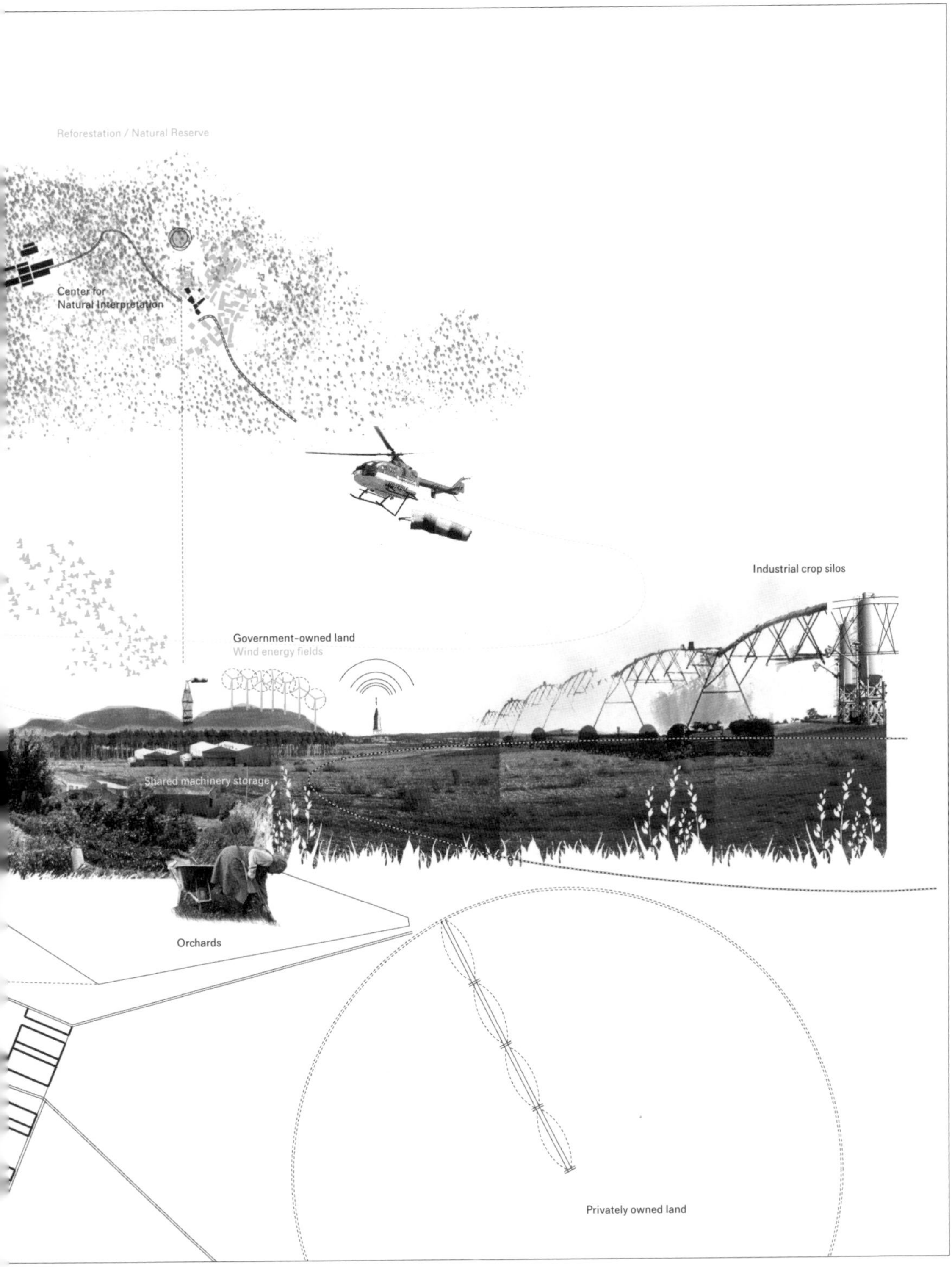
Reforestation / Natural Reserve
Center for
Natural Interpretation
Industrial crop silos
Government-owned land
Wind energy fields
Shared machinery storage
Orchards
Privately owned land

LESS AND MORE: ON THE POLITICAL POTENTIAL OF A VIRTUAL ARCHITECTURE

ADRIAN BLACKWELL

LESS AND MORE: ON THE POLITICAL POTENTIAL OF A VIRTUAL ARCHITECTURE

ADRIAN BLACKWELL

The contemporary world has been irrevocably refashioned by the rise of information technologies. It is only through the process of informatization and the explosion of computing power that post-Fordism's spatial and temporal forms can be surveilled and regulated.[1] New spaces have been structured by global supply chains based on outsourcing and subcontracting, while present temporality is tied to the contingencies of just-in-time production and precarious labor. The increasingly complex networks that organize our economic and social relations are so closely tied to technological advances that contemporary politics appears imprisoned by them. The bylines of the neoliberal ideology that emerged in the 1980s have been Margaret Thatcher's call that "there is no alternative" and Francis Fukuyama's claim that we have reached "the end of history," in terms of economic and political change.[2] Events such as the terrorist attacks in the United States on September 11, 2001, which seemed to move American politics toward a new authoritarianism, and 2008's economic crisis, which threatened to usher in a new Keynesianism, were both used by governments around the world as opportunities to deepen the hegemony of economics over politics. We live in an era whose apparent digital immateriality and flexibility only serve to further concretize a political system governed by the logic of the market.

The rise of information technologies has also significantly impacted architectural education and practice, making the computer the essential tool for the design and realization of buildings. In the early 1990s, the digital revolution finally affected tools of representation, as computer-aided design became the necessary means for architectural drafting. By the turn of the new millennium, computer-aided manufacturing added new complexities and capabilities to the interface between design and construction. Over the past decade, data visualization and mapping have produced novel analytical tools that position architects to expand their practices into parallel fields.[3] These three significant changes have opened up new possibilities for design and paved the way for the architectural renaissance of the last global real estate boom.[4] This intersection of architecture and economics is no coincidence, as the over-inflated property market that burst in 2008 was simply the urban dimension of neoliberalism's financial turn.[5] During this period of both technical and financial innovations, transnational design practices were closely tied to the whims of capital.

Many students, theorists and practitioners have described the informatization of architecture as a turn toward "the virtual" in an attempt to polemicize and theorize the new powers offered by digital practices.[6] In this context, the virtual does not simply refer to the digital as opposed to the physical realm, but also alludes to the liberatory potential these new tools of deterritorialization allow in terms of formal experimentation, construction processes and geographic scale. "Virtuality" refers here to the facility with which digital

1
This digital space has become so crucial to global political and economic processes that the U.S. government issued a "Department of Defense Strategy for Operating in Cyberspace" in July 2011.

2
Margaret Thatcher famously used the phrase "There is no alternative," shortened to TINA, to refer to her policies of economic liberalism in the early 1980s. The phrase "the end of history" was used by Francis Fukuyama to refer to the new status quo of economic liberalism in the early 1990s. See Francis Fukuyama, *The End of History and the Last Man* (New York: Free Press, 1992).

3
For examples of this phenomenon, see David Gissen, "Architecture's Geographic Turns" in *Log* 12 (Spring/Summer 2008): 59–67.

4
Dan Lewis, "The End of the Global Real Estate Boom?" *World Finance*, May 13, 2008, http://www.worldfinance.com/home/final-bell/the-end-of-the-global-real-estate-boom (accessed May 25, 2014).

5
Fredric Jameson, "The Brick and the Balloon" in *The Cultural Turn: Selected Writings on the Postmodern, 1983–1998* (London and New York: Verso, 1998), 162–190.

6
Robert Somol and Sarah Whiting, "Notes around the Doppler Effect and Other Moods of Modernism," in "Mining Autonomy," *Perspecta* 33, (Spring 2002): 72–77.

tools have enabled the construction of new geometries, freed from the straitjacket of linearity; to experiments with the fabrication of custom components, rather than standardized ones; and to the ability to map territories, unconstrained by simple site observations.

However, as much as these tools expand and unmoor architecture from its modernist paradigms, there is also something troubling in these theorizations of the incredible flexibility of contemporary practices. As Hal Foster points out in *Design and Crime*, deterritorialization can just as easily refer to the mobility of finance capital as it can to the freeing of meaning from rigid or oppressive ideologies and practices.[7] The inherent liberation assumed in most contemporary architectural experimentation, whether this experimentation indulges in new form-making as urban spectacle or new practices of territorial management, is nothing other than the "freedom" of the market promised by the contemporary consensus. What neoliberalism's freedom really refers to is the opening of borders to capital, goods and services, while labor is more strictly disciplined through the dismantling of unions and the expansion of precarious working arrangements such as contract, part-time and piece work, guest workers, and migrant labor. This new liberalism has resulted in an unprecedented process of "accumulation by dispossession" overseen by supranational organizations such as the International Monetary Fund and the World Bank, and a resulting re-entrenchment of class power.[8] It is a political tragedy for architectural practice that it has enthusiastically celebrated this wholesale theft by creating playgrounds for the new rich and infrastructure for the contemporary paradigm of logistics. Despite references to Gilles Deleuze, the "virtual" that is being used in most architectural discourse today has very little in common with the philosopher's forty-year development of the concept. In the face of neoliberalism's flexibility, the virtual has lost its meaning as an affirmation of political potential.[9]

THE SPECIFIC ARCHITECTURE OF THE VIRTUAL

In order to rethink the political relevance of virtual architecture, it is important to reexamine the theory of virtuality that Deleuze developed while reading Henri Bergson's *Matter and Memory* in the mid 1950s.[10] For Bergson, virtuality was associated with the concept of memory, which itself had a definite architecture that he illustrated in a famous drawing of a cone. In Bergson's diagram, the cone sits upside down on a plane, which stands for a person's "actual representation of the universe." In contact with the plane, the narrow apex of the cone is the body's conscious present, perceiving and acting in the world, while the wide "base" of the cone that hovers above represents all of one's recollections as a "motionless past" or what Bergson called "pure memory."[11] At the apex, memories are contracted to form diagrams for motion, while at the base, memories exist fully expanded

7
Hal Foster, *Design and Crime: And Other Diatribes* (New York, London: Verso, 2002), 24.

8
See David Harvey, *The New Imperialism* (Oxford: Oxford University Press, 2003), and *A Brief History of Neoliberalism* (Oxford: Oxford University Press, 2005), 16. See also Gérard Duménil and Dominique Lévy, "Neoliberal Income Trends: Wealth, Class and Ownership, in the USA," *New Left Review* 30 (2004): 103–133.

9
See Daniel Barber, "Militant Architecture: Destabilizing Architecture's Disciplinarity," *The Journal of Architecture* 10, no. 3 (2005): 245–253.

10
See Gilles Deleuze, "Bergson 1859–1941," and "Bergson's Conception of Difference," in *Desert Islands and Other Texts 1953–1974*, ed. David Lapoujade (New York: Semiotext(e), 2004), 22–51. Both texts were originally published in 1956, but Bergson's "Conception of Difference" was written in 1954 and delivered as a paper at a Bergson studies conference in that year.

11
Henri Bergson, *Matter and Memory*, trans. N. M. Paul and W. S. Palmer (New York: Zone Books, 1988), 152.

as "singularities," specific experiences with names, dates and locations attached to them. Individuals are unable to carry pure memories to consciousness, nor can they actually see the motor-diagrams that move their bodies; rather, they draw on intermediate sections through the cone, which contain memories existing somewhere between full contraction and full relaxation. Bergson describes us as constantly ascending and descending through these levels, actualizing our memories in present action and virtualizing our perceptions in memory. This motion is what Bergson calls a true idea of time, duration, a time of movement, undivided into units or frames, where past and present co-exist.[12]

Henri Bergson's Cone of Memory

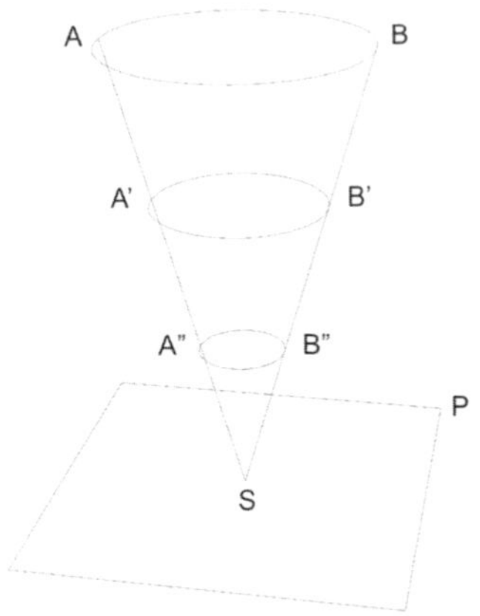

For Deleuze, this cone, cut by "a thousand repetitions of our psychical life,"[13] is the scene of the circuit between the virtual and the actual. Where, for Bergson, the concept of the virtual always describes memory and duration, Deleuze develops a theory of the virtual itself, seizing on the word "virtual" because of its denotations in common usage. Today, "virtual" means something that "is so in essence or effect, although not formally or actually,"[14] but this current definition is derived from two distinct sources. The first comes from the medieval Latin *virtualis*, derived from virtus, which means "strength" or "power."[15] For the scholastics, virtuality corresponded closely with potential force. The second sense originated in the eighteenth century, when the word was used to describe optical images produced through reflection and refraction. As a result, "virtual" came to be associated with a pure image in opposition to a physical thing.[16] For Deleuze, drawing on both of these roots, the virtual refers to the unconscious potential or power of ideas, a potential attributed to the very fact that they are not yet actualized or made present.[17] In order to render the concept more precise in a philosophical context, Deleuze makes three important claims concerning the virtual. First, he argues that the virtual should not be opposed to the *real*, because it is itself fully real.[18]

12
Henri Bergson, *Creative Mind: An Introduction to Metaphysics*, trans. Mabelle L. Andison (New York: Dover Publications, 2007), 10–11.

13
Ibid., 162

14
Oxford English Dictionary, s.v. "virtual."

15
Pierre Lévy, *Becoming Virtual: Reality in the Virtual Age*, trans. Robert Bononno (New York: Plenum Press, 1998), 23.

16
Ibid.

17
Deleuze makes it clear that despite his engagement with the discipline of psychology, Bergson is primarily using the concept of the unconscious as an ontological concept, not a psychological one. See Gilles Deleuze, *Bergsonism*, trans. Hugh Tomlinson and Barbara Habberjam (New York: Zone Books, 1988), 56.

18
Deleuze argues that only the virtual is, that the actual is always becoming, while the virtual as a space of duration is the home of being. The virtual is real in the same sense that the past possesses reality. See Deleuze, *Bergsonism*, 55.

Instead, it should be opposed to the *actual*, or the present. However, the virtual and the actual do not exist in dialectical contradiction, but rather constitute two tendencies of a repetitive relay. In consequence, and despite their apparent opposition, the Deleuzian concept of the virtual does not dismiss or devalue the actual, but rather posits *actualization* as a central event of virtuality: a moment of creation when the complex relationality of ideas in the virtual is divided into singular and distinct entities. Second, Deleuze warns us not to confuse the virtual with the possible. Their first important difference is in their external relations: unlike the virtual, which possesses reality and faces the actual, the possible is opposed to the real.[19] The second distinction between them is internal: Deleuze argues that the possible is derived retroactively from the real,[20] and as such it resembles the real, and realization is a process governed by the principles of similarity and identity. In contrast to this, actualization proceeds according to "differenciation,"[21] and as a result always produces something new and unpredictable.[22] Finally, quoting Proust, Deleuze insists that the virtual is "ideal without being abstract."[23] As Bergson's example of memory makes clear, the virtual houses "singularities," incorporating specific dates, names and places, and thus it is never abstract.[24] Rather, the virtual is ideal, a space of potential ideas, where thoughts form in the movement of memories.

If we are to import Deleuzian terms like "the virtual" into architectural discourse, we also need to acknowledge the reason such concepts were developed to begin with. Deleuze uses the concept as a fundamental building block for his philosophy, which acts as a militant challenge to the domination of society by the hegemonic forces of the family, the economy and the state.[25] For Deleuze, the political promise of the virtual is its potential to create a new form of politics. In their innovative work, *Empire*, Michael Hardt and Antonio Negri use Deleuze's philosophy to argue that the virtual consists of a "set of powers to act (being, loving, transforming, creating) that reside in the multitude."[26] They name the virtual a *constituent* or emergent power, in opposition to the *constituted* power of the law or state.

VIRTUAL ARCHITECTURE

It should be clear by now that the political stakes of a virtual architecture have nothing to do with computers per se. Many contemporary uses of the concept in relation to digital and parametric architecture are, in fact, directly opposed to Deleuze's understanding on all three counts listed above. They are often actual, not virtual; possible, not real; and abstract, rather than ideal. First of all, digital drawing and fabrication are both actual rather than virtual because they are fully available to consciousness in the present. Second, most current uses of data and mapping make use of possibility and probability as statistical information, and as a result their projections can only resemble

19
The possible is opposed to the real because it does not exist; it has no being. Deleuze argues, rather, that the possible is derived retroactively from the real as a backward projection. See Deleuze, *Bergsonism*, 98. Bergson distinguishes between two senses of the possible: a negative sense in which the word simply means that there is no barrier, and a positive sense in which it implies that the result of an idea could have been known in advance. Bergson criticizes this second definition of the possible, and Deleuze follows this argument in his writing on Bergson; see Bergson, *Creative Mind*, 10.

20
Deleuze, *Bergsonism*, 98.

21
Deleuze often uses the word "differenciation" instead of "differentiation," for the process of actualization, in order to more clearly distinguish it from the differential condition of the virtual. See Gilles Deleuze, "How Do We Recognize Structuralism?," in *Desert Islands and Other Texts*, 180, and Gilles Deleuze, *Difference and Repetition* (New York: Columbia University Press, 1994), 207.

22
For a very clear reading of these concepts, see Paul Patton, *Deleuze and the Political* (London and New York: Routledge, 2000), 36.

23
Deleuze, *Desert Islands and Other Texts*, 179. Also quoted in Deleuze, *Bergsonism*, 96.

24
In *A Thousand Plateaus*, Deleuze and Guattari appear to claim the opposite when they say that existing linguistic models are not abstract enough, but this merely refines their critique of the specific form of abstraction referred to above, one which remains static and spatial, rather than being put into motion. Gilles Deleuze and Felix Guattari, *A Thousand Plateaus: Capitalism and Schizophrenia*, trans. Brian Massumi (Minneapolis: University of Minnesota Press, 1987), 7.

25
For a description of the potential of Deleuze and Guattari's political militancy as a program for architecture, see Barber, "Militant Architecture: Destabilizing Architecture's Disciplinarity."

26
Michael Hardt and Antonio Negri, *Empire* (Cambridge: Harvard University Press, 2000), 357.

a future real. Finally, digital architecture is abstract rather than ideal because it is founded in purely technical constraints of numerical data and specific software that often overcode its ability to foster new ideas. All of these factors set contemporary architectural procedures in opposition to the Deleuzian politics of the virtual, where politics is always the practice of producing what is currently invisible or impossible.[27]

On the other hand, all architecture engages the virtual in two fundamental ways. As a practice, architecture is a project of imagining a different world, and as a result it involves the constant actualization of ideas. Moreover, even after construction, architecture remains empty in the sense that its uses can always be rearticulated; because of this, it always remains an unfinished space of political desire, disagreement and deliberation.[28] These two attributes constitute both architecture's political potential and its fundamental virtuality.[29]

However, this potential needs to be rethought, not simply in terms of architecture's ontological virtuality, but as a means of practicing architecture differently.[30] In *Design and Crime*, Foster has used Karl Krauss's concept of running-room (*Spielraum*) to designate a space for criticism within the near total subsumption of contemporary capitalism.[31] The virtual is another way of designating this *space for play* in its indetermination. A virtual architecture would take this literally, providing unprogrammed space for appropriation and creation within the neoliberal city, a spacing that is a function of the fact that a virtual architecture is always, in some sense, not actualized. This investigation will use four exemplary architectural projects to examine four dimensions of a virtual architecture that confront the paranoid logic of neoliberalism: the Landhausplatz in Innsbruck as an exhumation of the urban unconscious, the decolonization of P'sagot in Palestine as a destruction of existing boundaries, an architecture school in Nantes as a site for events, and an urban interstice in Paris that reconfigures architectural practice as political praxis.

LANDHAUSPLATZ: THE EXHUMATION OF THE URBAN UNCONSCIOUS

For Bergson, memory remains unconscious until it is actualized in either memory images or movement. Similarly, Deleuze emphasizes the unconscious nature of virtuality as its productive potential.[32] In *Nietzsche and Philosophy*, he argues that active force is always unconscious, while conscious force is always reactive.[33] Active force is fundamentally creative because it involves the production of something new; as a result, it must come not from the self-conscious mind but from the unreflective actualization of virtualities. In *Capitalism and Schizophrenia*, Deleuze and Félix Guattari radicalize Jacques Lacan's argument that the unconscious is "extimate," or outside us in language, by positing that the contemporary capitalist unconscious

27
For a discussion of the idea of politics as a project of realizing the impossible, see Jacques Rancière, *Disagreement: Politics and Philosophy* (Minneapolis: University of Minnesota, 1999), 131–133.

28
Lacan makes this point in his seventh seminar. Jacques Lacan, *The Ethics of Psychoanalysis: 1959–1960* (New York: Norton, 1992), 135–136.

29
Antoine Picon has expanded on these two features, arguing that five specific aspects of architecture, "design, order and proportion, ornament, structure and space ... may help us to understand the medium's virtual content." Antoine Picon, "Architecture, Science, Technology and the Virtual Realm," in *Architecture and the Sciences: Exchanging Metaphors*, eds. Antoine Picon and Alessandra Ponte (New York: Princeton Architectural Press, 2003), 300.

30
In *Architecture from the Outside*, Elisabeth Grosz argues that the key to a new conception of architecture might be to apply to space Bergson's (and Deleuze's) rethinking of time as duration, in order to consider space as "multiple, differential and specific." But while Grosz provides an ambitious challenge to architecture, her interpretation of the virtual has often been absorbed in an apolitical play of forms that appears in many trajectories of contemporary design claiming the influence of Deleuze, which make use of "succession, layering, folding and entwining." Elizabeth Grosz, *Architecture from the Outside: Essays on Virtual and Real Space* (Cambridge: MIT Press, 2001), 128.

31
Foster, *Design and Crime*, 16.

32
In "Bergson 1859–1941," Deleuze writes: "The past is therefore the in-itself, the unconscious, or more precisely, as Bergson says, the virtual." In "How Do We Recognize Structuralism?," Deleuze emphasizes this: "Structures are necessarily unconscious. ... Perhaps the word 'virtuality' would precisely designate the mode of structure or the object of theory, on the condition that we eliminate any vagueness about the word." See Deleuze, *Desert Islands and Other Texts*, 29, 178, 181. In *Bergsonism* he points out that Bergson viewed the unconscious as ontological, not psychological. See Deleuze, *Bergsonism*, 56.

33
Gilles Deleuze, *Nietzsche and Philosophy*, trans. Hugh Tomlinson (New York: Columbia University Press, 2006), 39–42.

is exposed rather than hidden. According to Lacan, there is no repression in the psychoses of paranoia and schizophrenia. The schizophrenic is defined by what he calls "foreclosure," the failure of the process through which an individual's desire is subjected to the symbolic authority of the father: the name-of-the-father.[34] Deleuze and Guattari argue that capitalism suffers foreclosure, describing it as a schizophrenic regime of signs defined by desires that always circulate on the surface, unencumbered by Freud's deep structure of the psyche. In this state, instead of desire being defined by lack and appearing only under exceptional circumstances, the unconscious becomes productive, "desiring-production" itself.[35] Deleuze and Guattari seek to turn this condition against itself through a process they call "Schizoanalysis,"which activates this exposed unconscious as a connective tool, capable of assembling new collective subjectivities.

The Landhausplatz, a public square in the Tyrolian capital of Innsbruck, Austria, was redesigned by LAAC Architekten, Stiefel Kramer Architecture and the artist Christopher Grüner in 2011. The project engages the city's collective unconscious by exposing four historic monuments as witnesses of the Nazi occupation of Austria.[36] Filling the narrow north face of its triangular form is the provincial government building of Tyrol, whose reduced neoclassical façade was designed between 1938 and 1940, during the German occupation. Opposite this monument to fascism stand three counter memorials. In the center of the square is a postwar French monument, later rededicated to all those who died liberating Austria, which was built in a style that uncannily mirrors the Nazi elevation it faces. Beside this monument is a much smaller sculpture erected in 1997 to commemorate the victims of Innsbruck's Kristallnacht. Attached to the entrance of the government building is a plaque commemorating Franz Mair, a high school teacher who led the local resistance movement against the Nazi occupation. Since their fabrication, the three monuments have been subject to multiple misunderstandings. The monument to Austria's liberation has been persistently misread as a Nazi construction, while a continuous debate has been waged over the meaning and language of the other memorials, with the Franz Mair plaque being rewritten three times and a local conservative newspaper criticizing the Kristallnacht sculpture's high cost and unclear design process.[37]

Once an unruly collection of paving, grass, paths and planting beds, the redesigned square's surface is cast in white concrete, which unifies the space materially, and highlights the contrasting objects placed upon it. Curving shapes fold up from the surface, forming waves of concrete that serve as seating, planters for trees, plinths for the disputed monuments, and a fountain. Slight variations in treatment differentiate the surface: a trowel finish for walking, a sandblasted exterior at its folds, and a polished facet on the horizontal planes where its folds are cut. Without any of the recognizable tropes

34
This concept names a series: the noun "Father"; his last name, now your name; his first name spoken by your mother, as her object of desire; and the prohibition, his "No" ("non" sounds exactly like "nom"). See Jacques Lacan, *Seminar III: The Psychoses 1955–1956*, ed. Jacques-Alain Miller, trans. Russell Grigg (New York: W. W. Norton and Company, 1993), 193, 306.

35
See Gilles Deleuze and Félix Guattari, *Anti-Oedipus: Capitalism and Schizophrenia*, trans. Helen R. Lane, Robert Hurley and Mark Seem (Minneapolis: University of Minnesota Press, 1983). The book's first page begins with a description of desiring production, but the description of capitalism as a schizophrenic regime of signs is one of the central themes of both *Anti-Oedipus* and *A Thousand Plateaus*.

36
Descriptions and images of this project can be found at LAAC, http://www.laac.eu/en/projects/landhausplatz-eduard-wallnoefer-platz, and at Stiefel Kramer, www.stiefelkramer.com, both accessed July 24, 2011.

37
The remaking of the plaque followed different sides of a debate over whether the occupation should be called an "oppression," whether it should simply refer to a liberation without naming what the city was liberated from, or whether it should simply say "non-freedom." Details of the square's history can be found at "Spuren des Anchlusses 6: Um Das Landhaus," http://klavierzimmer.blogspot.com/2008/01/spuren-des-anschlusses-6-um-das.html. Hannes Stiefel also explained this history in a lecture at the University of Toronto for the John H. Daniels Faculty of Architecture, Landscape and Design on March 3, 2011.

of a park, the space becomes disorienting and its monuments take on the status of naked signs on a continuous slab. The redesigned square is at once transformed into an assemblage of memory images that continually contest their meanings against the emptiness of the square, and a simple surface that provokes the bodies of its users to produce new sensorimotor diagrams.[38] The square itself acts as a virtual plane, undifferentiated yet differential. As if under the rotating lens of a camera or telescope, the monuments as memory images emerge in stark focus against the indistinct, somatic ground of the square.

38
To date, most of its users appear to be skateboarders.

39
Bergson, *Matter and Memory*, 169.

40
Gilles Deleuze, *Difference and Repetition*, 35, 304. For a discussion of the "univocity of Being," see pages 35–39.

41
Deleuze, *Bergsonism*, 55.

42
Bergson, *Matter and Memory*, 39.

LAAC Architekten, Stiefel Kramer and Christopher Grüner, Landhausplatz, Innsbruck, Austria, 2011

DECOLONIZING P'SAGOT: VIRTUALIZATION AS THE DESTRUCTION OF EXTANT BOUNDARIES

Bergson argues that every slice through the memory cone contains all recollection at different levels of contraction or expansion, or, to use his words, in "different mixtures."[39] Each section therefore represents duration as the coexistence of the past in the present. This coexistence, or simultaneity, marks the virtual as the univocity of being.[40] For Deleuze, the present is never *being* because it is always *becoming*: only the virtual *is*.[41] In this context, duration acts as an indetermination, or temporal spacing between perception and action. This "zone of indetermination"[42] is the differential, or internal difference, of the virtual. In other words, the virtual is difference-in-itself, intensive difference, rather than the extensive difference that we find in actual spaces or between actual objects.[43] This zone of intensive difference is what we try to access through every movement away from the subject as a point of identity, whether such movement is through love, solidarity, intoxicants or meditation. In the first chapter of *A Thousand*

43
Deleuze, *Desert Islands and Other Texts*, 29.

Plateaus, Deleuze and Guattari define the plateau as "a continuous self-vibrating region of intensities whose development avoids any orientation toward a culmination point or external end."[44] Though they cite Gregory Bateson, the "plateau" also resonates with the planes that Bergson cuts through his cone of memory. Deleuze and Guattari describe the virtual plane as a table on which concepts are arranged in relation to one another.[45] Its horizontality is what guarantees its nonhierarchical character and the possibility of creating unexpected connections between ideas.[46] The construction of this virtual plane of consistency, or immanence, is a project of deterritorialization, which itself is simply another word for virtualization.[47]

Decolonizing Architecture is a research group consisting of Sandi Hilal, Alessandro Petti and Eyal Weizman, who are centrally interested in the deterritorialization of colonized spaces. They primarily work in the occupied territories of Palestine, and their first "laboratory" in 2008 investigated the Israeli settlement of P'sagot at the far northern tip of Jerusalem, directly adjacent to the most urbanized areas of the Palestinian cities of Ramallah and al-Bireh. The settlement itself dominates the landscape from the top of the hill, looking down on its Palestinian neighbors. Its cul-de-sacs and single-family, two-story houses with sloped roofs affirm its spatial connections to suburban Jerusalem, while asserting its extreme difference from the dense housing in neighboring al-Bireh.[48]

Working with Italian architects Salottobuono and Situ Studio from New York, Decolonizing Architecture proposed a speculative architectural project to decolonize P'sagot.[49] The project, which was suggestively organized under the concepts *deparceling, ungrounding, unhoming*, and *unroofing*, imagined a radical virtualization of the settlement that was designed to undo its current pose of domination through both subjective and spatial deterritorialization. *Deparceling* proposes returning to the much larger lot sizes defined by 1954 property lines, effectively cutting some existing houses in half while collecting many others into single properties. *Ungrounding* suggests breaking up the ground plane and reorganizing it according to use over time. Weizman argues that the existing organization of territories is substantively structured by a thin section of a few centimeters above and below ground. If this ground could be pulled up, the way the territory is used could be rethought. Together, *deparceling* and *ungrounding* would challenge both the sovereign property of the state and the private property of the market as the twin foundations of capitalist urban development.[50] Finally, *unhoming* and *unroofing* present two strategies for connecting the remaining solitary suburban houses with spaces for collective use that appropriate elements of the existing architectural typologies and lifestyles found today within Palestinian camps. The final design for P'sagot radicalizes the process of decolonization, from a simple act of reappropriation to an attack

44
Deleuze and Guattari, *A Thousand Plateaus*, 22.

45
Gilles Deleuze and Felix Guattari, *What Is Philosophy?* (New York: Columbia University Press, 1994), 35.

46
Like Bergson's plane, the plateau is flat. As Deleuze and Guattari say, the virtual has n–1 dimensions. It is produced through the subtraction of the one (subject, father, despot), insofar as it dominates the multiple. Deleuze and Guattari, *A Thousand Plateaus*, 21.

47
Éric Alliez, *The signature of the world, or, What is Deleuze and Guattari's philosophy?*, trans. Eliot Ross Albert and Alberto Toscano (New York: Continuum, 2004), 87. Alliez quotes Pierre Lévy on virtualization as deterritorialization.

48
All information about the site and project comes from Decolonizing Architecture's website, http://www.decolonizing.ps, accessed May 18, 2011, and Salottobuono, *Manual of Decolonization* (Milan: A+M Bookstore Edizioni, 2010).

49
Salottobuono, *Manual of Decolonization*.

50
For a clear description of conflicting ontologies of property, see Shiri Pasternak, "Property in Three Registers," in "Property," *Scapegoat: Architecture / Landscape / Political Economy*, Issue 00 (Fall 2010): 10–17.

on the architectural foundations of both the subjective fantasy of the autonomous suburban family and the objective domination of territory as property. By breaking down the boundaries of state, market and family, this sequence of proposals rethinks the ways that architecture could be virtualized through the experimental construction of undifferentiated, yet generous spaces.

Decolonizing Architecture Art Residency (DAAR)/SITU Studio, *Unroofing*, 2010

ARCHITECTURE SCHOOL IN NANTES: A SITE FOR EVENTS

Bergson's understanding of the relationship between perception and memory proceeds according to two forms of division: one which corresponds to the divergent and composite nature of the virtual, and the other which is actualization itself, the "vital impetus" (*élan vital*) of differenciation that divides the totality of the virtual into singularities.[51] In the first, intuition serves as a method for locating true differences in nature, dividing things according to the "articulations of the real."[52] Bergson refers to Plato's example of the good dialectician, "the skillful cook who carves the animal without breaking its bones, by following the articulations marked out by nature."[53] However, Bergson is not a dialectician; he is not interested in opposition or contradiction, so these differences in nature cannot be actual. Instead, they remain virtual, such that thought merely tends toward them, rather than being split between them. As Deleuze says, "only tendencies differ in kind."[54] The virtual itself is oriented by these tendencies, with pure memory and pure perception acting as its polarities.[55] The second form of division is the actualization of the virtual. Bergson claims that sensation comes to consciousness through selection.[56] If matter is the sum of all possible images, then we can perceive matter only by sensing a smaller number of its possible images. This means that perception is driven by a process of *subtraction*, whereby our body lets those images which do not interest us pass by. This selection is governed by memory: in other words, through our experience, we learn what to perceive and what to ignore.[57] Likewise, specific memories are themselves triggered by present perceptions.[58] All our actions

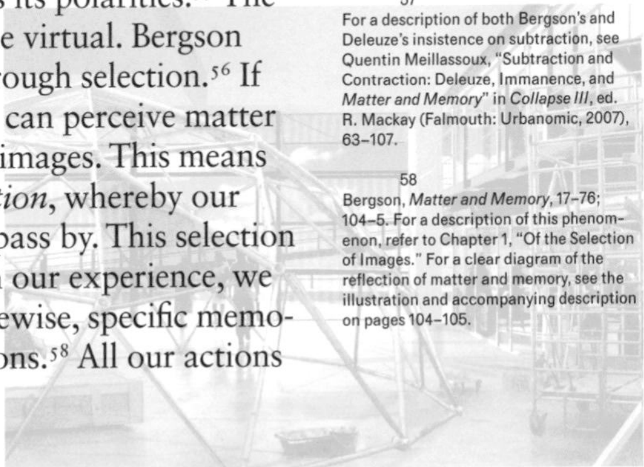

51
Constantin V. Boundas, "Deleuze – Bergson: An Ontology of the Virtual," in *Deleuze: a Critical Reader*, ed. Paul Patton (Oxford: Blackwell, 1996), 91.

52
Deleuze claims that Bergson uses intuition as a method. Bergson contrasts intelligence and intuition, arguing that the problem with intelligence is that it fixes time in order to analyze things; by contrast, intuition is a way of thinking within movement, and within the true continuity of space and time. Only intuition understands differences in nature, because only intuition can examine this continuum and determine its internal differentials, or differentiation (as opposed to its differenciation). See Bergson, *Creative Mind*, 22–23.

53
Henri Bergson, *Creative Evolution*, trans. Arthur Mitchell (Mineola, New York: Dover, 1998), 156.

54
Deleuze, *Bergsonism*, 22.

55
Deleuze, *Desert Islands and Other Texts*, 26–27.

56
Bergson, *Matter and Memory*, 36–38.

57
For a description of both Bergson's and Deleuze's insistence on subtraction, see Quentin Meillassoux, "Subtraction and Contraction: Deleuze, Immanence, and *Matter and Memory*" in *Collapse III*, ed. R. Mackay (Falmouth: Urbanomic, 2007), 63–107.

58
Bergson, *Matter and Memory*, 17–76; 104–5. For a description of this phenomenon, refer to Chapter 1, "Of the Selection of Images." For a clear diagram of the reflection of matter and memory, see the illustration and accompanying description on pages 104–105.

59 A clear description of this project can be found in Anne Lacaton and Jean-Phillipe Vassal, *Lacaton & Vassal* (Paris: Editions HYX / Cité de l'architecture et du patrimoine, 2009), 122–135.

are the result of, and a response to, the coexistence of these selections from the present and past.

In their architecture school in Nantes (2009), French architects Lacaton & Vassal begin with a cut.[59] They split the building in two, producing a space of maximum contraction for the essential functions of the body, and a space of maximum expansion for unknown actualizations to come. The plans for each part of this radically bifurcated space are completely different. The space of maximum contraction is a reprise of *Existenzminimum*; its rooms are based on detailed diagrams of washrooms, offices and studios, developed through iteration from other plans. By contrast, the space of maximum expansion is indefinite, undivided and disorganized; these open areas wrap and loop around the functional spaces, passing easily between inside and outside and joining ramps that run from the ground to the roof. Where the first set of spaces is typological, the second set is topological.

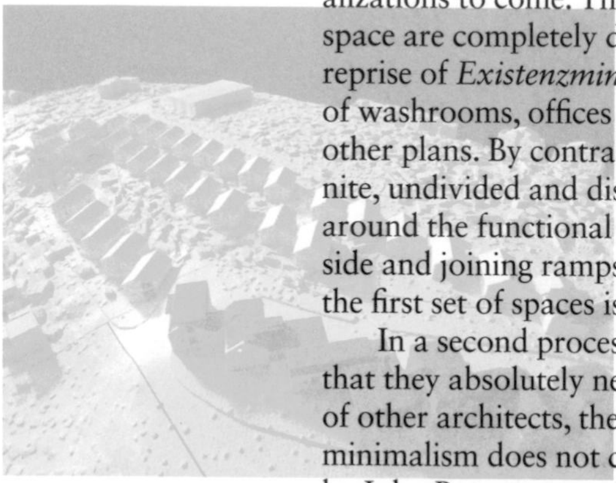

In a second process, Lacaton & Vassal select only those materials that they absolutely need for construction. Compared with the work of other architects, their work is radically reduced. However, their minimalism does not conform to the purely visual strategy practiced by John Pawson, nor does it follow the controlled expression of materiality seen in the architecture of Tadao Ando. Instead, they select only everyday materials that are normally covered, such as precast concrete slabs, exposed electrical systems, greenhouse glazing and corrugated steel panels. The building's expanded areas are not even heated, so some normative functions, such as uniform protection from the weather, are eschewed to produce a building which is in many respects not fully actualized as architecture.

These two selection processes, one acting at the level of organization, the other at the level of material, form a system of symbiotic effects. Lacaton & Vassal's buildings are materially minimal yet spatially maximal; the inexpensive materiality of the building is exactly what allows the architects to construct a larger building. Since the user's basic needs are satisfied, the remaining expanse is left to the school's students and faculty for the invention of new uses. In this way, Lacaton & Vassal follow a simultaneous logic of addition and subtraction, where the deletion of finishes facilitates a radical generosity

Lacaton & Vassal, School of Architecture, Nantes, France, 2009

of space. This process maximizes the virtuality of their architecture, leaving events of actualization to the building's inhabitants.

ECO-INTERSTICE: ARCHITECTURAL PRACTICE AS POLITICAL PRAXIS

Bergson argues that all perception is learned. We do not simply perceive; rather, perceptions call forth memories and are bound to them in order to create images and actions. Our actions become familiar through the repetition of this sequence until we have built a sensorimotor diagram and our body becomes capable of acting without reflection.[60] Following Bergson, Deleuze argues that "the actual and the virtual coexist and enter into a tight circuit, which we are continually retracing from one to the other."[61] The virtual is always being actualized and the actual virtualized, and both these movements are forms of becoming: a virtual becoming that Deleuze and Guattari call "becoming-other,"[62] and an actual "becoming"—becoming *something*. Every becoming is also an improvisation. Repetition is fundamentally creative because everything that returns from memory is a singularity, and every time this loop repeats, it repeats differently. Deleuze calls this experimental process of repetition "transcendental empiricism,"[63] and his entire philosophical project enacts this method of learning through repetition, testing and intuition. This is why, in the last book they wrote together, Deleuze and Guattari argue that we need a "pedagogy of the concept," to save us from the fall from the "encyclopedic" toward "commercial professional training."[64] Without using the word, Deleuze calls for a form of praxis, theoretical knowledge and practice, fused in a differenciating and differential circuit.

Atelier d'architecture autogérée (Studio for Self-managed Architecture, henceforth abbreviated as AAA) is a network of architects and researchers who immerse themselves in an iterative practice. Their projects are distinguished by their slow development in relation to a specific site, and by their collaboration with a local public using common materials and limited means. *Le 56 / Eco-interstice* is an architectural and landscape intervention that they facilitated in an empty space between two Paris apartment buildings. The project involves four distinct zones. A small, two-story building at the front of the lot serves as an operable wall to the garden, the project's interface with the street, and features a quieter and more private space for community activities on the second floor. A paved outdoor area for public programs, a garden for food production and a greenhouse for winter farming at the back of the lot make up the other three components of the design. The active duration of the design and construction project was three years in length, beginning with a highly contingent occupation in 2006, and following with the construction of a growing array of permanent amenities each year until 2009. The design was not immediate, but instead responsive to the evolving conversations

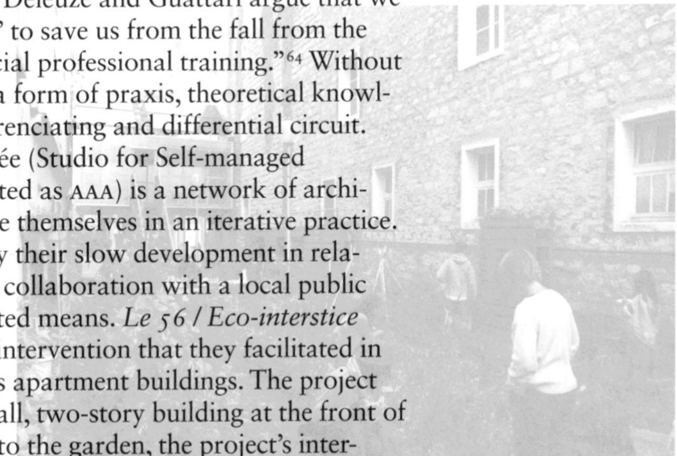

60 The French word "repetition" also means "rehearsal."

61 Gilles Deleuze, "The Actual and the Virtual," in Gilles Deleuze and Claire Parnet, *Dialogues II*, trans. Hugh Tomlinson and Barbara Habberjam (New York: Columbia University Press, 2007), 151.

62 For a discussion on becoming, see the section entitled "Memories of a Bergsonian" in Deleuze and Guattari, *A Thousand Plateaus*, 237–239.

63 For a discussion on Deleuze's pragmaticism, empiricism and practice, see Jeffrey Bell, "Charting the Road of Inquiry: Deleuze's Humean Pragmatics and the Challenge of Badiou," *The Southern Journal of Philosophy* 44 (2006): 399–425.

64 Deleuze and Guattari, *What Is Philosophy?*, 12.

65
See "1837: Of the Refrain" in Deleuze and Guattari, *A Thousand Plateaus*, 310–350.

66
Urban Tactics, accessed May 19, 2011, www.urbantactics.org.

that occurred between the participants. The project holds an empty space in the city open for collective appropriation rather than private control. Like squatting, this process involves the repetition of habitual use as a way to defend an interstice in the urban fabric from appropriation by the market. Use acts as a refrain that marks and claims territory.[65]

The project focuses on the concept of ecology, which is one clear example of an actualization-virtualization circuit. AAA's use of the concept aligns with the basic tenets of urban political ecology because it includes both people and environmental justice. The group's drawings illustrate the latent flows that circulate through the garden: different users, air, water and energy. This exploration of *emergence* can be directly contrasted with popular uses of the concept in current architectural discourse, which emphasize formally expressive effects of self-organization or ecological processes without addressing their social and political consequences. For AAA, emergence is about "self-management": a concept that carries with it a series of political histories and experimental practices. Rather than emphasizing digital technologies and representational techniques, these architects focus on the activist potential of self-management by paying attention to the expertise of nonarchitectural actors. For them, the practice of architecture itself is a way of collectively discovering a new politics.[66]

Atelier d'architecture autogérée,
Le 56 / Eco-interstice, St. Blaise, France, 2006

LESS AND MORE: TOWARD A VIRTUAL ARCHITECTURE

Deleuze developed the concept of the virtual in the mid 1950s, at the height of Fordist Keynesianism, in an attempt to circumvent the philosophical and political status quo. He listed the three chief attributes of this concept with little modification in "The Actual and the Virtual," a short text he left unfinished at the time of his death in 1995. This piece threw his concept into a new milieu, creating the possibility for a renewed relationship between his philosophy and contemporary politics.[67] Certain representatives of the contemporary left have argued that Deleuze's philosophy seems now to have so precisely prefigured certain dimensions of post-Fordist capitalism that we should abandon his work as little more than an apology for it.[68] However, Deleuze himself claimed a critical difference between his concept of virtuality and its misuse in the hands of technocrats, politicians and their architects. The concept remains a political weapon which insists on the radical horizontality of the virtual in the face of neoliberalism's punitive precarity. It attacks gender, race and class distinction through deterritorialization, names the event of actualization as the creation of new paradigms of thought in place of capitalism's repetition of the same, and finally claims the cycle of actualization and virtualization as a *praxis* through which new forms of life can be invented. LAAC Architekten and Stiefel Kramer Architecture, Decolonizing Architecture, Lacaton & Vassal and Atelier d'architecture autogérée have each designed projects that harness this conception of the virtual as a primary aesthetic strategy. What characterizes these projects as a set is their indeterminacy, minimalism and generosity in the face of the violent militarization, spectacular excess and voracious appetite of contemporary urbanization.

67
Deleuze, "The Actual and the Virtual," in Deleuze and Parnet, *Dialogues II*, 148–152.

68
See Slavoj Žižek, *Organs without Bodies: Deleuze and Consequences* (New York and London: Routledge, 2004), 183–186.

Sponge Urbanism

Troy Schaum
and
Rosalyne Shieh

> The conception of a void arises... when consciousness, lagging behind itself, remains attached to the recollection of an old state when another state is already present.
> —Henri Bergson[1]

Situated within the Rust Belt, Detroit is America's most infamous "shrinking" city.[2] In March 2010, Mayor Dave Bing announced his intent to "right-size" Detroit through a combined strategy of large-scale demolition, population redistribution and targeted rehabilitation; under his plan, ten thousand derelict houses would be demolished within three years.[3] Blighted swaths of the city would be razed to make room for fields and farmland, and residents would be relocated to strengthen "more viable" neighborhoods. This approach represents an ideological shift from the post-industrial urbanism of continuity and extensiveness to a series of overlapping zones that invoke a well-worn polynuclear, center-periphery model.

The specifics of the plan remain vague, but taken at face value, the vision projected is top-down and retrograde: a tabula rasa approach based on an ideal notion of the city that tacitly presumes that urbanism requires density, and that the basic unit of density is built form.[4] Under this logic, open lots and unoccupied buildings can be seen only as emblems of loss in an attritive slide toward porosity. Yet, this perspective condemns us to the limitations of prejudgment: seeing only what is missing prevents us from seeing what is already there.

Perhaps we can learn to recognize cities like Detroit, which not only have ceased to grow but are undergoing an unprecedented rate of population and economic decline, as infrastructurally connected and prepared sites rather than remnants of entropic urban dysfunction. In order to work through this conceptual reorientation

1
Henri Bergson, *Creative Evolution* (London: MacMillan and Co., 1922), 298.

2
The 2010 U.S. Census Report documented 713,777 residents in Detroit, charting a precipitous 25 percent drop (down from 951,270 in 2000) over the last ten years, and measuring less than half of its peak population of 1.8 million in 1950.

3
David Runk, "Detroit Looks at Downsizing to Save City," *The Washington Times*, March 9, 2010.

4
For an extended and cogent articulation of the need for a theorization of open space, see Albert Pope, "The Primacy of Space," in *Ladders* (New York: Princeton Architectural Press and Rice University School of Architecture, 1996), 1–13.

we propose a combination of alterations, insertions and constructions within an existing neighborhood on Detroit's northeast side. By testing these transformations at the smallest unit of dereliction and occupation—the single lot—we investigate a strategy for bringing about a new, multidirectional order that emerges from within the existing system.

Detroit requires an urban strategy that can direct and organize the accrual of an increasing amount of emptiness. Sponge Urbanism imagines Detroit's neighborhoods as a porous framework within which infill and blankness, form and space, the material and the immaterial simultaneously produce the city. This methodology facilitates the transition from a condition where unoccupied parcels are seen as voids between buildings to one where the city is a thick,

General view of neighborhood, Detroit, Michigan.
Photograph by Catie Newell

horizontally extended substrate within which islands of built form are suspended. In this future state, the infrastructure-rich yet vacant plots and structures of Detroit can be conceptualized as variegated, productive surfaces with a range of potential activities and uses. To accommodate this heterarchical view of urban space, we propose an alternative to the platted street grid. At present, the existing grid forms rectilinear blocks that are massed at the perimeter to reinforce the lines of the streets. Sponge Urbanism transforms these blocks into a distributed and multidirectional system that emerges bottom-up from numerous local insertions, constructions and realignments.

Aerial view of project site: a modest neighborhood on the northeast side of Detroit, Michigan

VOIDS TO FIELDS

Fields lend an unprecedented legibility to the shrinking city. Where a compositional representation of the city would relegate vacant lots as omissions in a preexisting fabric, a mapping of available infrastructural amenities across open lots might recast these same spaces as potentials toward a future that is distinct from the city's past. Such a representation produces an understanding of the post-industrial city as extensive and continuous, thus reintegrating the false dialectic of solid/void, built/unbuilt and density/decline that has simplistically plagued our understanding of "shrinking cities." Describing Detroit as a field may help us to release ourselves from a corrective model of progress and recast what were previously seen as spaces of absence as material full of potential.

Representations both make visible what exists and project new possibilities across fields of difference. The process is one of working from effects or relationships toward the objects and material conditions that produce them. The basic premise of Sponge Urbanism is that of *radical inclusion*—we are not limited solely to the performative, symbolic, semantic or compositional. Instead, we seek to develop a generative diagram that operates simultaneously among all of these registers with a mixture of established and inventive representational approaches.

In this project, formal and informal criteria meet in a master diagram that serves as an open repository for drawings of, into and out of the site. We begin by projecting a field of multiple, divergent, local vectors onto a plan of the existing neighborhood. These multidirectional vectors suggest scalar and perceptual relationships that relate to yet supersede the existing geometry of the neighborhood. The diagram is scaled to a grain slightly larger than existing lot widths to project the eventual lower density of built form, while the vectors follow the existing grid and add a projected rotational overlay. This overlay becomes a scaffold of field orientations that directs the placement of nodes, attractors or points of programmatic intensity. The points guide interventions of construction, incision or alteration. Energy resources are located at points where environmental forces are highly concentrated and distributed along existing utility lines. Productive landscapes are defined along water lines that straddle cisterns supplied by rainwater and snowmelt. Wind towers take advantage of the newly open landscape and low building heights to collect energy and tie into remaining fragments of the municipal grid.

The master diagram assumes that private property is retained by current inhabitants at approximately 50 percent. The small but vibrant Bengali community that currently makes up the greater population of this particular Detroit neighborhood is largely responsible for keeping it safe and viable. We propose that the other 50 percent of vacant homes and empty lots be divided into smaller units and ganged into larger parcels in order to accommodate a broader mix of landscape and built uses.

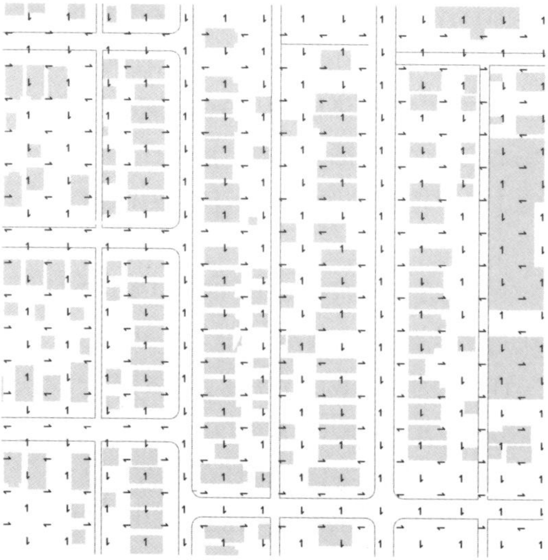

Field vectors

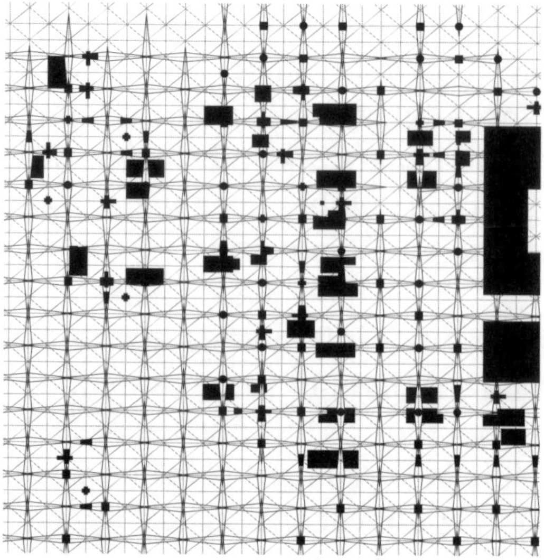

Scaffold and nodes

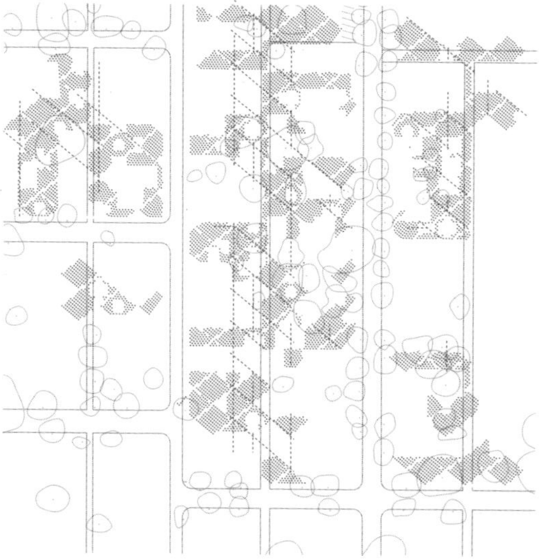

Infrastructure and surfaces

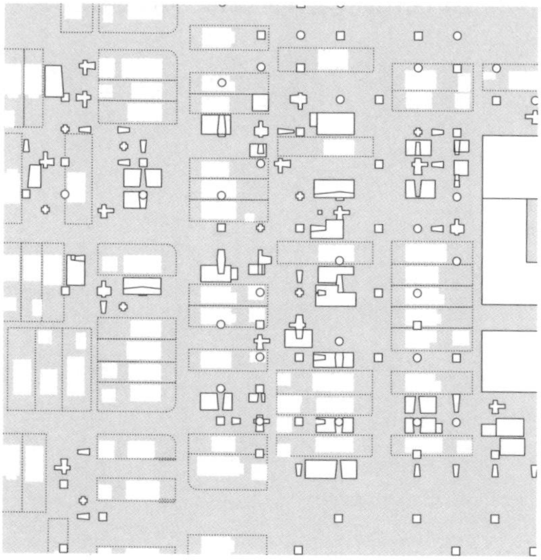

Ownership

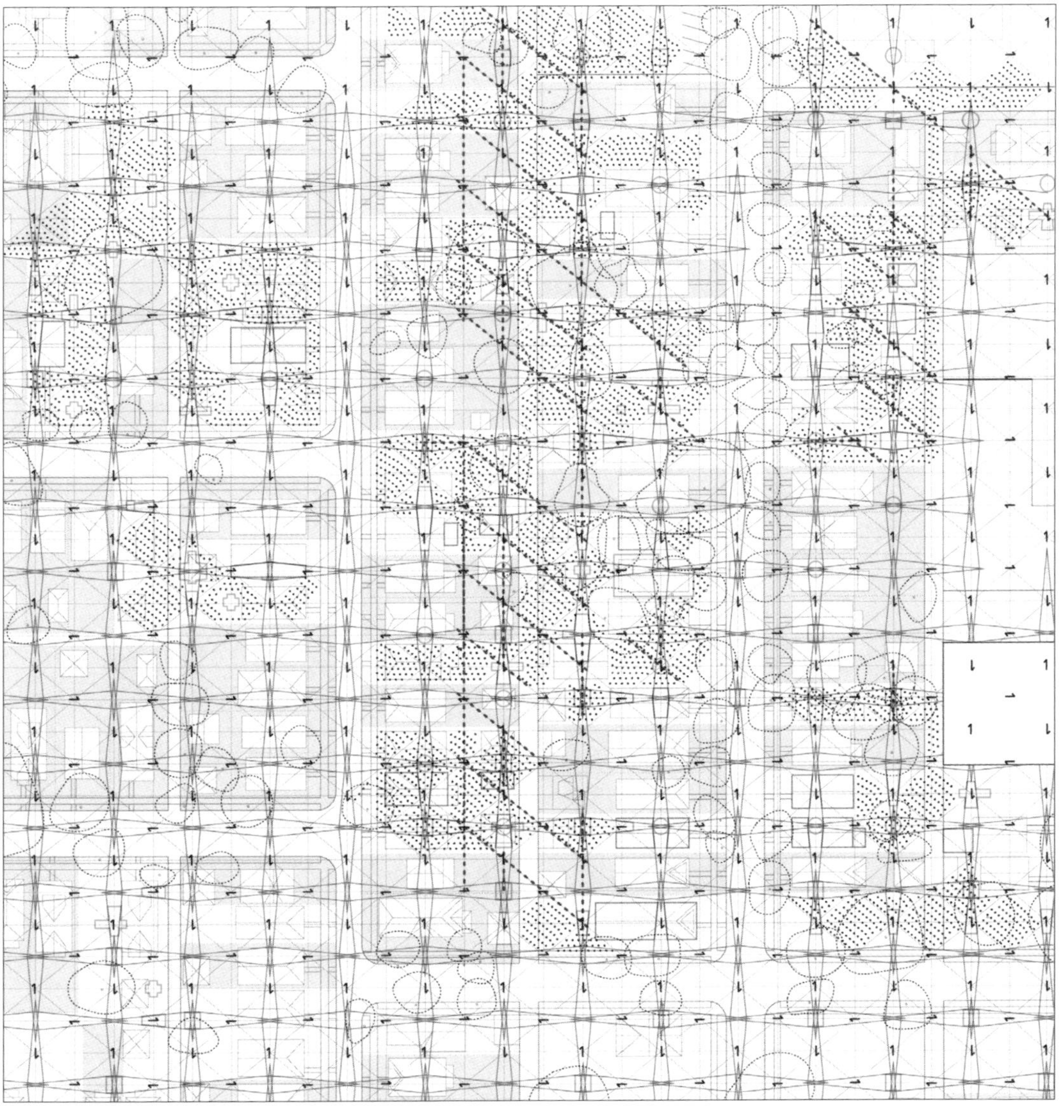

Master diagram with descriptive and projected systems layered

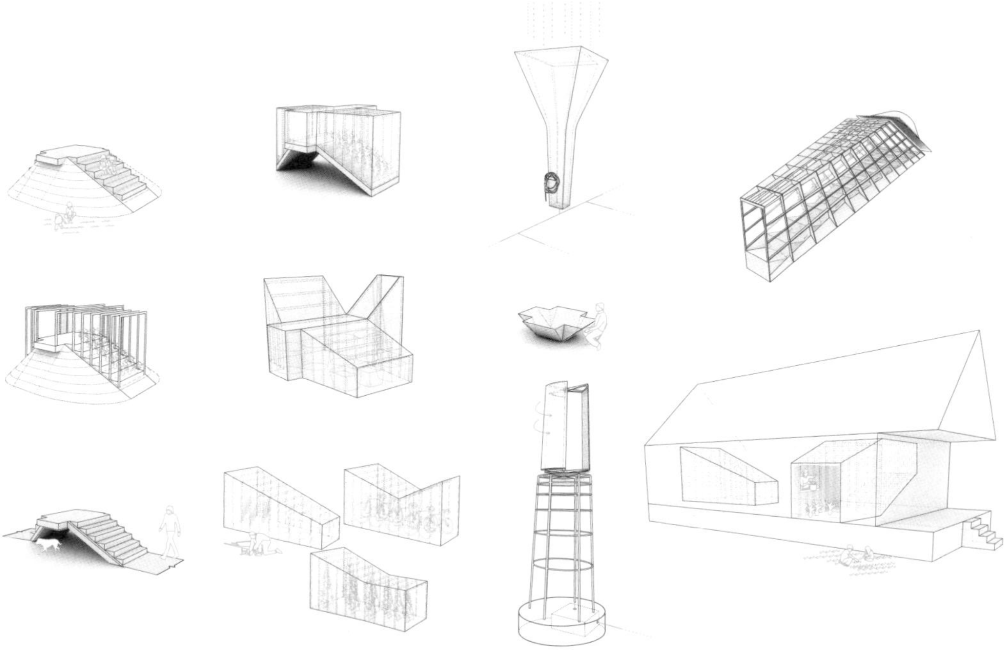

Formal Interventions: Catalogue of Types

Landforms:
Activity Mound, Greenhouse Mound, Bridge

Spatial Objects:
Greenhouse Bridge, Storage Shed, Multi-Purpose Sheds

Hubs:
Cistern Tower, Picnic Table, Turbine Tower

Constructions:
Cinema Sleeve, Fresh Air Sleeves

TYPOLOGICAL INTERVENTIONS

Sleeves, mounds, sheds and towers make up a catalogue of formal interventions that include alteration to existing structures, redistribution and sculpting of the ground, insertion of objects and the point collection and distribution of resources. A field-like, multidirectional organization can grow from these parts and emerge from within the neighborhood through the new local relationships they engender. Voids become spaces of occupation and activity as well as shared open areas.

As a formal object that directs an effect or use, each of the interventions defines a type. The qualities associated with each type range from spatial to programmatic and utilitarian to aesthetic. Each type organizes a territory larger than its material limits: inhabitable

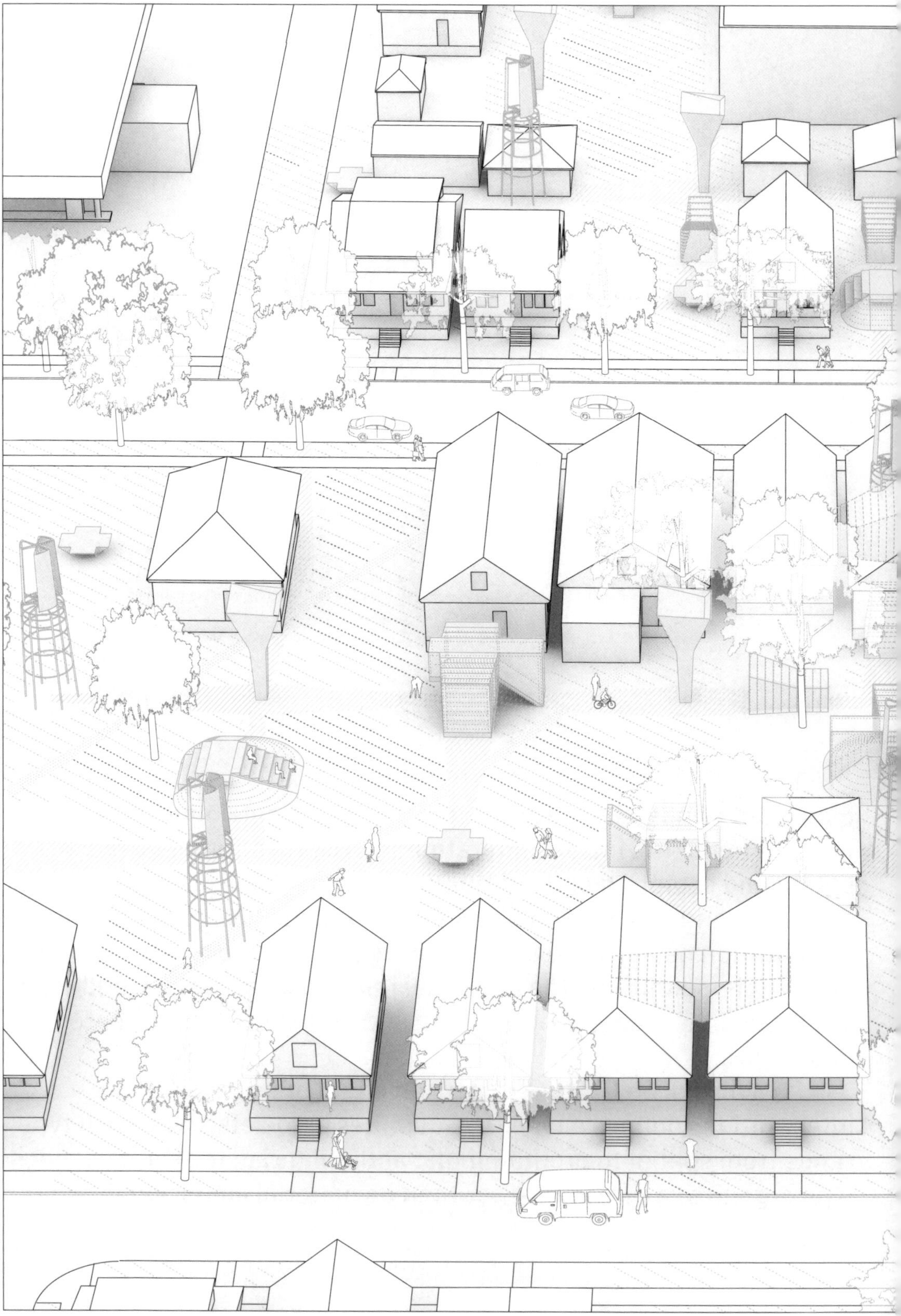

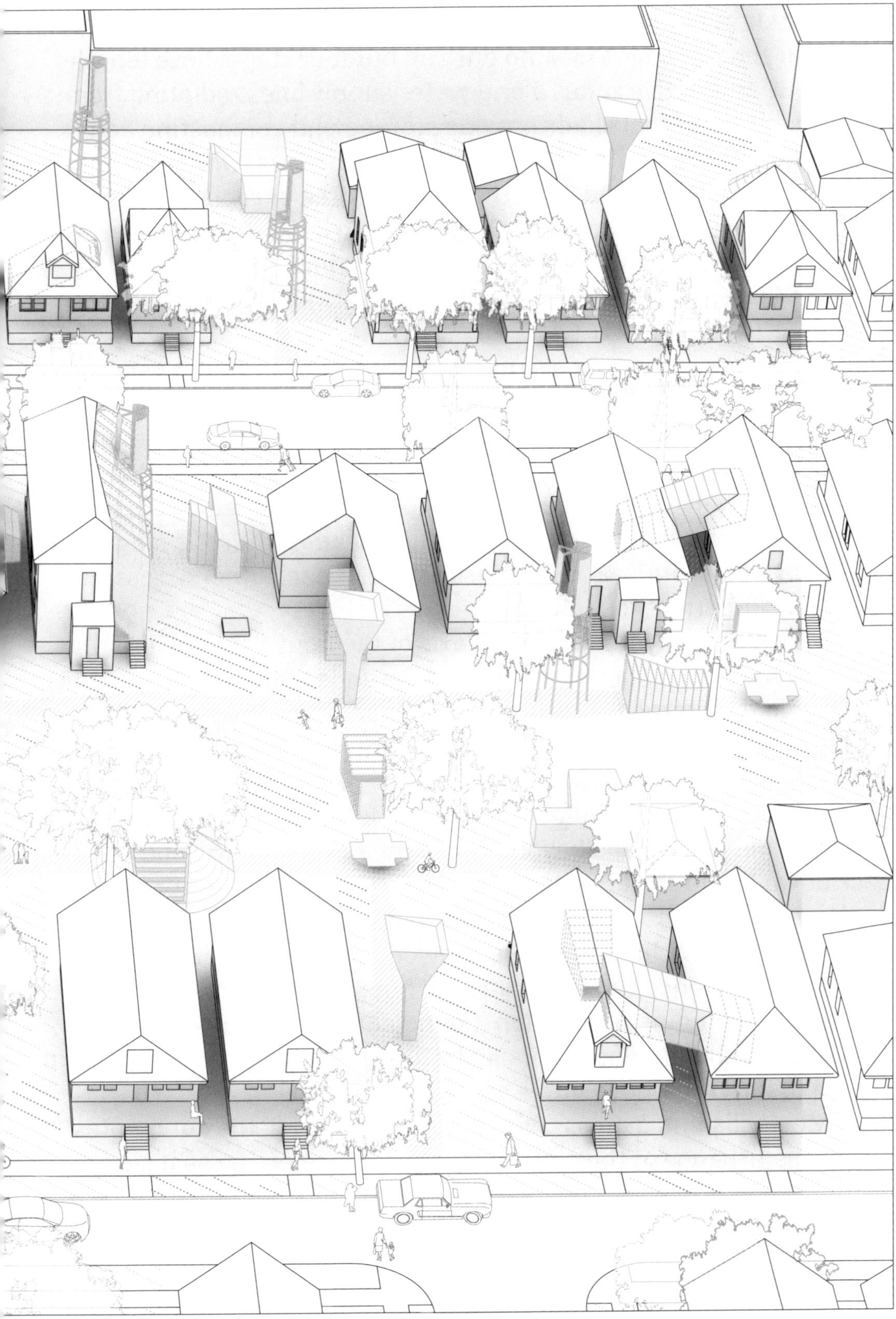

sleeves redirect light through existing houses; raked seating creates an indoor theater space looking onto an outdoor stage; hose lengths sweep out productive zones along water supply lines radiating from cisterns; bike and tool sheds provide storage and composting centers keyed to catchments of gardens and residences; windmills are placed according to wind patterns and reinforce or replace municipal utilities. Surfaces are created and considered as part of the logic of building-scale structures and infrastructural lines.

PROTOTYPE: ABOUT FACE

We were able to construct a single prototype, called *About Face*, at 13178 Moran Street, an inconspicuous single-family house located within the neighborhood on Detroit's northeast side.[5] The existing urban fabric in this area is tightly packed and rationally organized: a grid of sidewalk-lined access streets is further defined by porches offset across easements; each residential façade features a single door flanked by windows. The houses stare at each other across the street like imperfect reflections.

By turning away from the long axis of the house and the existing city grid, the *About Face* sleeve prototype adds two new faces to the building and reciprocally focuses its surroundings on a new axis. The insertion cuts diagonally from the north side of the first floor through to the roof, terminating at a slumped acrylic window that opens onto the southern sky. The window's seamless, bubble-like form allows a person to move her head beyond the plane of the roof to get a view back down to the street. The volume rises upward along steps that diminish incrementally in height, producing seating of varying sizes along its slope. Within the sleeve, viewers face what will be the new open space left once the fire-damaged house next door is demolished. The remaining foundation mound can be repurposed as a stage, or the sliding glass door can be closed and used as a projection screen to turn the sleeve into a contained theater.

By establishing a cross-axis through the house, the cut creates a local disturbance in the city fabric. Each house on the east side of Moran Street is in shade on its north side, making a regular pattern

5
About Face was constructed with generous support from the Architecture Fellowship Program at University of Michigan, Taubman College of Architecture and Urban Planning, 2009–2010.

Site of *About Face*, before construction. Photograph by Catie Newell

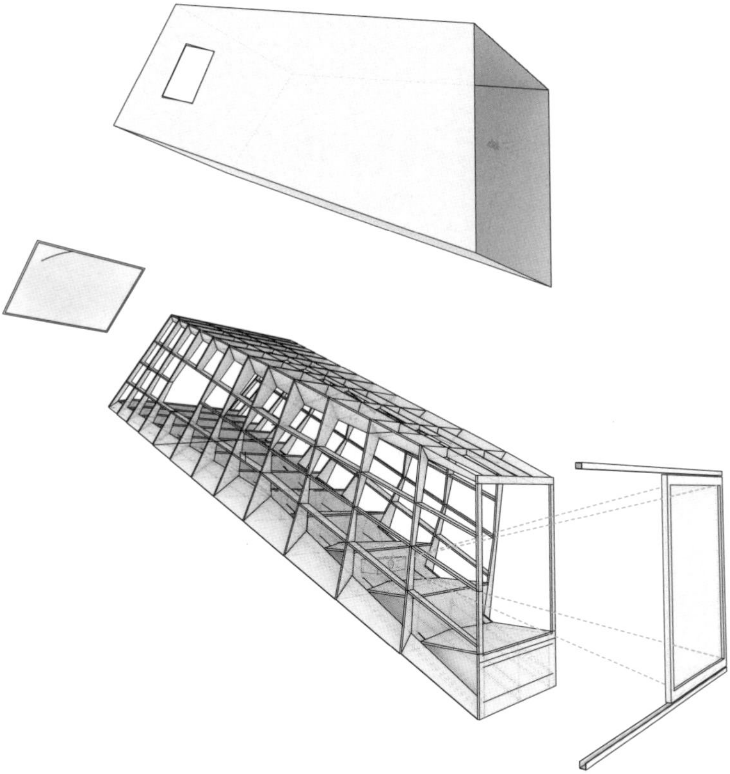

Exploded axonometric vinyl mesh sign
5' × 6' seamless, slumped acrylic bubble window

Milled plywood lattice frame
Housing for projector
Projected surface/sliding glass window

About Face, Detroit, Michigan, 2010

of alternating light and shadow. The room cuts a path for light to enter into the house during the day, and illuminates the volume between the house and its neighbor at night. The new cross-axis readies the house to turn away from the street and face its more distant neighbor across what will be an open lot.

Local rotations produced through surgical removals and strategic insertions in the urban grid introduce a preliminary investment of atmospheric intensity into what had been a residual space. If multiplied across the neighborhood, such interventions may precipitate a new, multidirectional, sponge-like organization that grows from within the existing fabric and acknowledges the latent potential at all positions within the urban field.

About Face, Detroit, Michigan, 2010

Interior view, *About Face*, Detroit, Michigan, 2010

CONCLUSION: INVISIBLE POTENTIALS

Detroit is a paradigmatic and particularly visible case of the shrinking city, but as global and local economies continue to shift, the ability to constructively think through the rapid deintensification of urban areas is critical not only for cities in the American Rust Belt but for cities everywhere. The "building down" of cities requires a conceptual reorientation that does not refer to an ideal defined by density. We need to move beyond a corrective model that diagnoses open spaces as voids within the city, and instead, choose to see and represent open space as a positive condition. Field theory has been instrumental in extending our awareness and acceptance of immaterial and invisible forces that can shift, realign and intensify over time, but for architecture, an expansion of design criteria beyond the traditional study of form must first register in the expansion of representational criteria. In other words, to leverage an expanded field of possibilities, we must first visualize them as such. Representational

techniques that favor massing and figure-ground reductions must be expanded with representations that differentiate open space into surfaces and environments with specific properties that afford different occupations and activities. Detroit has the potential to become an unprecedented paradigm of urbanism based on the extensive and the open, adaptable to both building up and building down. The key may be to stop focusing on what is missing and to start mining what already exists in order to imagine what could be.

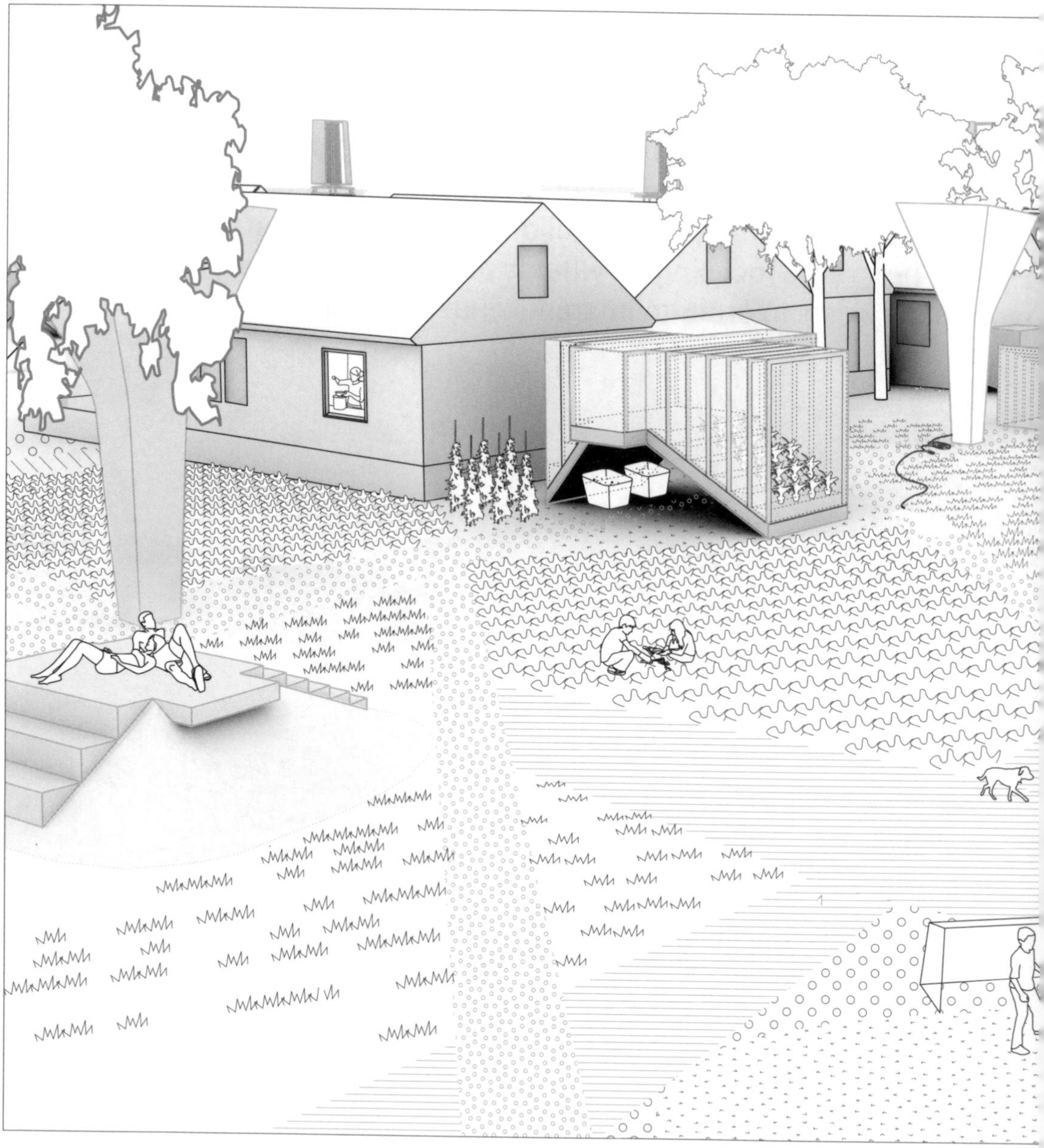

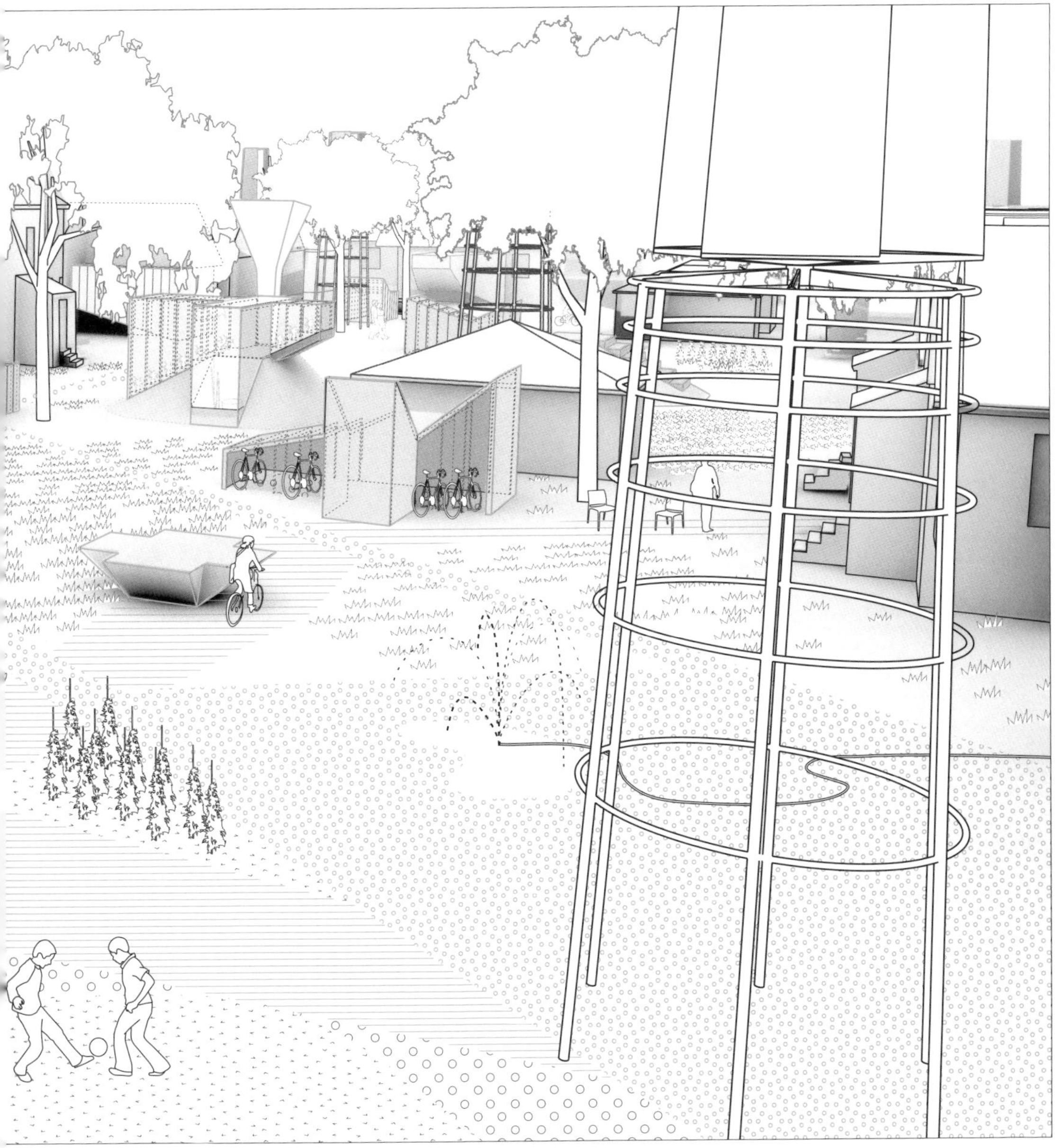

CONTENTIOUS ELECTRONICS/ RADICAL BLIPS

OLGA TOULOUMI

In 1970, *Architectural Design* dedicated its June issue to the Osaka Expo, the first world exposition to be held in Asia. Among the articles covering the expo's metabolist phantasmagoria was a concise but analytic report with the inflammatory title "Architecture versus the Movies, or Form versus Content" by the young British architect and critic Martin Pawley. Throughout the article, Pawley engineered juxtapositions with the intent to entrench the disciplinary boundaries of what he believed his field to be; "architecture," "form," "hard" and "laws of mass and force" existed only as opposites of "media," "content," "soft," and "laws of perception." He noted:

> If the environment of the future is to be created according to the principles governing perception rather than those of construction; if the exhausting tramp over acres of concrete is to be avoided ... then the design of the environment, with its accompanying software, is going to become *de facto* [the] province of systems and media men, electronics and computer experts, film directors and editors, photographers and yes, shopfitters. Architects who cannot manipulate sound and projection systems and their associated optics and electronics will be about as much use as demonologists in a cancer research hospital.[1]

For Pawley the postindustrial age, with its production of electronics and commodification of information, was pulling experimental architects away from questions of form and toward ephemeral architectures of content. Pawley found this shift particularly problematic because he believed the radical separation of envelopes from interiors and buildings from media endangered the totality of the architectural project. Casting the Osaka Expo as the culmination of a failed attempt to comprehend the futures that the postindustrial age entailed for architecture, he suggested that architects reconsider not only the media content of architecture but also the architecture of content itself. He called upon architects to address the electronic realities of the postindustrial age, radicalize architectural thought and practice, and shore up the discipline's precarious boundaries.

1 Martin Pawley, "Architecture versus the Movies, or Form versus Content," *Architectural Design* 40 (1970): 292.

Cover of Martin Pawley, "Architecture Versus the Movies or Form Versus Content," *Architectural Design*, vol. 40 (1970)

Pawley was not the first to notice the impact that systems thinking, communication technologies and media at large was having on architects educated in the United States and Japan. Anticipating that media technologies would transform not only the production of the built environment but also the modalities of its inhabitation, designers and architects who aspired to define the future of the field deeply engaged with cybernetics and media theory. The postwar confluence of systems thinking and human engineering coincided with the development of ever more invisible networks of global communication and the automation of industrial production. In response, architects replaced machines and commodities in design inquiry and pedagogy with information.

The Osaka Expo provided a major opportunity to investigate the futures that media technologies and electronic content could bring to architecture—an anticipatory role that was promoted by Japanese industrialists. After World War II, the Electronics Promotion Law had given the Japanese consumer electronics industry a great boost, resulting in the rapid growth of companies producing radios, televisions and other electronic products. The introduction of computers and automated production triggered discussions of an "information society," with Japan's Economic Planning Agency and the Industrial Structure Council, an advisory group put together by the Ministry of International Trade and Industry (MITI), issuing reports that outlined the information utopias of postwar Japan.[2] These reports celebrated information as the new commodity for calibrating cycles of production and consumption and ultimately reorganizing life in the postindustrial age.[3]

The information revolution affected the humanities at large as well. Apart from industrialists as well as in conversation with them, academics and scholars throughout the 1960s also speculated on the transformations the postindustrial society would entail for humanity. The 1967 *Daedalus* special issue "Toward the Year 2000: Work in Progress" featured Daniel Bell and his think tank arguing that societies did not constitute organic or "unified systems" but rather multivalent entities.[4] That same year, the Oslo conference "Mankind 2000" launched a global effort to establish a speculative "future studies research" community around the narratives of change of the electronic age.[5] In 1968 the Tokyo symposium "Perspectives on Postindustrial Society" debated the structures that shaped the information society.[6] Kyoto University professor Tadao Umesao argued in his seminal "Theory of Information Industries" (1963) that the "information society" was to be the inevitable culmination of the information revolution in production and labor. According to Umesao, this revolution would inaugurate the "ectodermal" stage of society, where the human-environment system would be organized around the circulation of knowledge.[7] When Umesao proposed the "information society" as

2
Tessa Morris-Suzuki argues that in the late 1960s reports such as *Japan's Information Society: Themes and Visions, Policy Outlines for Promoting the Informisation of Japanese Society*, and the 1971 *Plan for an Information Society* were all widely circulating documents that articulated Japanese economy and society as a future "computopia." See Tessa Morris-Suzuki, *Beyond Computopia: Information, Automation and Democracy in Japan* (London: Kegan Paul International, 1988), 7, 29. She goes on to argue that these documents announced an "information capitalism" of automated labor; see chapter 5.

3
Computerization Committee, *The Plan for an Information Society: A National Goal Toward Year 2000* (Tokyo: Japan Computer Usage Development Institute, 1972), 10.

4
The initial special issue of *Daedalus* was later published as a separate book by MIT Press. See: Daniel Bell and Stephen R. Graubard, eds., *Toward the Year 2000: Work in Progress* (Cambridge, MA: MIT Press, 1997), xi.

5
Robert Jungk and Johan Galtung, *Mankind 2000* (London: Allen & Unwin, 1969).

6
Yujiro Hayashi, ed., *Perspectives on Postindustrial Society* (Tokyo: University of Tokyo Press, 1970).

7
Umesao offers an account of this first article in: Tadao Umesao, "Keynote Address: Information and Communication in the Comparative Study of Civilizations," *Japanese Civilization in the Modern World XIV: Information and Communication, Senri Ethnological Studies* 52, ed. Tadao Umesao, Harumi Befu, Josef Kreiner (Osaka: National Museum of Ethnology, 2000), 1–2. Youichi Ito discusses the impact of Umesao's article in Youichi Ito, "Birth of Joho Shakai and Johoka Concepts in Japan and Their Diffusion Outside Japan," *Keio Communication Review*, 13 (1991).

the intellectual concept around which the expo would be organized, the Japan Expo Committee and the Japanese industries it represented enthusiastically assented.[8]

In response, the architects and officials involved in the expo proposed a radical reframing of the event's exhibition strategies. In a world where the human could "avail himself of the modern communication system to be kept informed," the committee noted, "exhibitions can no longer impress and stimulate visitors by novel items of display."[9] Rather than exhibiting machines as the concrete *objects* of technological progress, the officials proposed to exhibit their *performance*: to envelop the public in "environments" of technological affect. Essentially, this decision separated "information" from the channel economy that produced it, interpellating it as the very condition of immateriality. In other words, the Osaka Expo construed worldliness as an ecology of systematically produced and broadcast informational flows.

However, the "information society" that the Theme Committee ultimately aspired to construe differed from purely technocratic visions of the future. With the Cold War defining much of the political climate and memories of Hiroshima and Nagasaki still haunting Japan, the public was skeptical of the technological utopias projected by industrialists and corporations. Aware of the criticism surrounding narratives of progress and mechanization, the committee introduced the qualitative modifier "harmony" to endow the expo with a sense of humanity. The Bureau International des Expositions (BIE) immediately endorsed this modifier as essential to the emerging global community and "mankind."[10]

Architecture and planning played central roles in endowing the expo's informational ecologies with narratives of "harmony." The appointed designers Uzo Nishiyama and Kenzo Tange both contemplated ways in which the master plan could produce a harmonious unity from the multitude of corporations, nations, institutions and publics involved in the event.[11] Construing the expo as a model "city of the future," Nishiyama proposed that the plan be organized around a central "Festival Plaza," which was to be a combination of the Italian urban piazza and a festival program.[12] This decision placed the public sphere at the center of the future city, suggesting that the automated production and electronics to be exhibited in the pavilions would enable strong global ties among postindustrial communities.[13]

When Tange took over the master plan, he transformed Nishiyama's "Festival Plaza" core, with its loose arrangement around a central empty space, into an immense space frame of servomechanisms and cybernetic control. Christened the "Invisible Monument," the space frame endowed the public sphere with an infrastructure of mainframe computers, control rooms, telecommunication cables and closed circuit TV: a "reservoir of information and communications,"

8
The chairman of the committee was Seiji Kaya and the vice chairman was the writer Takeo Kuwabara. See Nihon Bankoku Kahurankai Kyokai, *Japan World Exposition, Osaka, 1970: Official Report*, vol. 1, no. 58, 62. (Subsequent citations of this source will be to *Osaka, 1970: Official Report*.) It should be noted that architecture was always implicated in such visions for the future. For example, in 1970, the year of the expo, the Japan Society of Futurology expanded their annual conference's usual program to include the city and media theorist Yujiro Hayashi and the architects Kisho Kurokawa and Kiyonori Kikutake. Together, Hayashi, Kurokawa and Kikutake proposed that architects and planners could become the programmers of a "multi-channel" postindustrial age. See Japan Society of Futurology, ed., *Challenges from the Future: Proceedings of the International Future Research Conference* (Tokyo: Kodansha, Ltd., 1970).

9
Nihon Bankoku Kahurankai Kyokai, *Osaka, 1970: Official Report*, 62.

10
Ibid., 40–44, 58, 60.

11
Osaka, 1970: Official Report, vol. 3, 159–160. For a discussion of Nishiyama's contributions to the master plan, see Andrea Yuri Flores Urushima, "Genesis and Culmination of Uzo Nishiyama's Proposal of a 'Model Core of a Future City' for the Expo '70 Site (1960–1973)," *Planning Perspectives* 22 (October 2007): 396–398; and Hyunjung Cho, "Expo '70: The Model City of an Information Society," in "Expo '70 and Japanese Art: Dissonant Voices," *Review of Japanese Culture and Society* 23 (December 2011): 57–71.

12
For a discussion of Nishiyama's contributions to the master plan, see Andrea Yuri Flores Urushima, "Genesis and Culmination of Uzo Nishiyama's Proposal of a 'Model Core of a Future City' for the Expo '70 Site (1960–1973)," *Planning Perspectives* 22 (October 2007): 396–398; and Cho, "Expo '70: The Model City of an Information Society," 57–71.

13
Misa Odanaka and Yukha Miura have meticulously translated the original Japanese documents to English; see Shu-kai Chousa Houkokusho [Landscape Investigation Report], *Research of a Comprehensive Production Mechanism Using Water, Sound, and Light in Exterior Spaces Centered on the Festival Plaza*, 17. Among the accounts of Kenzo Tange's contributions to architecture, most critical to my project were Zhongjie Lin, *Kenzo Tange and the Metabolist Movement: Urban Utopias of Modern Japan* (London: Routledge, 2010); Cho, "Competing Futures: War Narratives in Postwar Japanese Architecture, 1945–1970" (PhD diss., University of Southern California, 2011); and Seng Kuan, "Tange Kenzo's Architecture in Three Keys: As Building, as Art, and as the City" (PhD diss., Harvard University, 2011).

as Tange called it, that was intended to spatio-temporally "unify" humans and nonhumans through art and technology.[14] Significantly, by obscuring the material infrastructure of communication to the point of invisibility, Tange argued that "software," or exchanges of information, would replace the "physical hardware of culture" in the production of new knowledge.[15] Ultimately, this rhetorical liquefaction of information as an immaterial abstraction, particularly as articulated inside pavilions throughout the expo, was instrumental in the fiction of communication as a force of unification that the Japanese industrialists and technocrats hoped to fabricate.

Tange's team was joined by Arata Isozaki, who was entrusted with the preliminary report on the "invisible monument" they designed for the central piazza. Tange and Isozaki found Nishiyama's concept of a "festival" potentially helpful. During the 1960s, groups such as Archigram and architects such as Yona Friedman had been casting responsiveness and participation as a matter of mobile and transformable structures. Departing from these paper architectures, Tange and Isozaki displaced participation from the realm of form to that of program.[16] Rather than mobile and transformable structures, the two architects proposed a megastructural triangulated space frame that would retreat into the background of the expo visitors' experience even while it enclosed the totality of such encounters. Within the context of the communication age, what the Festival Plaza would render simultaneously invisible *and* monumental was the very infrastructural logic of the postindustrial information age.

To furnish their technological frame with the myth of a harmonious globality, the two architects turned to music. They argued that their "invisible monument" would unite individual "voices" in a composed collective.[17] Isozaki explained:

> The sound of music further shakes the people, further unifying the song, the dance, and the prayer. In this way each person melds into an enormous collective that surpasses the individual. The power of the moving collective that surpasses the individual shakes the mysterious curtain, and further shakes it—the light moves around bewilderingly, enclosing the ring of people. Suddenly! An excited dancer jumps out into the center of the ring, dancing wildly. The soloist calls a partner, and the duet melts into the group dancing, and the cheering of the people swells, and the rhythm intensifies. Eventually, the sky and the earth slowly opens its doors in the crossing of light, amongst the roaring rhythm, the fierce sound of music and voice of prayer, and that "enormous thing" and all the tribes gradually show themselves on the festival plaza, as if to pour out from the depths of the earth, or to descend from the heavens and the sky, or to seep out of the shadows. The "enormous thing" that appeared out of invitation is once seated,

14
Kenzo Tange, "The Basic Concept of Expo '70," in *Structure, Space, Mankind: Expo '70. Committee of the Second Architectural Convention of Japan* (Osaka: The Second Architectural Convention of Japan, 1970), 14; and Houkokusho, *Research of a Comprehensive Production Mechanism*, 11, 93.

15
Kenzo Tange and Noboru Kawazoe, "Some Thoughts about Expo '70: A Dialogue between Kenzo Tange and Noboru Kawazoe," *Japan Architect: Japan World Exposition, Osaka 1970* 45, no. 5 (May 1970): 29–33.

16
Houkokusho, *Research of a Comprehensive Production Mechanism*, 25.

17
Ibid., 18.

and interacts with the people through sympathy and song. Its transcendental existence speaks to the people, and in turn the people speak to the transcendental thing.[18]

In this imaginary scenario, Isozaki not only envisioned the experience of globality as immersive, but also located sound—and, in particular, music—as its vital component.

The two architects did not restrict themselves to metaphors and illustrative future scenarios. They also planned the Festival Plaza so that it would critically revise nineteenth-century theatrical spaces and their constructed divisions between real and imaginary space, program and form, events and envelopes. "Theaters and concert halls today try to create a conclusive microcosm within a small, closed space," contended Isozaki.[19] Deeply entrenched in the Japanese avant-garde and its exchanges with the U.S. and continental experimental scenes, Isozaki instanced a wide variety of "expanded" practices in art and music to exemplify how temporal events and synchronization would stratify the environmental condition under the space frame. Jacques Polieri's Total Theater and Maurizio Sacripanti's mobile seats;[20] E.A.T.'s *9 Evenings*; the Philips Pavilion and its *Poème Électronique*; Allan Kaprow's Happenings; Jean Tinguely and Niki de Saint Phalle's work for the French Pavilion; Buckminster Fuller's geodesic dome for the Montreal Expo; Nicolas Schöffer's spatiodynamic mobiles; László Moholy-Nagy's environmental modifier; Stan Vanderbeek's expanded cinema practices; and Philip Johnson's work for the 1964 New York Exposition all became precedents for transgressing media-specificity and signified events capable of moving beyond "a fixed space, time, or style."[21] In keeping with this fabricated genealogy, Isozaki and Tange proposed mobile equipment, loudspeakers, moveable seating and adjustable prosceniums to modulate the space and adapt to diverse program specifications.[22]

Isozaki saw this approach as moving toward what he termed a "soft architecture." He explained:

> In 1970 the expression of progress by means of huge monuments has become a thing of the past. We now find our excitement in precision, exactitude and systematic complexity. We want mobility, organization and unity. The excitement of the coming decade will derive from change, mobility, stimulation and all the technology that makes that possible. Architecture has become a medium in itself determining an environment for its inhabitants. In addition to space it must take time into account. Architecture must now take on multiple meanings: its presence can no longer be determined by form; rather it must be flexible and responsive to the flow of time and the needs of a succession of occasions. I call such an architecture "soft architecture."[23]

18
Ibid., 19–20.

19
Ibid., 112.

20
Ibid., 78.

21
Ibid., 111.

22
Ibid., 111.

23
Isozaki quoted in Pawley, "Architecture versus the Movies," 293.

24
Arata Isozaki, "Invisible City," in *Architecture Culture 1943–1968*, ed. Joan Ockman (New York: Rizzoli, 2007), 403–406.

25
Ibid., 406–407.

26
Marshall McLuhan, "The Invisible Environment," *Canadian Architect* 11 (1966): 71–74; and Marshall McLuhan, "The Invisible Environment: The Future of an Erosion," *Perspecta* 11 (1967): 165.

27
McLuhan, "The Invisible Environment: The Future of an Erosion," 165.

28
Ibid., 164.

29
Ibid., 165.

For the young architect, invisibility constituted a crucial characteristic of the postindustrial age. Isozaki had been rehearsing this idea since the publication of his article "Invisible City" in the 1967 issue of *Tenbou*. Transposing Norbert Wiener onto the built environment, he pronounced the city of the future a "system model," cybernetics its design method, and the designer the "pilot" who would mediate between the present "reality" and the "hypothesis" to organize the future.[24] For Isozaki, the city was a matter of "urban composition" and the synthesis of "totally invisible systems."[25]

This focus on invisibility as a fundamental condition of the information age was deeply connected with the architectural reception of media theory. During the mid 1960s, Marshall McLuhan had been contemplating the "invisible environment" in a series of articles published as a follow-up to his seminal book, *Understanding Media*. First in *The Canadian Architect*, and later in *Perspecta*, McLuhan explicitly presented his view on what makes an "environment" to the architectural community.[26] He noted that environments "are not just containers, but [...] processes that change the content."[27] "This is another mysterious feature about the new and potent electronic environment we now live in," he explained. In McLuhan's empiricist model of knowledge, where human subjectivity is constituted by the interruptive workings of such processes, there was no outside vantage point from which to perceive the environment to which one was subjected. "The really total and saturating environments are invisible. The ones we notice are quite fragmentary and insignificant compared to the ones we don't see," he noted.[28] The environment, which McLuhan saw as technologically determined, remained invisible until a new technology produced new environments that rendered the old one visible while becoming undetectable in turn.

McLuhan's invisibility was directed at processes and networks. In other words, for McLuhan the environment was not a "thing," an object with a visual presence that could be documented, but rather a process with both territorial and temporal characteristics.[29] In his theory, "environmental" was a modifier that underlined the technological conditioning of humanity as a totality within which everyone was enfolded. What remained invisible for him were the processes that produced this totality: the infrastructure at work.

McLuhan's technological positivism emerged from his analysis of new and old media: the telephone, radio, television. In his first book, *The Mechanical Bride: Folklore of Industrial Man* in 1951, he pointed at the audimeters that broadcast companies used to research their audiences and market value and declared this kind of human engineering was "inconspicuous," although central to the world of the "industrial man." Following Margaret Mead's line of argument in *Male and Female*, he claimed that audimeters were for the media theorist what the "object" was for the anthropologist: a source of information and data regarding the life of the "tribe," further entrenching the Western construction of "primitivism" within new ideas of globality.[30]

However, between the publication of *The Mechanical Bride* and *The Gutenberg Galaxy*, in which McLuhan would pen the words "global village," transpired almost a decade of phenomenal silence.[31] During this hiatus, McLuhan engaged in a series of seminars on the "new media of communication" and published articles in the short-lived journal *Explorations* with a group of colleagues at the University of Toronto.[32] McLuhan used the seminar to confront what he saw as a tendency toward "participation in a process, rather than apprehension of concepts." He noted that mass media placed a new emphasis on "visual-auditory communication" for the youth of his time, who he found could not "follow narrative" or "bear description," but rather loved "landscape and action."[33]

The opportunity to further explore this "audio-visual" tendency of a media environment that produced "processes" arrived when one of McLuhan's colleagues, Carl Williams, presented a lecture entitled "Acoustic Space," published in *Explorations* the following February of 1953.[34] In the article, Williams claimed that auditory space "has no boundaries in the visual sense," is democratic and responsive, is instant, "lacks the precision of visual orientation," "fills space" and is deep and immersive. Williams proclaimed the universe the "potential map of auditory space."[35] McLuhan found Williams's placement of the visual and the acoustic register as opposites convenient, for it allowed him to theorize the electronic age as an acoustic regime, where the infrastructure remained removed and hidden from the atmosphere created. In fact, he felt so close intellectually to the argument that when he republished the article as part of a collection of essays from the eight volumes of *Explorations*, he whipped off Williams's name and replaced it with his own and that of another University of Toronto collaborator, Edmund Carpenter.[36] The new version of the article would read more like a general theory on electronic media and the "oral tribes" they necessitate than the personal observations of a psychologist on the functions of hearing.

Two years after this anthology and following the dissolution of the group, McLuhan published *The Gutenberg Galaxy*, the fruit of almost a decade of thinking and talking media and modalities of perception. Departing from Karl Popper's understanding of the "tribal community" as a safe place and a closed society, McLuhan claimed that the "electronic age" was sealing "the entire human family into a single global tribe."[37] This "human family" inhabited a "space resonant with tribal drums," where computers replaced libraries and individuals connected with one another with a "technological brain for the world."[38] He anticipated that the world of "simultaneous information movement and total human interdependence" would suspend

30
Marshall McLuhan, *The Mechanical Bride: Folklore of Industrial Man* (1951; repr., New York: Vanguard Press, 1967), 49–50.

31
For a critical biography of McLuhan, see W. Terrence Gordon, *Marshall McLuhan: Escape into Understanding; A Biography* (New York: Basic Books, 1997); and Philip Marchand, *Marshall McLuhan: The Medium and the Messenger* (Cambridge, MA: MIT Press, 1997).

32
McLuhan and his colleagues, Carl Williams, Tom Easterbrook, Jacqueline Tyrwhitt and Ed Carpenter, had won a Ford Foundation grant to study "Changing Patterns of Language and Behavior and the New Media of Communication" in 1953. They decided to invest the funds in their journal. See "Report of the Ford Seminar at Toronto University, 1953–1955," Ford Foundation: Correspondence, Reports, Financial Matters, 1953–1959, Marshall McLuhan Fonds, National Archives of Canada (MMF-NAC), Box 204, Folder 26.

33
Letter from Marshall McLuhan to Harold Innis, 1951. Correspondence with Harold Innis, MMF-NAC, Box 27, Folder 2.

34
Carl Williams, "Acoustic Space," *Explorations: Studies in Culture and Communication* 5 (1954), 15–21.

35
Ibid.

36
Edmund Carpenter and Marshall McLuhan, "Acoustic Space," in *Explorations in Communication: An Anthology*, ed. Edmund Carpenter and Marshall McLuhan (Boston: Beacon Press, 1960), 65–71.

37
Marshall McLuhan, *The Gutenberg Galaxy: The Making of Typographic Man* (Toronto: University of Toronto Press, 1962), 8–9

38
Ibid., 31–32.

judgment and adopt an "open field" modality.[39] Although the concept was appropriated in narratives about an inevitably harmonious future for humanity, McLuhan's "global village" looked anything but that. He predicted that the "new electric galaxy" would create collisions, alienation and displacement, new conditions of international conflict and trauma.[40]

McLuhan did not intend to celebrate the invisible condition of the technological environment. He chose an architectural audience for his article precisely because he believed that architects and artists could potentially reveal the otherwise imperceptible conditioning of the electronic age. Indeed, in his article he invited architects and artists to turn invisibility into the subject matter of their projects; to take a critical position and create "anti-environments" of Happenings and events that would reveal the processes of mediation.[41] This revelation was crucial in McLuhan's phenomenological framework, where new knowledge could emerge only from the experience of an environment or an event. Art and design offered a concrete opportunity for making apparent what technological and political processes were concealing from view.[42]

McLuhan's ideas had a strong impact on the architectural community. In 1966, John Johansen decided to demonstrate to architects exactly how the electronic revolution McLuhan was discussing would affect architecture per se. He asked architects to imagine "building and man as [a] Cyborg," and to design their buildings as extensions of men.[43] Firmly convinced of the importance of McLuhan's tenets, Johansen published his manifesto for an electronic architecture in three different journals and sent copies of it to numerous others. When Jonathan Barnett of *Architectural Record* received Johansen's article, he decided to test its claims, so he reached out to McLuhan and numerous other architects to solicit responses. While McLuhan insisted that "[e]lectronic space is ... tactile and auditory," and that the role of the architect is to "program the environment itself as a work of art,"[44] however, architects did not seem so willing to let go of the architectural object. John Hejduk characteristically claimed, for example, that "as long as men have eyes ... there will be space that a man can see," and consequently an architecture that frames this gaze.[45] What seemed to be at stake was the definition of architecture as either the programming of an experience or the design of a building, as either environment or object: content or form.

A younger generation of designers who were already theorizing architecture as the "extension of man" was less dismissive. In a 1969 issue of *Architectural Design* dedicated to the work of recent graduates in London, Martin Pawley himself tried to parse architecture as a sensorial experience that "can listen, see, smell, touch and remember," while Chris Dawson, his classmate from the Architectural Association, declared that he had learned to "luv [sic] McLuhan" and "not care

39 Ibid., 276.

40 Ibid., 278–279.

41 McLuhan, "The Invisible Environment," 165.

42 Jonathan Barnett, "Architecture in the Electronic Age," *Architectural Record* (March 1967): 151.

43 John M. Johansen, "An Architecture for the Electronic Age," *Design* 10 (September 1966): 20.

44 Cited in Barnett, "Architecture in the Electronic Age," 150.

45 Ibid., 151.

about concrete and form."[46] Similarly, in their "Mind Expanding Program," launched in 1967, the Viennese firm Haus-Rucker-Co. experimented with a variety of technological "extensions" for futuristic subjectivities. They produced a series of structures that ranged from helmets to capsules, which they continued to implement and exhibit until the early 1970s. Designed as "environmental transformers," these structures interfaced between users and their surroundings, altering their immediate sensorial world and promising to offer an escape from dull everyday life.[47] In collaboration with his wife and electroacoustic music composer Franca Sacchi, Milanese architect-turned-artist Ugo La Pietra created a series of installations that he retrospectively called *Le Immersioni*.[48] La Pietra designed his electroacoustic PVC helmets as a critique of the museum and the institutional environments of the art world.[49] These experiments culminated in the work of Walter Pichler, associated with both La Pietra and Haus-Rucker-Co., who turned the transparent techno-utopias of other architects into opaque nightmares of self-induced, inescapable feedback loops, criticizing the subjectivity that mass media were producing through television and the big broadcasting corporations.

Interestingly enough, the critical reception of McLuhan's call materialized mostly in either paper architecture or art projects. In theory, architects enthusiastically embraced the dissolution of the object in favor of programming environments. With plug-in structures, blobs, helmets and the like, experimental architects visualized the designing of experience and implicated the production of form with electronic content and media technologies. In practice, however, their work continued to uphold the concept of the container within which everything else happens. Be it the endless grid of Archizoom, the mind-expanding program of Haus-Rucker-Co., or the immersive environments of La Pietra, a designed object still defined the limits and limitations of this experience, and hence the boundaries of an electronic architecture.

What architects found difficult to visualize, composers had already incorporated as part of their critique of both serialism and the institution of academic music education. Studios like Westdeutscher Rundfunk (WDR), Radiotelevisione Italiana (RAI), and Nippon Hōsō Kyōkai (NHK), just to name a few, provided composers with rich infrastructure, equipment and experts to aid the development of new modes of composition and new means of recording and modulating sounds, thus initiating new alliances between music and the sciences. To these composers, the only obstacle remaining for the realization of multisensorial environments was actual architecture itself: the performance space. Deeply involved in criticizing the modernism realized by the serialists for not breaking with the institutional ties of academia and the Western canon, these circles of experimentalists aimed to radicalize the experience of music. Frustrated by the limitations and restrictions of the available spaces, they asked for new, responsive and

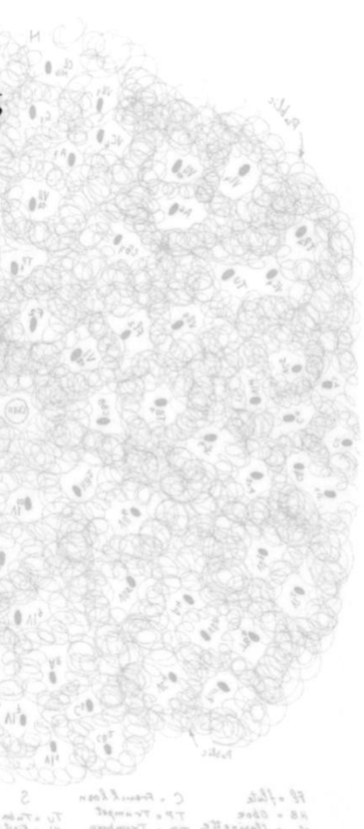

46
Martin Pawley, "The Time House," and Chris Dawson "Home Comforts" *Architectural Design* 44, no. 3 (March 1969): 140–141.

47
"FLYHEAD. A day like any day–dreary. You may buy a revolver, sit down and wait for a miracle or put 'flyhead' over your head and enjoy everyday life." See Haus-Rucker-Co., "Favola," *Domus* (June 1969): 18–19.

48
Ugo La Pietra, in discussion with the author, December 2010.

49
Ugo La Pietra, *Ugo La Pietra: Habiter la Ville* (Orléans: Editions HYX, 2009), 62.

adaptive architectures that would bring the audience right into the middle of music production, subverting the spectacular element of music performance and interrupting the construction of a bourgeois audience built on attentive audition.

Karlheinz Stockhausen was one of the first to contemplate such alternative architectures. "Music in Space," a lecture he delivered at the Internationale Ferienkurse für Neue Musik in Darmstadt, called for composers to make "space" part of their experimentations. In the essay version of his talk, Stockhausen envisioned venues where the composer could program the distribution of sound sources and publics alike in an effort to reinvent "concert-going" as "art-gallery" visiting.[50] Pointing at the exhibition complex, he proposed concert halls where electronic programs would play in feedback loops throughout the day, in much the same way that artworks are exhibited in museums.[51] Stockhausen endowed his idea with a specific form that prescribed universal value:

> In the middle of this spherical chamber, a platform, transparent to both light and sound, would be hung for the listeners. They could hear music, composed for such adapted halls, coming from above, from below and from all directions.[52]

50 The article constituted a transcription of two lectures Stockhausen delivered at American universities during the period he visited the United States in 1958. See: Karlheinz Stockhausen, "Two Lectures," *Die Reihe* 5 (1961): 59–82.

51 Ibid., 69.

52 Ibid.

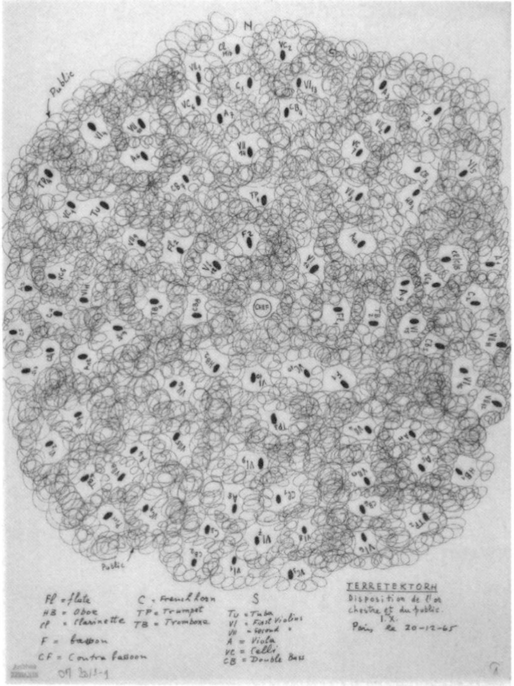

Iannis Xenakis's sketch of the positions of the performers and audience for Terrethektorh, 1966

Greek composer Iannis Xenakis, who had collaborated with Le Corbusier in the design of the Philips Pavilion for the Brussels Exposition of 1958, also dedicated a major part of his work to investigating the spatialization of his music. Beginning with the Philips Pavilion, he would continue experimenting with the physical existence of the temporal event that music was. In his 1966 composition, *Terretektorh*, for instance, the orchestra was dispersed within the audience, forcing unexplored levels of intimacy on both the audience and the performers while the conductor in the center orchestrated the event.

In the Osaka Expo, composers found the perfect opportunity for further exploring new performance space possibilities. To produce the "harmony" that the Japan Expo Association promoted as the necessary corollary to progress, officials encouraged composers to work with engineers and architects in creating worlds of signals. In turn, these collaborations forced architects to confront the changing nature of their profession because multidisciplinary groups challenged the totality of the architectural project. This nascent shift was particularly apparent in the virtual lack of dialogue between the forms of pavilions and the contents of their interiors. Put together, the electronic environments and their envelopes often seemed at odds with one another, with the architectural project frequently reduced to overt symbolism and crude illustrations of networks and globes.

Stockhausen was introduced to the architect-in-chief of the winning proposal for the German Osaka Expo pavilion, Fritz Bornemann, in the summer of 1968. The Federal Republic of Germany was putting together an ambitious spectacle under the leadership of Klaus von Dohnányi, and Stockhausen seemed the obvious person to talk about music.[53] At the International Festival of New Music in Darmstadt, Bornemann explained the plan to have four buried exhibition halls opening up to an outdoor amphitheater. The theme was "Gardens in Music."[54] Grasping the opportunity to realize his dream concert hall, Stockhausen proposed they turn the open amphitheater into a spherical auditorium with the audience placed in the center of an audiovisual envelope.[55] Bornemann agreed, since this would give him the opportunity to experiment with an architectural gimmick that was particularly important after Buckminster Fuller's celebrated geodesic dome for the 1967 Montreal Expo.[56]

Fritz Bornemann, Interior of the West Germany Pavilion, Osaka, Japan, 1970

53
Paul Sigl, "Raum-Klang-Impressionen," *Arch Plus* 149–150 (April 2000): 119.

54
Karlheinz Stockhausen, "Osaka-Projekt," *Arch Plus* 149–150 (April 2000): 122.

55
"German Pavilion," in *Osaka, 1970: Official Report*, vol. 1, 214.

56
Karlheinz Stockhausen, "Kostenvoranschlag," *Texte zur Musik*, vol. 3 (Köln: M. Dumont Schauberg, 1971): 170–172.

When *Hinab-Hinauf*, the ambitious thirteen-minute electroacoustic extravaganza Stockhausen proposed, was rejected on the grounds of cost, the composer replaced the piece with a simpler electronic music program.[57] Two miniature sensor-globes controlled by the composer would modulate the output of sound and light, thus reinstating the composer's control of the total event while making a formal nod to the notion of globality.[58] In fact, for *Pole*, one of the pieces performed inside the dome, Stockhausen divided his "spherical theater" into two hemispheres controlled by two performers at audiovisual war with one another, simulating contemporary Cold War politics.[59] In doing so, he reduced the envelope to a symbol that ironically qualified his own claims to universality.

57
Meaning "Down-Up" in German, "Hinab-Hinauf" referred to the movement of sound from high to low frequencies and of light from darkness to bright light. See Karlheinz Stockhausen, "Licht-Raum-Musik: Hinab-Hinauf," in *Texte zur Musik*, vol. 3, 157.

58
Fritz W. Winckel and Manfred Krause, "Acoustical and Electroacoustical Arrangement for the Dynamically Focused Room," *Journal of the Audio Engineering Society* 20, no. 3 (April 1972): 198–206, 198.

59
Karlheinz Stockhausen, *Pole: Nr. 30 Und Expo: Nr. 31*. (Kürten, West Germany: Stockhausen-Verlag, 1975).

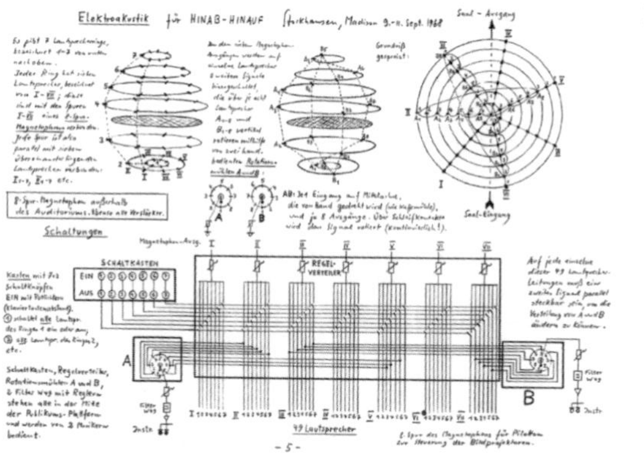

Karlheinz Stockhausen, Diagram of *Hinab-Hinauf*, 1968

Program and form were even further separated from one another in the Japanese Iron and Steel Federation (JISF) pavilion. For the architecture, JISF hired Kunio Maekawa, who had already designed the Japanese Pavilion for both the Brussels Expo and the New York World's Fair of 1964.[60] For the programming, the company hired Toru Takemitsu, an active participant in the mixed-media and intermedia Tokyo scene, to articulate an artistic vision for the "song of steel." Inside Maekawa's cubic core, Takemitsu sought to reinvent the theatrical experience against the architecture that defined it. What did "art gain by dividing the space within […] walls," he wondered.[61] He criticized theaters and concert halls for promoting "the quantitative architectural space of division," and he proposed instead a singular "qualitative perceptual space" that he called a "Space-Theater."[62]

With the help of Japan Electron Optics Laboratory and NHK, Takemitsu's team divided the auditorium into clusters of almost a thousand loudspeakers, mounted on the ceiling and embedded below the seating area.[63] When bathed in lasers and surface light, the spherical loudspeakers mounted on the ceiling would turn the auditorium into a small planetarium. Takemitsu claimed that the Space-Theater would allow the audience to become "travelers" passing through

60
Kunio Maekawa and Hiroshi Matsukama, ed., *Kunio Mayekawa Retrospective* (Tokyo: Bijutsu Shuppansha, 2006), 171–180. Kunio Maekawa was an apprentice in Le Corbusier's office before returning to Japan and opening his own practice. Kenzo Tange, who was the master architect of the Festival Plaza, was Kunio Maekawa's student. For an overview of Japanese modern architecture, I used David B. Stewart's account: David B. Stewart, *The Making of Modern Japanese Architecture: From the Founders to Shinohara and Isozaki* (Tokyo: Hodansha International, 2002), 107–163.

61
Toru Takemitsu, "Nature and Music," in *Confronting Silence*, trans. and ed. by Yoshiko Kakudo and Glenn Glasow (Berkeley, CA: Fallen Leaf Press, 1995), 17–18.

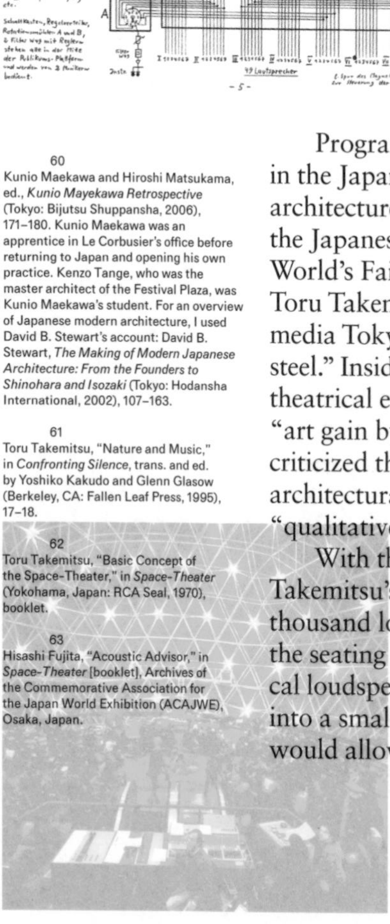

62
Toru Takemitsu, "Basic Concept of the Space-Theater," in *Space-Theater* (Yokohama, Japan: RCA Seal, 1970), booklet.

63
Hisashi Fujita, "Acoustic Advisor," in *Space-Theater* [booklet], Archives of the Commemorative Association for the Japan World Exhibition (ACAJWE), Osaka, Japan.

different "time zones" of sound and experience.[64] Visitors would be able to move freely within this electroacoustic space, and even if they should choose to sit still, the shifting sonic landscape around them would compensate for their immobility.[65] Rotating and changing directions, the loudspeakers would adjust to each composer's program to immerse the audience in an ever-changing soundscape.[66]

64
Toru Takemitsu, "Fundamental Principles of the Space Theater," in *Space Theater* [booklet].

65
Ibid.

Toru Takemitsu with Kunio Maekawa, Interior of Space-Theater for the Japanese Steel Iron Federation, Osaka, Japan, 1970

Iannis Xenakis, Diagrams showing the timing of the loudspeaker sound projection for "Hibiki-Hana-Ma," n.d.

During the expo, the Space-Theater would lower and shift loudspeakers either manually or electronically and turn the mirrors of the central robotic structure, adjusting the infrastructure to the environmental program.[67] Programming for the Space-Theater included

66
"Reproducing a 'Ground Breaking World of Sound,'" *Tekkou-kan Nyu-su* [Iron and Steel Hall News], no. 1 (March 1, 1969), Tekkou-kan Nyu-su [Iron and Steel Hall News], ACAJWE, Osaka, Japan.

67
"Acoustic Equipment of the 'Steel Pavilion,'" *Tekkou-kan Nyu-su* [Iron and Steel Hall News], no. 5 (July 1, 1969), *Tekkou-kan Nyu-su* [Iron and Steel Hall News], ACAJWE, Osaka, Japan.

Takemitsu's own "Crossings," Iannis Xenakis's "Hibiki-Hana-Ma," and Yuji Takahashi's "Veguen."[68] The three pieces were looped throughout the expo along with specially created visual effects. The Steel Pavilion became the biggest surprise of the expo, since there was nothing in the austere, cubic form of Maekawa's brutalist composition to announce the programming that had taken over the interior.

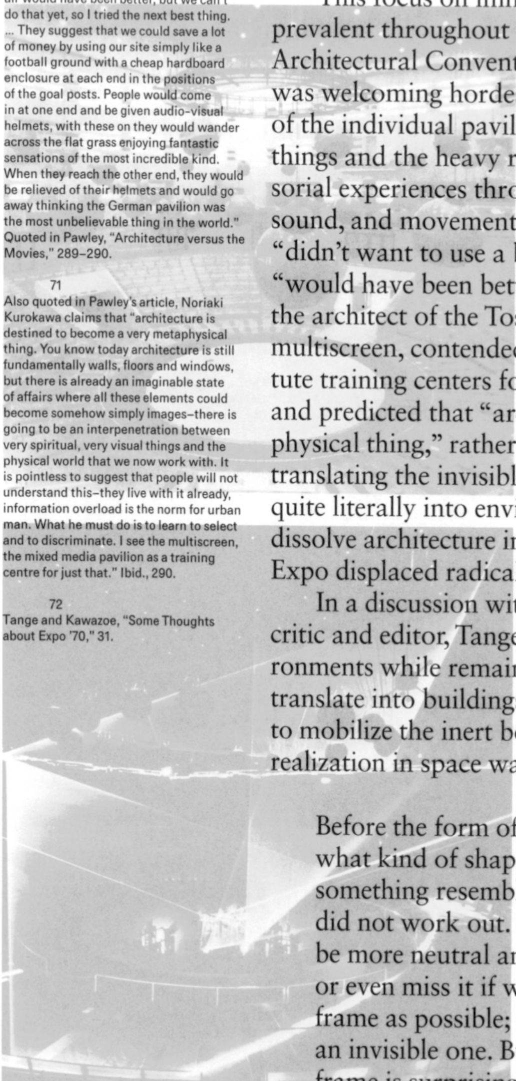

This focus on immersive informational environments was prevalent throughout the Osaka Expo pavilions. At the Second Architectural Convention of Japan, which took place while the expo was welcoming hordes of visitors, Tange applauded the producers of the individual pavilions for "going beyond simple presentation of things and the heavy reliance on motion pictures," and producing sensorial experiences through the "extensive use of photography, lights, sound, and movement."[69] Bornemann proclaimed that he originally "didn't want to use a building at all"; but "[r]adar frozen air," which "would have been better," was not yet available.[70] Noriaki Kurokawa, the architect of the Toshiba IHI pavilion, with its tetra-frame and 360° multiscreen, contended that audiovisual environments would constitute training centers for human survival amid information overflow and predicted that "architecture is destined to become a very metaphysical thing," rather than just "walls, floors and windows."[71] In translating the invisible condition of communication infrastructure quite literally into environments of sound and light that aspired to dissolve architecture into thin air, the architects involved in the Osaka Expo displaced radicality from architectural form to content.

In a discussion with Noboru Kawazoe, the Japanese architectural critic and editor, Tange welcomed the move toward "flexible" environments while remaining skeptical of how such flexibility would translate into buildings. For Tange, this discrepancy between the desire to mobilize the inert body of architecture and its "surprisingly solid" realization in space was all the more evident at the Festival Plaza:

> Before the form of the roof was decided, people would ask me what kind of shape it would have, and I usually said that I wanted something resembling clouds. But in the final analysis, the idea did not work out. I actually wanted to erect a frame that would be more neutral and self-effacing, that people might not notice or even miss it if were gone. I wanted as flexible and simple a frame as possible; if it could have been done, I would have liked an invisible one. But after building the roof, I learned that a space frame is surprisingly solid and not nearly as flexible as I had hoped it would be.[72]

For Kawazoe, these experiments harbingered the "collapse of architecture," which was, as he noted, a "touchy subject." The "softness" of the Festival Plaza was manifested more in the mobile units, the

68
Space-Theater [booklet]; and Takemitsu, *Space-Theater* (Yokohama, Japan: RCA Seal, 1970), booklet.

69
Tange, "The Basic Concept of Expo '70," 17.

70
Martin Pawley attributed the following quotation to Fritz Bornemann, the architect of the West Germany Pavilion: "I didn't want a building at all. Radar frozen air would have been better, but we can't do that yet, so I tried the next best thing. ... They suggest that we could save a lot of money by using our site simply like a football ground with a cheap hardboard enclosure at each end in the positions of the goal posts. People would come in at one end and be given audio-visual helmets, with these on they would wander across the flat grass enjoying fantastic sensations of the most incredible kind. When they reach the other end, they would be relieved of their helmets and would go away thinking the German pavilion was the most unbelievable thing in the world." Quoted in Pawley, "Architecture versus the Movies," 289–290.

71
Also quoted in Pawley's article, Noriaki Kurokawa claims that "architecture is destined to become a very metaphysical thing. You know today architecture is still fundamentally walls, floors and windows, but there is already an imaginable state of affairs where all these elements could become somehow simply images–there is going to be an interpenetration between very spiritual, very visual things and the physical world that we now work with. It is pointless to suggest that people will not understand this–they live with it already, information overload is the norm for urban man. What he must do is to learn to select and to discriminate. I see the multiscreen, the mixed media pavilion as a training centre for just that." Ibid., 290.

72
Tange and Kawazoe, "Some Thoughts about Expo '70," 31.

"environmental equipment," the robots, the moving lights, the loudspeakers and the transformable seating areas than in the space frame itself. "I feel that the entire EXPO, from master plan to individual pavilions, is an attempt to produce just such communications relations between human beings and their environment," Tange noted, professing Expo '70 to be a mere "first step."[73]

[73] Ibid., 32.

Despite its effort to anticipate the future that the postindustrial age of automation and information would bring, the Osaka Expo is mostly remembered as the swan song of metabolism, before the oil crisis put such experimentation to a halt. However, as a historical moment, the expo and the period leading up to it were rich in debates on the social and aesthetic aspects of the information revolution. Within these discussions, architecture was called upon to participate in the myth-making of information as an abstraction detached from the very material infrastructure that produced it. In detaching infrastructure from environment and consumption from the production of information, the architects and composers discussed here construed the postindustrial age as an inescapable surround of information intake. Removed from the public eye, the infrastructure, along with the politics informing its processes, acquired a new level of invisibility that would actually outlive Expo '70. In more ways than one, the Osaka Expo provided the ground zero of contemporary confusions between the infrastructural realities of global communication, be it radio, the telephone, or television, and their ephemeral presentation in the form of instances of community.

As for its architecture, throughout the Osaka Expo, the more intense the discourse on the dissolution of the architectural object was, the more monumental the pavilions ended up being. It seems as if, in practice, architects actually agreed with Pawley's heroic definition of architecture as the formalized matter of a framing device. During the Osaka Expo, electronics were contentious precisely because they challenged the modernist paradigm of what architecture is and what architecture does. And even though architects searched for the methods and tools to break the constraints of their own field, what ended up being the most radical of all were the sonic blips.

If We Wake Up to Find We Have Been Too Well-Trained

A CONVERSATION BETWEEN JOHN HARWOOD AND JOHN J. MAY

JOHN HARWOOD In architecture, questions of automation have almost exclusively centered on the location and limits of *design*—in the first case, as a generative set of logical statements capable of automatically producing design, and in the second, as a way of marking out the inviolable subjective status of the architect through an appeal to disciplinary modes of knowledge. It's easy to miss the basic representational problem posed by this relationship: Any investigation of the relationship between automation and architecture cannot be parsed from the larger representational crisis posited by the concept of "real time." Our work shares a fundamental suspicion of this noun and adjective, which are never defined either in technical, philological or critical terms. My appropriately packaged Apple *New Oxford American Dictionary* states that "real time" is "the actual time during which a process or event occurs," which hardly separates it from time itself. The term only communicates a doubt that time still exists if not reified by digital means, and expresses the difficulty the computing apparatus has with processes and events.

John J. May Let's isolate the definitional language you've referenced—that of "actual time" and "time itself." I am immediately wary of such language.

JH Absolutely. This notion of "time itself" indicates a persistent nostalgia for an analog model of time, already evinced in the work of Marx and the writings of the earliest architectural theorists,[1] that is concerned with the problem of reconciling basic problems of meaning to an increasingly disorganized awareness of chronology. This can be labor time, but it can also be a "phenomenological," "lived" time. The value of the concept of analog time lies solely in its capacity to sustain the power and efficacy of digital time. The discourse that produced "real time" as a moniker requires "actual" time as a foil, but the very proposition precludes taking the ideal of an analog time seriously. This is one of the major flaws with one of the most rigorous theories of media available, Friedrich Kittler's *Gramophone, Film, Typewriter*, which, despite all of its histrionics regarding the convergence of digital media, still privileges the auratic properties of analog media.[2] I find it ironic that Kittler chastised Foucault so vehemently for being incapable of writing the discourse network of 1900, and yet Kittler himself short-circuited the most important historical period for the proliferation of electronic media by refusing to theorize and historicize the period stretching between the electrification of the "developed world" and World War II. It's as if establishing the historical emergence and importance of electrification, and the digitality that it prefigured, required some kind of atavistic backdrop.

Another way of thinking about this problem of "real time" is through the question of the phenomenology of technics. In architecture, there is an insidious tendency to assume that Heidegger is attempting to fix some kind of pretechnical essence, to separate the human being from its technologies and uncover some putatively true mode of authentic life that is obscured by modernity. One finds this poor reading in the various strands of the architectural reception of

1
The Renaissance theorists of architectural history imagined an architectural time *before* rules and measures were necessary. See Alexander Nagel and Christopher S. Wood, *Anachronic Renaissance* (New York: Zone, 2010), 159–174.

2
Friedrich Kittler, *Gramophone, Film, Typewriter*, trans. Geoffrey Winthrop-Young and Michael Wutz (Stanford, CA: Stanford University Press, 1999).

phenomenology, which Jorge Otero-Pailos has recently historicized.[3] I think that no one has been more effective at disarming this interpretation than Samuel Weber, who shows decisively in his essay "Upsetting the Setup" that the technical demand for representation undermines the very subject/object relations it continually establishes.[4] That is, in Heidegger's terms, "technics institutionalize themselves," which means that there is no pretechnical moment, but only a history of a continual process of becoming-technical.

3 Jorge Otero-Pailos, *Architecture's Historical Turn: Phenomenology and the Rise of the Postmodern* (Minneapolis: University of Minnesota Press, 2010).

4 Samuel Weber, "Upsetting the Setup: Remarks on Heidegger's 'Questing After Technics,'" in Weber, *Mass Mediauras: Form, Technics, Media*, ed. Alan Cholodenko (Stanford, CA: Stanford University Press, 1996), 73.

JJM We're clearly better served by comparing various *species* of time, which, in this ongoing process of becoming-technical, are always overlain upon and competing with one another. We might say that real time amounts to a kind of permanent military encampment of electrical discontinuity—of *signalization*—which inserts itself as a representational regime between mechanical time and the inevitable uncertainty of lived life; a species of time in which the present moment is discontinuously regulated against both the known past and all probable futures. That definition only holds if we admit that those subconcepts ("present moment," "known past" and "probable future") have by now also been defined in electrical terms as data, information, signal and so forth.

And yet, real time stems from a logic that predates the fully realized techniques it implies. Unlike mechanical time, which followed from a haphazard history of technical experiments, the logical framework of real time was laid out long before it was ever instrumentally realized. Its possibility was inaugurated by the probabilistic revolution, which posited an increasingly comprehensive cosmology to compensate for the failures of classical mechanics since the seventeenth century. Isn't this where the dream of a "statistical abstract" commensurate with the world itself was first born? And surely that dream included a kind of master analyzer capable of undertaking a process of knowing—calculating the relative likelihood of all probable outcomes, viz., a God. And so we have "the record" and "the process," or *recording* and *processing*.

JH Yes. The statistical abstract is both a temporal problem for the scientist and the historian, and is the fundamental representational crisis posited by real time. There is no rational basis for real-time technologies without this tautology. One might take any example—the need to coordinate rail schedules in order to transport goods, or the need to "protect" one geographical area from aerial bombardment by planes or missiles that come from another. In either case, the basic shared issue is how one understands the difference between the seventeenth-century problem of commensurability between scientific and quotidian observations of time, and the realization of *models* of the reciprocity between records and processing. For me, this is a technical question, and the fundamental aim of the doctrine of *automation*.

JJM ... and more specifically between the doctrine of automation and the formation of an almost anti- or non-modern subjectivity. Whereas the mechanical clock gave rise to a mechanistic cosmology that was to become the theology of progressive modernity, it was a probabilistic cosmology—and more specifically, a statistical view of nature—that led to the electrical clocks of real time, which were latent as magical dream devices in the statistical tables of the early modern bureaucracy. What has always struck me as remarkable about this story is that it's a cosmology that belongs to the psychology of the ancient gambler, whom we can now finally recognize—thanks to a period of extraordinary historical work around these topics, by Ian Hacking, Gerd Gigerenzer, Theodore Porter, Peter Galison, Lorraine Daston and others—as a kind of protomodern risk manager.

Despite this work, however, there is a genealogy that, as far as I know, remains unwritten: a philosophical history of the real time-space of reflexive modernity that is, at least in part, also a pathography of the gambler. Certainly some of Ulrich Beck's work approaches this synthesis—for example, in his excavation of what he calls "the self-refutation of bureaucracy," and the "victory of industrialism over itself."[5] As remarkable as that work is, however, he tends not to drive his descriptions down to the level of, say, the short but brilliant expositions Georg Simmel produced on various types and qualities of modern subjectivity (the stranger, the blasé and so on) at the outset of the previous century. A modified description of that kind would illuminate both the individual and the collective within a typological history committed to technological explication—not toward any sort of dumb determinism, but rather toward the dissolution of the subject/object mythos of modernity. The result would pathographically demarcate a subjectivity that is itself suspicious of the modern subject, and is always marshaling all available techniques to protect itself against that illusion. That seems to have been the mentality of the early modern "statists," who erected around themselves a massive statistical edifice as a managerial response.

5
Ulrich Beck, "The Self-Refutation of Bureaucracy: The Victory of Industrialism Over Itself," in Beck, *Ecological Politics in an Age of Risk* (Cambridge, UK: Polity Press, 1995): 73–110.

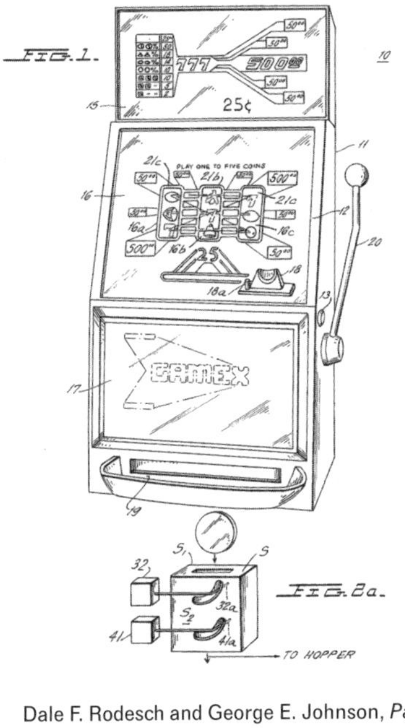

Dale F. Rodesch and George E. Johnson, *Patent for Electronic Slot Machine*, 1975

Whether or not that edifice was an ontology is no longer relevant: it has become one; we are *realizing* it. In any case, such a method would be far better than most sociological reasoning since Simmel, which today appears to be lost in the corridors of the contemporary scientific research university.

That project would entail showing that the rationality of modern bureaucracy (and by extension, of the computer and the corporation) is always already located in forms of speculative conjecture that are motivated by an intense sense of desperation—one capable of motivating a sustained exposure to risk, a sustained engagement with danger: "where there is danger, there also grows that which saves."[6]

It would also show that bureaucracy, as a way of thinking, understood long ago that modernity itself is a kind of desperate speculative conjecture. It's a form of certainty founded on false certainties and unstable concepts—a form of truth that finds its origins in the compulsion to lie. That's the gambler's truth, and its admission into histories of control technologies would immediately unmask the metaphysical skeletons of our technological lives, which we continue to insist are founded upon "reason" rather than belief—as though reason were not always already belief.

JH Yes. In the collaboration between the engineer Ove Arup and the Tecton Group on air-raid precautions in the Finsbury borough of London during the late 1930s, Arup developed a scheme that not only disproved the dominant and operative theory for protecting the populace against aerial bombardment—the so-called dispersal theory—but argued for defending the city both in literal, military terms and in ideological terms through the *architectural* analysis of risk. Arup's schemes for universalizing the application of risk analysis in urban and regional planning preceded the Beveridge Report, and the nationalization of risk by the welfare state that it presaged, by three years. It's an instance of an architectural intervention—complete with designs for buildings—helping to create a discursive field coherent enough to produce the welfare state. And Arup wasn't alone. The pages of *The Builder* during the war years were filled with architects, engineers and contractors arguing for risk management as a central activity of public policy and architectural thought.

Another shared concern is *logistics*. From my point of view, this is both a concept and a phenomenon concealed from view by the logic of management. Managerial theories and practices are primarily a-spatial; they simply process inputs and outputs with a view to establishing a static or dynamic equilibrium. Logistical theories and practices, by contrast, not only demand an instrumental end—e.g., achieving victory on the battlefield, profit in business or sequestration of carbon—but also must confront the basic concern and desire that *things* must be *moved* to particular *places*. Management, in other words, is ideological, whereas logistics is technical and spatial. To my mind, the latter should be the province and concern of architects, yet you seem to relegate logistics to "mere" instrumentalism.[7] Can you help me understand this move?

6
"Wo aber Gefahr ist, wächst / Das Rettende auch." Friedrich Hölderlin, "Patmos: Bruchstücke der späteren Fassung," in *Hyperion and Selected Poems*, ed. Eric L. Santner (New York: Continuum, 2002), 256.

7
John J. May, "The Logic of the Managerial Surface," in "Eco-Logics," *PRAXIS Journal of Writing + Building*, no. 13 (2012): 121.

8 Paul Rabinow, *Marking Time: On the Anthropology of the Contemporary* (Princeton, NJ: Princeton University Press, 2008), 26.

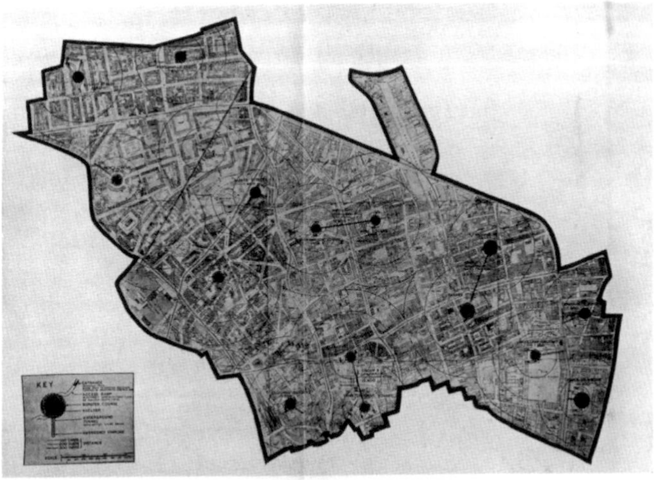

Tecton Group, Map showing the proposed position of air-raid shelters and tunnels in Finsbury Borough, 1939

JJM It seems crucial to make a distinction between those practices we might characterize as "logistical" and the conceptual-material substrate within which logistical processes toil. We can ask, for example, "Why do logistical processes seem to always be improving in their dedicated tasks?" Contemporary accounts that rest too heavily upon analyzing or describing logistical processes—including the well-known "systems" approach to urbanism—are unable to provide an adequate answer because their conceptual orientation can only submit variations on one kind of answer: that we are simply always becoming more technically proficient, more efficient, more skillful and clever in arranging and rearranging the furniture of the world.

However, such variations presuppose that we are not also simultaneously *working upon* that furniture and indeed upon "the world" itself, conceptually and materially. They presuppose that properly "scientific" efforts to explicate fundamental categories of existence—life, nature, being, etc.—have not also always contained within them a nearly simultaneous sideways glance toward efficacy and practical application. Even more unsettling to the Enlightenment mentality, the question arises of to what extent those properly scientific efforts are, in fact, secondary expressions of an age-old impulse toward subjugation. Or, to paraphrase Paul Rabinow: it may be that modern science and technology have all along had far more to do with "revealing potentials" than with "discovering essences."[8] Logistical analyses cannot possibly see the significance of this proposition.

In other words, it cannot be the case that logistical processes are simply becoming ever more adept at exercising themselves upon some sort of stable game board—though certainly *that's what appears to be happening to the eyes of the logistician*, who need only concern himself with *things* and *discrete places*. Rather, there is a reciprocal movement, for which such categories are little more than operational hurdles.

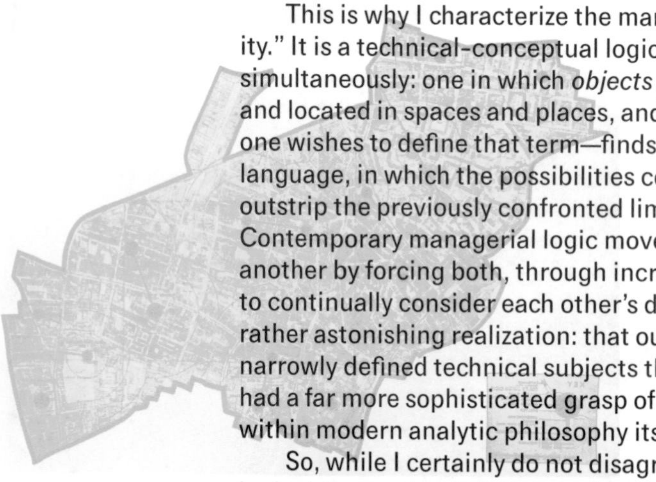

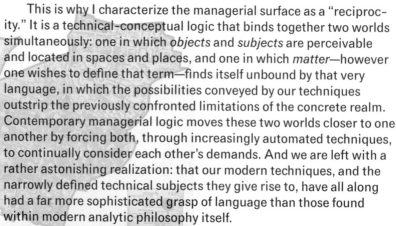

This is why I characterize the managerial surface as a "reciprocity." It is a technical-conceptual logic that binds together two worlds simultaneously: one in which *objects* and *subjects* are perceivable and located in spaces and places, and one in which *matter*—however one wishes to define that term—finds itself unbound by that very language, in which the possibilities conveyed by our techniques outstrip the previously confronted limitations of the concrete realm. Contemporary managerial logic moves these two worlds closer to one another by forcing both, through increasingly automated techniques, to continually consider each other's demands. And we are left with a rather astonishing realization: that our modern techniques, and the narrowly defined technical subjects they give rise to, have all along had a far more sophisticated grasp of language than those found within modern analytic philosophy itself.

So, while I certainly do not disagree that management is ideological, in my view, it is first and foremost techno-metaphysical. We might say that it recognized, long before the humanities or social sciences, that explanation is merely a specific form of description: that we have (in Bruno Latour's words) never been modern, and that certain precious and seemingly immutable conceptual distinctions have always been open to revision. Management has succeeded in reconfiguring life by recognizing that the concept of "life" is never more than an epistemic configuration situated at the intersection of complex instrumental assemblies—a configuration that can find itself appended to an enormous and expanding range of conditions.

We see this so clearly today in agricultural-managerial practices, which should surely be treated as a kind of advance scouting party for reflexive modernity more generally. The agribusiness corporation retains a masterful logistical command over its subject-objects, while simultaneously denying in its laboratories and marketing rooms that such subject-objects are governed by anything we might recognize as "essences." Nowhere do we see representation under greater stress than in this arena; nowhere is language straining so hopelessly to contain that which it claims to represent. It is this quality of opacity—the *sheen* of a purified ambiguity collapsing the space between epistemology and efficacy—that defines this logic as "surficial," and it is no accident that it takes precisely that visual form within the frame of the software interface.

JH Yes, the displacement of thought into the invisible realm of the "guts" of a computer, for instance, is not a simple matter of disappearance. This operation—necessary to the technical matrix of representation discussed above—is always accompanied by a *design* that presents us with a carefully constructed figure of that absence. Far from being a "black box," the intelligence that operates behind the screen of the interface is figured on and around that interface, providing the user with an image of the topology of machinic thought. The "white rooms" and "Miesian houses" of IBM's machines are a model of the networking of human beings and machines into a group subject—the "man-machine system"—that operates at multiple places and in multiple times, all within the present.[9] Heidegger is again crucial here, as is Kittler's provocative but often misunderstood dictum that "there is no software."[10] Although scholars have critiqued Kittler for his reductivism, they tend to miss his larger point, which is that the design of interfaces tends to conceal the technical "goings-on" of the machine behind multiple layers.

Likewise, in your work, you've articulated the logic behind the collapse of "statistical thought and statistical vision," by deploying an archaeology of instrumentation to make it clear that there is a *scopic* logic to sensing and control mechanisms, rather than viewing this collapse as the necessary and right *telos* of a technical process. Scopic logic is opposed to teleology. Whereas *telos* denotes the fulfillment of a process, *skopos* denotes the other form of rational fulfillment: *targeting*, a process of means-ends rationality, in which the targeter simultaneously establishes a firm distinction between itself and the target *and* collapses that distinction through the application of a teletechnology (a bow and arrow, or a Predator drone). In such targeting situations, conventional aesthetic relations—i.e., subject/object relations—are called into question even while they seem to be preserved. Scopic logic *covers over* a fundamental anxiety regarding the inadequate state of our knowledge of the world, and provides us with a secure vision of ourselves as separate from our enemies.[11] It is motivated and structured by the desire for statistical methods to stitch the world back together.

Despite the triumphalist claims echoing from the computer labs and mills in the basements of architecture schools, surface and raster are inseparable from one another. Erwin Panofsky and Hubert Damisch agree that the project of the three-dimensional or, better, pseudo-haptic representation is at bottom an effort at compressing space into a surface. Of course, this is hardly a new problem. I'm reminded of Damisch's statement, which I quote in the introduction to my book, that "an image constructed in perspective can be made perfectly coincident, optically speaking, with its object, such that it could be precisely superimposed over it or screen it out perfectly, *but only if it is seen from the fixed point of view of an observer who could take in both of them in one glance*."[12] One might add to that statement that even this little experiment still requires the viewer to transform her embodied eye into a mathematical point, with all of the strange acrobatics of thought that requires.

JJM We might consider, for example, the case of photogrammetry—defined in its literature as the art and science of deriving accurate measurements from two or more photographic scenes. It was an absolutely central technical practice through the nineteenth and into the first half of the twentieth century, and can claim credit for having radically extended the spatial reign of descriptive geometry. Although it is generally presented as an advancement within the history of cartographic techniques, in truth, the history of photogrammetry is basically the history of a dream of a fully automated metrological perception of the world, in which vision is immediately

9 John Harwood, *The Interface: IBM and the Transformation of Corporate Design, 1945–1976* (Minneapolis: University of Minnesota Press, 2011).

10 Friedrich Kittler, "There Is No Software," in Kittler, *Essays: Literature Media Information Systems*, ed. John Johnston (Amsterdam: OPA, 1997), 147-155.

11 See Samuel Weber, *Targets of Opportunity: On the Militarization of Thinking* (New York: Fordham University Press, 2005), especially chapters 1, 5 and 6.

12 Hubert Damisch, *The Origin of Perspective*, trans. John Goodman (Cambridge, MA: MIT Press, 1994), 151; author's emphasis.

and always a positivist metaphysics. But what we encounter along that history is that an insurmountable barrier to full automation resided, unseen, in the chemical structure of the photograph. For decades—nearly a century—cartographers and military technicians labored over the photograph on the assumption that it held the key to finally dissociating perception from the biological eye, but in every case they found themselves unable to erase the human factor within their instrumentation. In every case, the systems of stereoscopic production, no matter how elaborate, remained only semiautomatic because the photograph was unable to speak directly to the instrument, and vice versa.

What we find now, in the electronic image (unlike the chemical photograph), is a kind of seeing-knowing born directly from the womb of statistical metrology, so that in imaging, the "covering over," as you've called it, becomes a subocular, topological autocoalescing in which perception and statistical reasoning merge indistinguishably.

JH To return to where this conversation began, the difficulty arises when we attempt to connect this to the fundamental questions surrounding automation and autonomy in architecture. The visual equipment now central to architectural practice is best understood through the technical meanings that "automation" and "autonomy" carry in the disciplines beyond architecture. For instance, in the language of military theory, "autonomy" is understood not as selfhood or sovereignty, but as an expression of the spatio-temporal "distance" of an apparatus from a command-and-control hub. That is, autonomy in technical terms is measured out by degrees of intensity; it is considered topologically, and has nothing at all to do with discipline. Automation, on the other hand, is the process of articulating production as an apparatus that involves a control system. Architecture's efforts to articulate its own understanding of autonomy and automation have generally remained unmarked by a nuanced understanding of these phenomena. This is intensely problematic, since—as the example of an autonomous drone hinted at above indicates—the stakes of architecture's implication in autonomous, automated systems can be quite high indeed.

JJM Following from that, how does one bring technical meanings from disciplines beyond architecture to bear upon architecture itself? It seems to me that the search to discover precisely those connections, to elucidate and imagine their exact tangencies with *acts of making*—and the willfulness implicit in that vague phrase—is also to finally take up the question of the very possibility of "architectural theory" today.

I doubt, for example, that anyone considers your work or my work as situated within the category of architectural theory. Now, for my own part, I don't really care where they situate it, if at all. But it raises the question of why it wouldn't be considered as such, and what that reveals about the structure of contemporary architectural thought. The answer stems at least in part, I think, from the fact that our projects have no immediate instrumental use-value within the context of

13 See John May, "Under Present Conditions Our Dullness Will Intensify," *Project: A Journal for Architecture* 3 (Spring 2014): 18–21.

studio instruction. In other words, the problem with undertaking the sort of projects we've initiated is that they run directly counter to the entrenched institutional mentality of the '68 generation, who reflexively demand that all architectural production adhere to a form of intellection that is, at base, *juridical*. Within this psychology, "theory" is posited as the star witness at the trial of the architectural object, while the student-architect is forced into the position of a falsely sincere barrister whose obligation is to defend an object, no matter its poverty or guilt. One needn't look far to discover the wellspring of this psychology: the '68 generation was the first to be required to *speak* during their scholastic evaluations. This was not a feature of the Beaux-Arts pedagogic model, and it catalyzed a kind of unseen reversal within the architectural process that carries with it a concomitant demand that words be used as external legitimizations for a form of aesthetic expression that had never before required *justification*—description, even explanation perhaps, but never justification. The false tension between thinking and making we now face was actually set in motion nearly five decades ago when the latter was made subservient to a very specific brand of the former. That mentality now dominates all of architecture education, and I've wondered since I was a student whether "architectural theory" is capable of shedding the legacy of instrumental logic bestowed upon it.[13]

Within that context, does it even make sense to speak of "architectural theory" any longer? Or would we be better served—if only because theory itself is now a form of limited-liability self-institutionalization—to speak of the recreation of a philosophy of architecture? Or better still, might we posit work of this sort as belonging to an emerging *philosophy of design*? The question is not a simple matter of semantics, as some would say, but rather of the historical baggage now carried by an entire image of thought.

JH It is not semantics, but the semantic is at stake. Our work coincides at a certain crisis point, produced by a collision between philosophies: the relatively recent, utopian, and decisive ontologies of the digital (i.e., the demand that digital technologies present us with, namely, that every previous metaphorical regime be collapsed into a sequence of discrete codes, and the deontologies that are both necessary and absent in the face of the onslaught of these ontologies. What do we do when the previously thick, conflict-ridden, theological, political and materialist metaphorics are exhausted? What happens when a very specific brand of theory trumps "reality"?

The process of *naturalization* we are both mapping here and in our larger projects seems worthy of discussion. The premise that an archaic, operative and even instrumental notion of nature lies at the core of the most powerful, even insidious, aspects of (post)modern technologies of (post)political activity is only the tip of the consequential iceberg. Much more important, it seems to me, is the idea that scholarly activity—and especially scholarly activity that aims at any sort of political objective—should be focused not on removing the blindfolds of a particular class or subject position, not on debunking a rhetorical battlefield (e.g., the idea that some pure "nature" existed in the first place, as an inviolable ground against which our species or any other was figured), not on a claim of moral or ethical consistency and rectitude. Instead, both of us ask our readers to consider the fact that our most pressing task is to demonstrate that *representation is naturalization*.

JJM Can we focus very closely on your last statement for a moment?

JH Yes. The whole question of representation is, to follow the philosophical and anthropological push of figures like Bernard Stiegler, a matter of securing subject formation, where *subject formation is pursued through technical means*. It "works" by continuously updating ("refreshing," we might say today) the status of the individual in relation to a spatial field called "environment."

This is precisely what I find appealing in certain strands of media theory, in that it allows one to begin critique from a point of view that does not require a particular or privileged subject position. In media theoretical analysis, the subject is always already naturalized through a specific entanglement in media: the body is no longer sacred, since it is always already amputated, scarred and covered with technical prostheses; the mind is an effect of social interaction mediated by an ever-changing technical apparatus. Indeed, the subject is less important than the particular space that is opened up by calling the unity of the subject into question. It is this space that Heidegger was concerned to identify in "Building, Dwelling, Thinking," and that Marshall McLuhan offered up as a full-blown theory of "counterenvironment."

There is a danger here, though, and I do not want to imply that I embrace any old posthumanistic or deterministic theory of media, whether fearful or enthusiastic. For instance, I don't believe that we need to spend much time thinking or worrying about cyborgs, at least outside of the cinema multiplex. We have already learned this lesson, from a host of figures in the twentieth century who pushed us to abandon various received humanisms in favor of a technical understanding of subjectivity: Lewis Mumford, in his division of the modern human being into three technical subjective categories of "organ," "organic" and "organized"; McLuhan, in his more-or-less banal reading of ads, had already defined "the mechanical bride" in the 1940s; Claude Shannon and John Von Neumann had already set in motion the retheorization of thought as information through the 1930s, '40s and '50s; and so on.[14] Returning to one of our themes here, the issue is not one of worrying *whether* or celebrating *that* the human being is or is not becoming fundamentally technical, but rather (a) it has never been otherwise; and (b) the proper scope of critical analysis of this situation nonetheless remains an aesthetic question.

Let me clarify what I mean by that last assertion. The "counterenvironment" is an aesthetic concept that is not dependent upon a Kantian schema. A counterenvironment is produced through the use of one media apparatus to close out and reorganize others, and this spatial operation does not proceed in or on a stable Cartesian model of a priori "space." It literally produces space, and it does so through

14 See Lewis Mumford, *Technics and Civilization* (New York: Harcourt Brace and Company, 1934); Marshall McLuhan, *The Mechanical Bride: Folklore of Industrial Man* (London: Routledge and Kegan Paul, 1951); Claude Shannon and Warren Weaver, *The Mathematical Theory of Communication* (1949; repr., Urbana: University of Illinois Press, 1963); and John Von Neumann, *Theory of Self-Reproducing Automata*, ed. Arthur W. Burks (Urbana: University of Illinois Press, 1966).

a topological inversion. What is inside is outside, and what is outside is reorganized. Think of the fortress and the monastery. The fortress encloses a tiny amount of space in a maximally forceful way—with high concentric walls, arrow slits, murder holes and so on—in order to control and transform the space beyond. The monastery encloses an exterior space such as a cloister—through the use of arcades, landscaping and the crucial application of the mechanical clock—in order to transform the enclosed, exterior, natural space into a model of heaven-on-earth. Corporate architecture works the same way, albeit with a new media apparatus. In each case, the effect produced is *counterenvironmental*: it is a space that is produced over and against the surrounding space, secured—if only temporarily—through the concentrated application of technique, and it requires no stable subject to produce it. Indeed, any *impression* of the presence of a stable subject—whether monarch, church or firm—is only ever the effect of this strategic coordination of media, which is performed in a state of utmost individual and institutional anxiety about the viability of such a subject. So, the aesthetic coordination of subjects and objects here is an effect, and a temporal/temporary one.

JJM Perhaps it suffices to quote Michel Serres when he asked whether we "still have to prove that our reason is doing violence to the world."[15] But I'm interested in getting at the heart of this representation-naturalization problem. Can I pose your question in a somewhat modified form? Is it still possible to produce a "theory of representation" commensurate with the *ontological* prowess of our techniques? With our present capacity for rendering reality operational, can we still expect to formulate theories of representation capable of securing, as you say, subject formation?

15 Michel Serres, *The Natural Contract*, trans. Elizabeth MacArthur and William Paulson (Ann Arbor, MI: University of Michigan Press, 1995), 25.

JH If there's any reason to hold on to, or at least acknowledge, the staying power of humanism, it is implied by this question. I am profoundly skeptical of the idea that metaphysics can be thrown out like a baby with so much bathwater. I prefer to ask the question the other way around—and here I'm thinking of texts like Kant's "Prolegomena to Any Future Metaphysics"—and ask whether we have ever produced metaphysics in the first place?

But I wholly agree that the pressing problem that simulation poses for possible theories of representation is not to be ignored. I think, perhaps naively, that art and architectural history and "theory" can leverage a knowledge and awareness of media to critique the proposition put in place by operative theories of simulation. It is worth enumerating the inexorably genealogical connection of design to the technological regime of the managerial surface and the interface alike.

JJM Absolutely. Just as the immersion in capital during the previous two centuries required a parallel intellectual project concerned with the preservation of freedom (however one might define that concept), so too does our already well-underway technovisual immersion require the invention of concepts capable of orienting the bodily individual amongst all that seeks to rectify and regularize its composition from above and below.

I'm trying to fashion—if only for myself—a kind of road map that leads in two directions at once. First, at the practical level of everyday language, the now-mediated subject ought to have some recourse to ideas that by definition (by *design*) exclude *subjugation*, which always lingers, quite literally, just around the corner. I recognize the logical fragility of this proposition; it's a belief, not a certainty. Second, at the register of ontological language—where words are historical accumulations rather than anachronistic qualifiers—there must be a longer-range project that dedicates itself to the continual repositioning of thought in relation to the fact of daily existence. That might take many forms; in my case, it takes the form of problematics that are located at the intersection of architecture, philosophy and technology: a kind of ongoing experiment that tries to establish, over and over, tenuous adjacencies between philosophy and architecture, without ever resorting to an image of thought that instrumentalizes, reduces or trivializes either of those categories. Both must be taken seriously, on their own terms, and neither can be made to serve the other in any direct way.

So the disciplinary agenda of the work—insofar as there even is one, because it's never framed along those lines—is very simple: to work toward erasing the notion that architects are only capable of instrumentalizing thought in relation to objects, and in doing so erase its corollary: this now-pervasive sentiment in the field today (it's silent, but it's there) that somehow serious intellectual engagement, beyond mere technical acumen or observational pseudo-philosophy, runs counter to the production of newness in the world.

JH I'm not so sure how silent it is. That sentiment seems to me to have some very vocal champions.

But the kind of project you are outlining is a profoundly difficult task, for two reasons. As you point out, it is hard to know *how* to do it; and it is hard to produce a compelling narrative that will at once critique the production of newness for newness's sake, and in so doing open up space for vital new ideas and designs.

So, it's hard. But I am also encouraged by the possibilities that emerge from a re-articulation of method. Archaeologies of architecture's equipment provide us with a means of critiquing the new—which is often a matter, in the first instance, of explaining what is old about it—without foreclosing novelty in thinking or design. In such critiques, as in discourse analysis, the question is not of the production of an "autonomous" space from which to secure the rights to critique; instead, it is the acknowledgment of our own embeddedness that provides architectural critique with traction.

This is the sense in which architectural history and theory must remain "critical": it has to *explain* the fundamental complexities and ambiguities of that equipment, the ways in which it overdetermines historical and contemporary practices, without slipping into obfuscation. Architectural practice can remain critical in this sense as well, by refusing simple instrumentalization and instead producing work that upsets conventional uses of technology. Critique is, in its best form, constructive.

LANDSCAPES, SPACES, MESHES: A CULTURAL NARRATIVE OF DESIGN TECHNICS

ANDREW WITT

Theories of architecture are fundamentally connected to their particular accounts of design history. To date, most such accounts have been framed in terms of the political dynamics, communications and ambitions of specific architects relative to culturally situated projects. Here architects are assumed to be in privileged dialogue with each other and with the cultural postures through which theories are interpreted across time. Such cultural-ideological frameworks are practically foundational to architecture's disciplinary self-understanding, and particularly to any conception of professional autonomy. Yet, today, in a time of accelerating heuristic interaction between architecture and urbanism, ecology, and technology, such accounts feel distinctly incomplete. As a practice, we have yet to satisfactorily engage our transformative experimentation with design technology on its own historical terms.

Architecture does have a distinct technical culture, a tacit consequence of its fundamental engagement with the materials, structures and mathematics of form, and architects have historically developed or imported a range of conceptual and technical systems to address the elemental mathematical problems of formal description. These technical histories intersect with the political and authorial history of design only to ultimately diverge from it; any sense of their continuous development as discrete strains within design is thwarted by the cyclical cultural-ideological fashions of the discipline. Technical systems become repeat casualties of ideological revolutions, and each generation overturns the idols of the previous one. Designers are thus relegated to a cycle of technical dilettantism through historical ignorance. We are left with a collection of fragmentary technical archipelagoes, thematically unified under a project of formal control, but dated through their connection with failed political projects. Yet, technical problems are also generated by and generative of cultural concerns. The distinct history of the geometric design problem foregrounds otherwise unexamined tools of practice.

Consider the cultural history of the triangulated mesh, an analytic representation of landscape. A triangular mesh is a connected spatial latticework composed of points, lines connecting these points and triangular surfaces bounded by these lines. It is used to represent curved surfaces, and as such, it has played a particular role in architecture's recent fascination with surface geometry. Triangulated meshes can make landscapes out of spaces and spaces into landscapes. The articulated freeform surfaces of contemporary projects have all the complexity of geospatial terrain—each inflection and each fold must be planned, designed and analyzed. In design, complex surfaces accumulate whole sets of overlapping but unique mesh cartographies: maps of curvature, material stresses, environmental performance. In the field-like spaces described by mesh geometry, deformation is a watchword, but so is control: network maps calibrate a precise and constant interaction of design and engineering in the service of determined effect.

Meshworks extend and subvert the archetypal design apparatus of perspective projection. In the sightline connections between distinct observation points, the idealized, infinitely extended planar landscape of the Renaissance resolves itself into an undulating, articulated triangular mesh. Meshes are, in fact, composites of multiple perspective views. Each node is its own perspectival position, and the edges connecting these nodes form lines of sight. Through these several centers, the subjectivity of perspective is multiplied, forming a network of mutually connected and interlaced locations. The elastic symmetry and homogeneity of this local interconnectedness allows a radically inhomogeneous global form that is rational and self-consistent yet inflected and highly irregular.

Despite a history stretching back to the Renaissance, meshes are now strongly associated with design computation. They are treated as one instance in a burgeoning lexicon of abstract mathematical concepts that architects have adopted to quantify and describe digital forms. Mathematical concepts both broaden the content of architectural knowledge and challenge its notion of narrative: with new concepts come newly relevant conceptual histories, now woven into architecture in complication with heroic authorship and disciplinary autonomy. An archaeology of technical concepts can reveal the surprising connections of a coevolution of design with abstract mathematical systems.

Meshes have become a visual shorthand for architectural complexity itself. They are distinct visual themes in contemporary design, permutations of the delicate recursive subdivision inducing localized and inflected effects. A fascination with surface geometry and the ability of the mesh to abstractly represent folded space tempts designers to revel in its possibilities. The formal qualities of faceting endow meshes with a shimmering visual effect that is temporally and spatially dynamic. Such systems address deeply architectural themes such as the relationship of the part to the whole and the constraints of modular assemblage. Yet, meshes are as analytic as they are visual. As formal apparatuses, they are artifacts of an approach to spatial partitioning and control.

Due to its recurring role as a technical apparatus in diverse contexts, the mesh is also a cultural construct that reveals the normalizing preoccupations of the times that employ it. In fractious seventeenth-century Europe, meshes optimized the design of fortified cities and provided a graphic framework for maneuvers within militarized landscapes. In the nineteenth century, meshes abstracted and regulated commercial networks. Meshes later became the geometric shorthand for structural systems of curved shapes in the twentieth century. Today, they are used to represent and quantify a range of environmental,

A constellation of vaulted topological knots, discretized into even-parity triangular meshes.

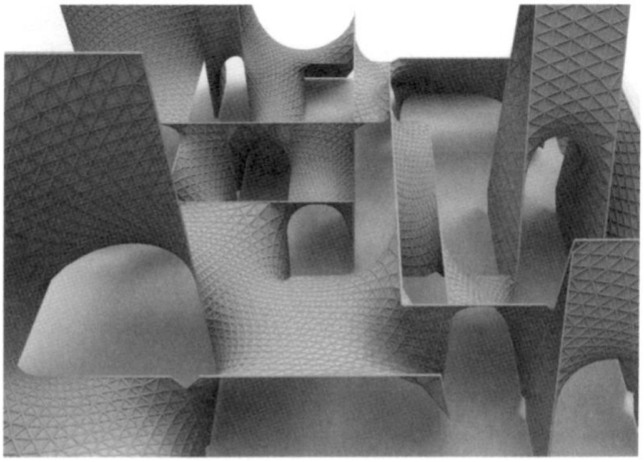

ecological and operational controls such as solar analysis, wind simulation and water-flow visualization. As abstract structures, meshes require a cultural orientation that invests each of their constituent nodes, edges and cells with specific meaning. Thus, meshes and other abstract heuristic methods have evolving semantic biographies. In turn, this conceptual development catalyzes the epistemic evolution of the discipline at large. Three specific cases illustrate this evolution, and the degree to which mathematical methods are bound up with historical projects.

1 Robin Evans, *The Projective Cast: Architecture and Its Three Geometries* (Cambridge: MIT Press, 1995), 44.

2 Josef Konvitz, *Cartography in France, 1660–1848: Science, Engineering, and Statecraft* (Chicago: University of Chicago Press, 1987), 9.

3 Janis Langins, *Conserving the Enlightenment: French Military Engineering from Vauban to the Revolution* (Cambridge: MIT Press, 2004), 66, and Konvitz, *Cartography in France*, 30.

THE PERFORMATIVE RECURSION OF MILITARY FORTIFICATION

Prior to the nineteenth century, cartography was an indispensable corollary of design. It functioned as a sort of geometric foil to architecture, using the same mathematical tools toward divergent ends. As Robin Evans explains: "While architecture provided the opportunity to force substance into geometric shapes, the allied business of surveying provided an opportunity to divest geometry of this same task as soon as it was turned from the designing of perfect architectural forms to the recording of imperfect ones."[1] Of course, the most provocative moments of this relationship occurred precisely when architecture and surveying were conflated around the particular operation of their mathematical tools.

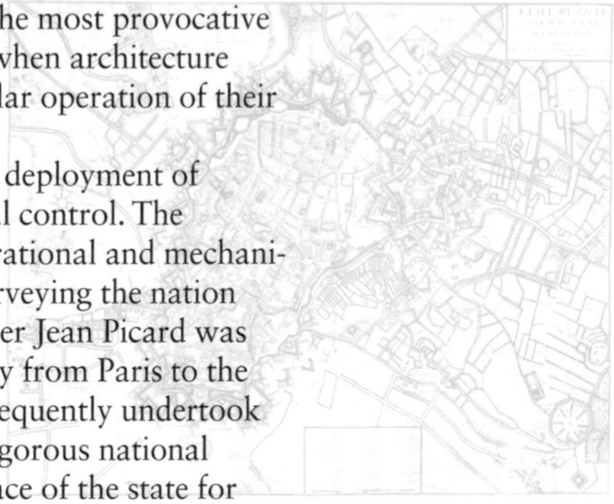

L'âge classique witnessed the first large-scale deployment of triangulation as a tool of cartographic and spatial control. The seventeenth-century French preoccupation with rational and mechanical systems influenced engineers charged with surveying the nation for military security.[2] While the French astronomer Jean Picard was the first to plot triangulated meshes systematically from Paris to the northern coast of France, the Cassini family subsequently undertook nearly a century of triangulation to complete a rigorous national cartographic survey—in effect, measuring the space of the state for the first time.[3] Fortification design applied the rational and geometric control of space to warfare. More performative than mere surveying, the design of fortifications was dictated by siegecraft stratagems and

4
Emilie D'Orgeix, "Fortification and Military Perspective in Seventeenth-Century France," in *Perspective, Projections, and Design*, ed. Mario Carpo and Frédérique Lemerie (London: Routledge, 2007), 140.

5
Ibid., 129

6
Konvitz, *Cartography in France*, 138, 142.

ballistic calculations. The preeminent practitioner of this geometric method was Sébastien Le Prestre de Vauban.[4] As the Maréchal de France during the reign of Louis XIV, Vauban's oeuvre included schemes for both defense and offense, but his most striking spatial contribution was to the design of urban-scale fortifications. Over a series of studies and projects for fortified towns between France and the Spanish Netherlands, Vauban developed a specific geometric approach to fortification subdivision: partitioning the landscape in such a way as to disrupt the progress of infantry while leveraging the elevated positions within the fortress to weaken attacking forces. This extensive subdivision of the landscape was accomplished through an intensive triangulation of the city wall itself. Its geometry was not only planimetric but sectional, drawing on the parabolic profiles of projectiles in order to calculate the proper elevation and ramp conditions for fortifications. The method depended on accurate surveying, as sectional variation in the landscape would materially affect architectural calculations.[5] This essential connection between the geometry of warfare and the geometry of landscape preoccupied engineers through the French Revolution.[6]

Faceted, fractalized fortifications could be characterized as one-dimensional meshes: triangulations generated from a single privileged perspective of segmented control. Although the forms themselves were two- and even three-dimensional, the underlying system was essentially a linear closed boundary curve. Yet, by translating the parameters of spatial control into a mathematical system of wall angles, combat trajectories, and ballistic arcs, the problem of state power was radicalized into a geometric formula. Thus, the abstract framework of the mesh became a vessel for cultural and ideological projects extrinsic to it.

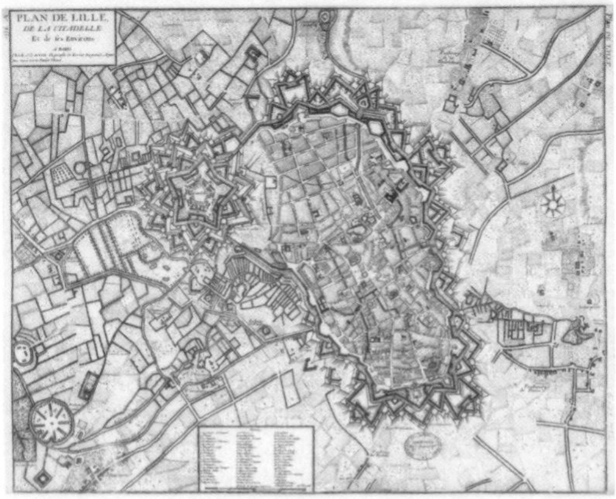

The proposed fortifications for Lille, France, were paradigmatic of the recursively triangulated geometry deployed to control the militarized landscape, as conceived by Vauban in 1668.

MATHEMATICAL SURFACES AND GEOMETRIC LANDSCAPES

In the nineteenth century, coordinated surveying expanded beyond military fortifications into an intricate network that organized cities, counties, regions and nations. Driven by both commercial and colonial demands for precise land and coastal surveys, extensive national mapping programs were set up in Britain, Germany and the United States. France, in particular, benefited from a state engineering corps already familiar with sophisticated terrain analysis.[7] With precise industrial survey instruments, these cartographic programs generated exact landscape-scale meshes and used the apparatus of perspective projection on an immense scale to quantize national terrain. Triangulation provided a newly abstract, purely mathematical representation of landscape that was homogeneous, self-consistent and elastic.

These methods were so seductively precise and so profoundly difficult that their study became a mathematical subdiscipline in its own right: geodesy. The development of cartographic methods was thus connected to the mathematization of surface geometry during the nineteenth century. For the first time, mathematicians were able to utilize precise characterizations for the quantitative curvature of curves, surfaces and curves on surfaces. Thus, beyond the quantification of landscape through surveys, the development of triangulation led to key discoveries in the geometry of curved surfaces. For example, the mathematician Karl Friedrich Gauss, to whom we owe the ubiquitous measure of nonstandard curvature, or Gaussian curvature, devoted a considerable portion of his career to geodesy and spatial surveying.[8]

Through triangulation, surveyors and planners mapped the complex surface of the earth itself in a purely abstract network of mutually coordinated perspective projections, tracing the planet's distortion as a doubly curved sphere. Locally relative and multifocal, the detail resolution of this framework was constrained only by quantitative requirements. These geodetic methods expanded the already deep connection between cartography and geometry, and the understanding of landscape became a mathematical endeavor.

Though they ostensibly remained matrices of engineering information asserting territorial control, nineteenth-century geospatial meshes began to take on a seductive visual quality. More than ever before, the mesh became an aesthetic object in its own right. The multiplied filaments adopted the intricate qualities of ornament. The mesh began to transcend its origin as a mere document and become a mesmerizing artifact of spatial permutation—a landscape of relativized space beyond the conventions of orthographic projection.

FULLER'S TOTALIZING MESHWORKS

If nineteenth-century cartography demonstrated the rich visual and operational control possible with meshes, it remained for designers to

7
Ibid., 9.

8
Félix Klein and Róbert Hermann, *Development of Mathematics in the Nineteenth Century*, trans. M. Ackerman (New York: Math Science Press, 1979), 14.

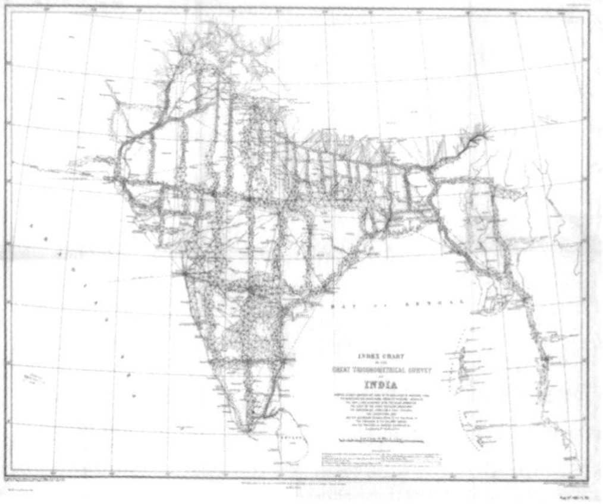

"1904 Index Chart To Great Trigonometrical Survey Of India." This plan shows the abstract relationship among stations, an aesthetic object with a reciprocal visual connection to the physical original.

9
David Hilbert, *Geometry and the Imagination* (London: Chelsea Publication Company, 1952), 218.

10
Siobhan Roberts, *King of Infinite Space: Donald Coxeter* (New York: Walker & Company, 2006), 178.

11
Max Bill, "The Mathematical Approach in Contemporary Art," *Arts and Architecture* 71, no. 8 (1954): 20–21.

fold these meshes into spaces. In the 1950s and 1960s, responding to a new understanding of complex structural and natural interconnectedness, architects and designers began using the frameworks of science to investigate design problems quantitatively. In this synthetic paradigm, the planet became an analog of the building, and the connected quality of terrestrial systems found concrete expression in structural space frames. Since modernism's neglect of Beaux Arts technical practices such as projective geometry led to the loss of rigorous geometric methods, this enterprising generation was left to themselves to reconstruct a logic for geometry in architecture.

At the same time, several developments in the mid-twentieth century reestablished visualization as a key dimension of geometry. The influential mathematician David Hilbert's posthumously published popularizations of geometry featured physical models of topological surfaces.[9] Among geometers, H. M. W. Coxeter almost single-handedly revived the visual study of polytopes, publishing several optically compelling books that found their way into architectural libraries. Coxeter became an interlocutor of Buckminster Fuller, and the two carried out parallel visual investigations of polytopic structures.[10] Nineteenth-century physical models of non-Euclidean surfaces were rediscovered and became objects of study for artists and designers such as Max Bill, Man Ray and others.[11] Geometry had found shape again.

Buckminster Fuller synthesized this renaissance of visual mathematics with an understanding of the mesh. In his work, we see the building as a complete ecology—a contained world in itself with the triangulated spherical landscape of the dome as its envelope. Appropriately, the architectural-scale microcosm was itself described by the perfect sphere of the geodesic dome. Yet, the simplicity of the ground plane folded back on itself is deceiving, as the old cartographic problems of measuring, controlling and correcting the curvature of the earth were now newly relevant for the architectural resolution of complex spherical fabrication problems. Fuller channeled a deep historical interest in subdivision and mapping by geodesics, and specifically mapping by the projective maps of simple platonic solids.[12] He was preoccupied with systems of measurement and pseudocontinuous physical phenomena. Through his various experiments with space frames and meshes, he attempted no less than the discovery of the shape of space itself. Fuller's particular brand of mathematics, "synergetics," canonized the basic unit of spatial meshes, the tetrahedron, as the fundamental geometric building block of the universe.[13]

H. M. W. Coxeter's diagram is an abstract mesh representation of a complex polytope. These same polytopes were used by Fuller in his geodesic domes.

By ascribing structural significance to the mesh and making it a proxy for the nodal configuration of space frames, Fuller moved it into three dimensions and intimated an approach to geometry that was both architectural and analytic.[14] This is a fresh permutation of the semantics of meshing: the reciprocal connections between triangular cells became a proxy for the dynamic forces of structure and nature.[15] Field-like yet strongly figural, meshes became a deductive and integrally unified solution to a simple question of enclosing space by the most efficient means. They created a compact and sewn-up world. Fuller's analytic skin of the dome was a precise landscape of industrial control: in his work we see the germ of our contemporary fascination with the mesh as a promise to control space itself.[16]

CONSTRAINT, CONTROL, WONDER

The cultural evolution of the mesh helps to contextualize contemporary computational geometry. Far from being unprecedented, today's experimentation draws on deep roots in the analytic history of design. In the case of the mesh, we see landscape as a simultaneous space of free action and constrained traversal, an operative field that shapes space itself. The current cartographic projects of computational

12 Buckminster Fuller, *The Critical Path* (New York: St. Martin's Press, 1981), 164.

13 Amy C. Edmondson, *A Fuller Explanation: The Synergetic Geometry of R. Buckminster Fuller* (3rd. edition) (Pueblo, CO: EmergentWorld Press, 2007), 34.

14 Fuller, *The Critical Path*, 209.

15 Edmondson, *A Fuller Explanation*, 263.

16 Ibid., 271.

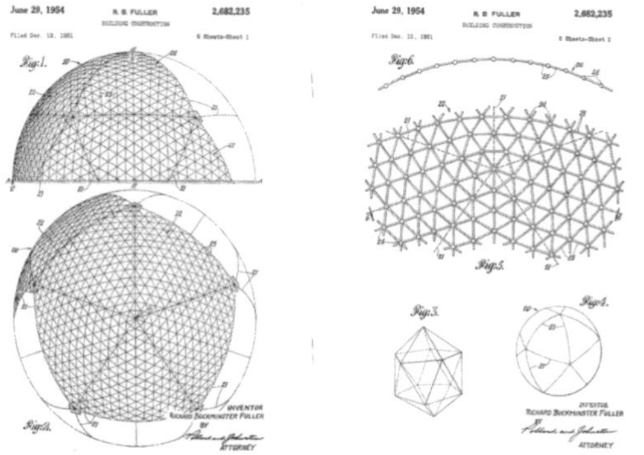

Diagrams from Buckminster Fuller's 1954 U.S. patent for the Geodesic Dome

design—mapping the phenomenal effects of parametric surfaces, or the constructability of distorted spaces, for example—are markers of design's specific state: it is increasingly invested in the heuristics of performative control, yet still resistant to acknowledging mathematics as an extension of design. This situation is in contrast with historical precedents. Instead of expanding the germ of an analytic puzzle into a framework for design, as did Vauban or Fuller, we tend to do the opposite: to see operative analytics as a dimension of engineering, a necessary verification for an ambition that is fundamentally visual. Yet, such historical projects were generative in their own way, calculating spaces and landscapes to satisfy metric performance criteria. The novel forms and daring ambitions of these projects attest to the fecundity of their inductive approach.

Norman Foster, Great Court, British Museum, 2000. The roof represents a paradigmatic modern use of the mesh, as the armature for a surface that oscillates between landscape and form.

I would argue that concepts and methods recur and evolve, and previous meanings assigned to these approaches are not so much invalidated or superseded as accumulated in a framework of correlated understanding. Our epistemic paradigm is thus connected to our historiographic model, and we cannot build robust theories of the first without carefully considering the second. A more rigorously historical approach might defend technological trajectories against both uncritical enthusiasm and unthinking critique. In the context of today's digital meshworks, for example, early critics were quick to point out the scalelessness of the screen and its tendency to incubate acontextual forms. Yet, cultural delight with the richness and complexity of these suspended and scalable world-forms predates the digital by hundreds of years. Meshes are part of cultural history. Understanding this context, we might be able to look past the so-called novelty of triangulated meshes and toward a recognition of their recurring role.

In the mesh we find the ultimate aesthetics of control: calibrated crystalline frames linking cellular regions of discrete dimensions and exactly contained capacities. This control creates an unnatural cage that bounds a dynamic landscape with fixed measures. With such artifice comes the possibility of estrangement, which explains the discomfort it induces. Estrangement is in fact a mechanism of cultural evolution, because it inaugurates the potential for wonder at our ability to contort and remap our environment. To an extent, we feel the same sense of wonder in occupying such a meshed surface as a world-in-itself that we experience when observing the miniature, which captivates not only because of its preciousness but also because it acutely refocuses our awareness on scale rather than context. By representing a garden as easily as a continent, and seeming to allow the same freedom to manipulate and transform both, the mesh induces estrangement through the mathematical rules of triangulation. Beyond this, the mesh also estranges at an epistemic level. Like other mathematical techniques applied to physical things, the mesh abstracts material and materializes abstraction. As diagrams, mathematical representations suppress the tactile and phenomenal properties of material—texture, provenance, mass. The mesh puts all objects representable by triangulation on essentially the same ontological level as physical territory. It enables the intellectual freedom to imagine transforming the most stable of given conditions. At the same time, it makes other, more relational material properties like elasticity and connectivity operable. Meshes thus function as a specific boundary condition between the abstract and the material.

This kind of technological estrangement amplifies interpretive and creative agency. In his essay "Art as Technique" (or more provocatively, "Art as Device"), Viktor Shklovsky claimed:

> The technique of art is to make objects "unfamiliar," to make forms difficult, to increase the difficulty and length of perception because the process of perception is an aesthetic end in itself and must be prolonged. Art is a way of experiencing the artfulness of an object; the object is not important.[17]

17
Victor Shklovsky, "Art as Technique," in *Modernism: An Anthology of Sources and Documents*, ed. Vassiliki Kolocotroni (Chicago: University of Chicago Press, 1998), 219.

The distancing of abstract artifice facilitates the kind of estranged wonder that exceeds mere novelty. Wonder is an active epistemic dislocation, a struggle to reframe understanding in the face of sublime experience. A culture needs the capacity to create forms appropriate to itself and the different futures it projects for itself. The elastic quality of mesh geometries encourages us to import our most radical imaginings from the virtual into the changeable spaces and scales of the physical human context. Thus, the conceptual devices of design artifice become a unique apparatus not only for the creation of new spaces but also for a new approach to the history of architecture itself.

PERFORMANCE REVIEW: IN PRAISE OF THE POSSIBILITY OF ARCHITECTURE

TREVOR PATT

PERFORMANCE REVIEW: IN PRAISE OF THE POSSIBILITY OF ARCHITECTURE

TREVOR PATT

> You are more than entitled not to know what the word "performative" means. It is a new word and an ugly word, and perhaps it does not mean anything very much.
> —J. L. Austin[1]

1 J. L. Austin, "Performative Utterances," in *Philosophical Papers*, ed. J. O. Urmson and G. J. Warnock (New York: Oxford University Press, 1979), 233.

It is difficult to know what is meant exactly when architecture is described as performative. Despite linguistic philosopher J. L. Austin's assertion otherwise, this ambiguity is usually taken to mean something profound and thus acceptably obscure. It sounds familiar and appropriate—hasn't architecture always been subject to performance criteria? —and yet still free of the ideological baggage which has accumulated around so many other terms. The appeal of a "performative" category for the architect, polemicist, curator or editor is readily apparent: it forms a large umbrella under which could be placed almost the entirety of contemporary architectural production. More opportunistically, "performative" enlivens the banal while giving weight to the frivolous.

In its most straightforward definitions, "performance" connects two opposed possibilities: the execution of a particular function and its indexical quality, which can be measured and improved, and the presentation of dramatic, even spectacular, productions. These polarities neatly reflect the objective, technological dimension of architecture as a physical entity as well as its purely subjective, experiential presentation. Little of the discourse on the performative focuses on these extreme positions themselves; rather, most concentrates on the relative degrees to which the two are co-present. Individual positions along this spectrum can be difficult to discern as each incorporates, implies, and, to some degree, relies upon the arguments it has absorbed from its neighbors.

Charting Performative Positions

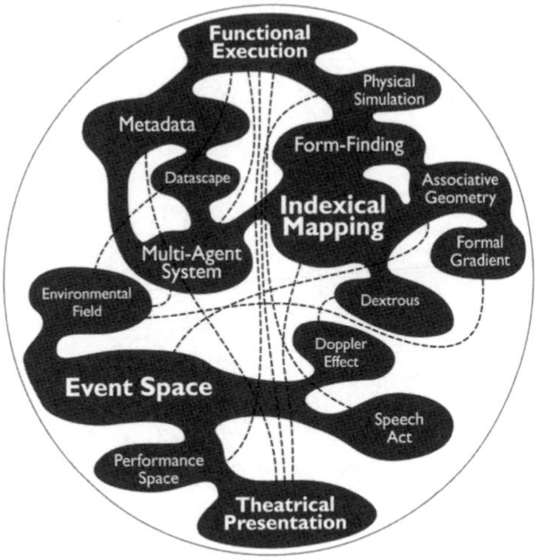

Closer to the indexical end of this scheme are architectural design methods that overlay engineering criteria with semantic coding, including information modeling, metadata, and more advanced techniques of computational form-finding that are often used in conjunction with associative geometry or parametric modeling.[2] Directed in tandem by analytic methods, these "high performance" design processes use the category of performance to refer to the configuration of systems and the expressive integration of internal forces; they are usually concerned with material and geometric behaviors under intensified, atypical conditions rather than simple operational metrics.[3] More explicitly narrative, if not yet dramatic positions recast quantitative metrics as actors in a scripted production. These actors are recorded indexically to produce transformational sequences that can be reread as a narrative of formal logics.[4] As in Peter Eisenman's use of the index,[5] the design process is narrativized through a series of operations which themselves become a form of performance while, in the case of algorithmic design, these operations also calculate and adjust to other performance capacities.[6]

2
See David Littlefield, *Space Craft: Developments in Architectural Computing* (London: RIBA, 2008).

3
Achim Menges, Michael Hensel, and Michael Weinstock, *Emergent Technologies and Design* (New York: Routledge, 2010), 56ff.

4
Holger Kehne and Jeff Turko, "Parallel Indexing: Infrastructure and Space," in "Digital Cities," *Architectural Design* 79, no. 4 (2009): 124–127.

5
See Wes Jones, "Big Forking Dilemma: Contemporary Architecture's Autonomic Turn," *Harvard Design Magazine: Design Practices Now* 1, no. 32 (Spring/Summer 2010): 8–17.

6
Antoine Picon, "Architecture as Performative Art," in *Performalism: Form and Performance in Digital Architecture*, ed. Yasha Grobman and Eran Neuman (Tel Aviv: Tel Aviv Museum of Art, 2008), 18–22.

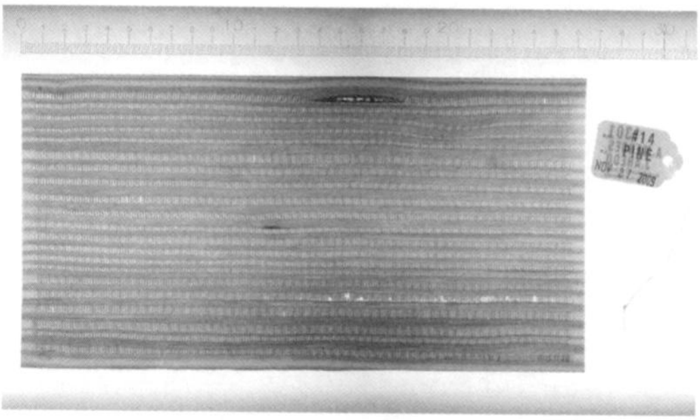

Jose Ahedo, *Microstructural Manipulations*, 2009. Cut patterns uniquely respond to growth patterns in pieces of wood veneer.

Conversely, from the antipode of dramatic performance emerge practices that are concerned with the formation of event-space.[7] Event-spaces can be characterized by their focus on the ambiences and imprecise spatial effects of actions as necessary elements. Their distinguishing feature is an emphasis on the temporal dimension of performance, which occurs in the reception of performance rather than in the design process.[8]

When invoked in the sense of Austin's performative utterances, statements that are neither factual nor rhetorical but operational, performance is meant to be a transformative political action instigated by the emergence of architecture.[9] As such, it is somewhat like an event-space with a similar emphasis on reception, though it is not restricted to the built environment; it becomes more representational, operating in a theatrical way to "capture desire and shape its transference by proposing a semblance of its object."[10] Whereas event-space requires engagement between the site and the performance to impress the affects of ambience, the performance in this second instance takes

7
Bernard Tschumi and Enrique Walker, "Bernard Tschumi, Fireworks," in *First Works: Emerging Architectural Experimentation of the 1960s and 1970s*, ed. Brett Steele and Francisco González de Canales (London: Architectural Association, 2009), 208–219.

8
This is opposed to the mathematical definition of "event-space" (or situation-space, parameter space, possibility space), which is an abstract topological field of all possible outcomes or configurations and would be more closely related to the concept of performance in the previous paragraphs. See Manuel DeLanda, *Intensive Science and Virtual Philosophy* (London: Athlone, 2002), 13–16.

9
R. E. Somol, "Green Dots 101," in "Rethinking Representation," *Hunch* 11 (2007): 28–37.

10
Alain Badiou, *Handbook of Inaesthetics*, trans. Alberto Toscano (Stanford: Stanford University, 2005), 5.

place in the emergence of representation and its effects beyond the architectural object.

Between the event and the index, then, lies a broad middle ground where reliance on technological actions and dependence on subjective actions are collapsed together into a new model. The exact nature of this performative type is ill-defined, in part because the correspondence between the structure enabling the action and its presentation is misaligned. On the indexical side, we find further formal approaches for integrating various regulating diagrams which no longer emphasize the legible precision of the trace but produce a novel and contingent negotiation of forces. Preston Scott Cohen describes these strategies as forms of "dextrous" architecture, "problematiz[ing] a task while multiplying the number of actions being performed at once."[11] On the event-space side is a proposal for an enactment of shifting conditions contingent on the "effects and exchanges" of the various components of the architectural program, as discussed in Robert Somol and Sarah Whiting's "Notes around the Doppler Effect."[12] Many other positions could be identified within the span between these two—some more formal,[13] some more environmental[14]—though all appear to have three characteristics in common: differentiation, affect and field conditions.

11
Preston Scott Cohen, "Dextrous Architecture," *Harvard Design Magazine* 29 (Fall/Winter 2008–9): 67.

12
R. E. Somol and Sarah Whiting, "Notes around the Doppler Effect and Other Moods of Modernism," in "Mining Autonomy," *Perspecta* 33 (Spring 2002): 72–77.

13
See Jeffrey Kipnis, "Performance Anxiety?" in "Foreign Office Architects," *2G* 16 (2001): 4–9.

14
See Gilles Clément and Philippe Rahm, *Environ(ne)ment: Approaches for Tomorrow*, ed. Giovanna Borasi (Milan: Skira; Montréal: CCA, 2006).

Preston Scott Cohen, *Lightfall*, Tel Aviv Museum of Art, 2011

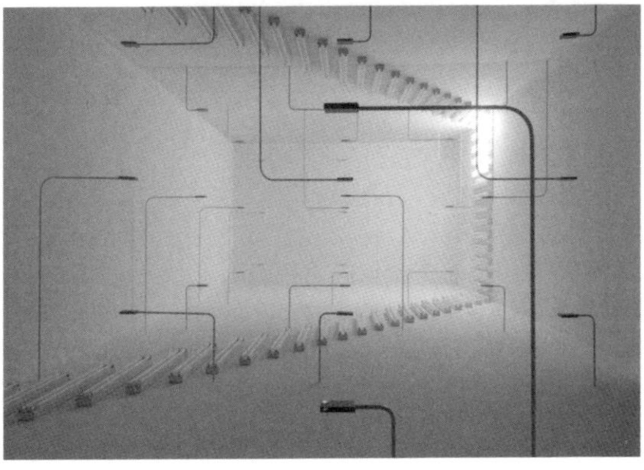

Philippe Rahm architectes, *Interior Weather*, Centre Canadien d'Architecture / Canadian Centre for Architecture, Montréal, 2006

Such a breadth of applications and possible uses (or misuses) of "performance" should make one suspicious, and growing anxiety over the use of such an imprecise term has, in fact, begun to appear in the discourse.[15] The source of this angst is the unfortunate irony that the single common feature of every invocation of performance is an appeal to *specificity* of one kind or another, and yet the terminology itself lacks the reflexive precision to distinguish from among its many meanings. If this imprecision registers as a genuine crisis, it is because the discipline's conception of itself is still deeply connected to an idealization of the production of specificity even as architecture has found itself moving toward "authorless" design and away from signification.

If, in fact, the role of the performative as a theoretical schema were to confirm or reaffirm architecture's own grounding in the specific, to quiet fears that authorlessness had taken command and to assert architecture's identity as creative enterprise, then it would be necessary to mark out more definitive areas of investigation. Perhaps we might even abandon the performative as a category altogether, and coin new and uglier names, as Charles Peirce famously did when he rechristened his philosophy as "pragmaticism," feeling "pragmatism" had been irreparably stretched out of shape.[16] The precise modes of particularity would need to be parsed in greater detail than the brief outline I've just presented, but would this amount to anything more than the laying out of new foundational myths?[17] What is more interesting is the extent to which the performative class has avoided the usual splintering of concepts into smaller and smaller niches, and instead, spans across various territories without barriers. It is as if everything which might be characterized as performative has been gathered together in a set from within which nearly any possible combination of characteristics is acceptable. In fact, no one definition provides enough material to fully support itself, but is, instead, thoroughly mixed up with other, only tangentially similar arguments. Thus, my paradoxical conclusion is that the methods by which architects today are attempting to assert the specificity of their work succeed only to the extent that they operate in the *absence* of that specificity. "Performative," then, is not a definitive adjective, but a rhetorical device which opens a space for a set of *un*defined interpretations. To paraphrase Paul de Man, this rhetorical field appears when our attempts to establish definitions are denied by the logics of the very methods used to formulate the qualities of the definition.[18]

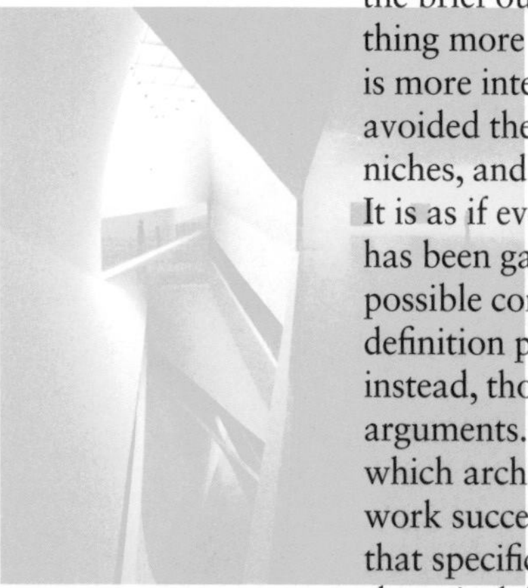

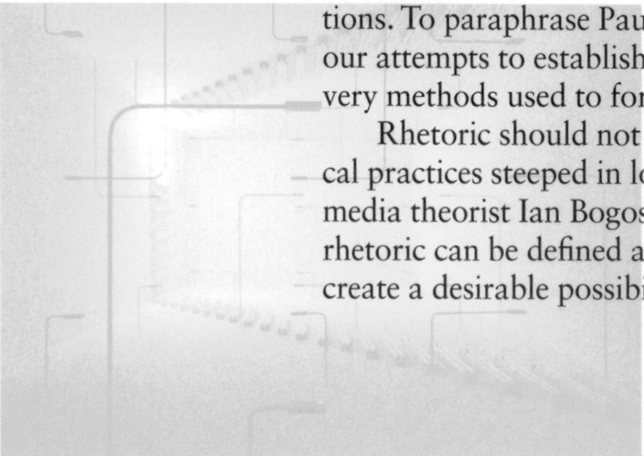

Rhetoric should not be understood as characterized by oratorical practices steeped in long-worn tropes and clichés. Rather, as media theorist Ian Bogost summarizes in his book *Persuasive Games*, rhetoric can be defined as the use of medium-specific techniques "to create a desirable possibility space for interpretation."[19] No longer

15
For examples of this anxiety, see the opening paragraphs of the following: Eran Neuman and Yasha Grobman, "Performalism: A Manifesto for Architectural Performance," 3–7; Yasha Grobman, "The Various Dimensions of the Concept of 'Performance' in Architecture," 9–13; Antoine Picon, "Architecture as Performative Art," 15–19; Sylvia Lavin, "Performing the Contemporary; or, Towards an Even Newer Architecture," 21–26; Eran Neuman, "The Collapsing of Technological Performance and the Subject's Performance," 33–36; all in *Performalism: Form and Performance in Digital Architecture.*

16
Charles Sanders Peirce, *Collected Papers*, vol. 5, *Pragmatism and Pragmaticism*, ed. Charles Hartshorne and Paul Weiss (Cambridge: Harvard University, 1934), §5.414, 416.

17
Peter Eisenman, "The End of the Classical, The End of the Beginning, The End of the End," *Perspecta* 21 (Spring 1984): 154–73.

18
Paul de Man, "Semiology and Rhetoric," *Diacritics* 3, no. 3 (Fall 1973): 27–33.

19
Ian Bogost, *Games: The Expressive Power of Videogames* (Cambridge: MIT Press, 2007), 20.

a legitimizing crutch but instead a means for expanding the field of reception, the architect's anxiety is suddenly rendered unnecessary.

While such imprecise terminology may have been an annoyance when treated as a matter of fact, when it is reformulated as a matter of rhetoric it raises a new question: given such permissiveness, why continue to retreat behind the temporary specificity of performances? If the rhetoric of specificity cannot survive without the very vagary that simultaneously undermines such claims, why doesn't architecture develop specific ways to work through the material of its nonspecificity?

What seems clear at least is that we must avoid the error of thinking of architecture as singular and objective. Instead, we must recognize that it is an assemblage of multiplicity and plurality. In his essay "Can We Get Our Materialism Back, Please?" Bruno Latour suggests that to fully understand an object's reality, we must explore the entire collection of contributing parts, the efforts required to assemble and maintain the assemblage, and the entities which exert those forces.[20] Latour calls this the "thick description of material," where the "thing" in question is expanded across the context which supports it in such a way that prevents the object from being reduced to a material essence independent of the actions and actors from which it was created.[21] As a result, "thick" material recognizes all the strata of an object's material actuality and the potential behaviors embodied therein.

The significance of the interactions between objects and other inanimate objects (together with an acknowledgement that objects are not *solely* defined by their relations) is central to a developing reemergence within philosophy of realism as a richer and more inclusive—but also more potent and more speculative—procedural and relational practice.[22] To give a simple and technical example, the wiring in a building is one part of that building's electrical system, which is itself part of a system for interfacing with a national power grid.[23] The wiring is also separately among the set of highly recyclable materials of a building, as evinced by its removal from any structure that remains vacant and unsecured for a long enough period of time.[24] Together these two systems connect local illicit economies to international commodities trading, energy production, and regional infrastructure, but may also affect the restoration prospects of a building, its public accessibility, or its likeliness to burn to the ground. This example illustrates not only the degree to which action and reaction are integral to the architectural object, but also the difficulty of disconnecting it from its environment when the full scope of interaction is collected. Any model that ignores the complexity of these assemblies will struggle to realize or even identify the physical and social situations that surround the object.

20
Bruno Latour, "Can We Get Our Materialism Back, Please?" *Isis 98*, no. 1 (2007): 140.

21
Latour's essay makes a significant distinction between "things," which are composed of thick material, and thin "objects." Things, following Heidegger, are assembled or gathered, whereas objects exist in an idealizing Cartesian *res* extensa. I will make no distinction, as other authors cited (especially Harman and Bryant) use the term "object" precisely to distance their definition from Heidegger's Ding, though their usage is closer to "thing" as Latour uses it than to "object."

22
See Graham Harman, Levi Bryant, and Nick Srnicek, eds., *The Speculative Turn* (Victoria: Re.press, 2011).

23
Jane Bennett, "The Agency of Assemblages and the North American Blackout," *Public Culture* 17, no. 3 (2005): 445–465

24
Timothy Williams, "Copper Prices and Incidences of Copper Theft Rise," *The New York Times*, February 7, 2011, A13, accessed January 20, 2012, http://www.nytimes.com/2011/02/08/us/08theft.html, and Steven Kurutz, "Criminal Recycling," The New York Times Magazine, December 9, 2007, accessed January 20, 2012, http://www.nytimes.com/2007/12/09/magazine/09criminalrecycle.html.

In the same way, we can learn to expand the event and unfold its internal complexity. For all its openness, the performative still offers only two models of event: the cause-effect event—whether formally predetermined[25] or dynamically sensor-based[26]—and the dramatic event of an enacted script.[27] In addition to these two models, we require a third framework capable of integrating improvisation, not for its own sake, but as an exploratory mode of being. While "thick" material is created by multiplying the number and sets of parts, events are thickened by the consideration of possible developments that exist at every moment but which need to be drawn out and supported.

This kind of questing improvisation is the sort more often found in dance, with its inherent connection to both time and space, than in architecture or even music.[28] Spanish flamenco dancer and choreographer Israel Galván's performance, *La Curva* (2011), is a compelling example.[29] Galván, dancing an almost unrecognizable flamenco, opens the piece by moving centrifugally over the stage. Initially unaccompanied, he first tests the acoustic potentials of the set. His dance alternates between still and small movements limited to fingertips or tiptoes, and fevered, stuttering, crescendoing staccatos. At times, slight gestures, such as tipping over a precarious stack of folding chairs, produce large sounds; at others, one action unfolds new possibilities: dropping a heavy metal sheet onto the ground creates a new material surface which, in turn, encourages different dance steps. Galván is not interested in playing a flamenco on the piano. Instead, he reconfigures the whole of his dance to see whether an assemblage of the steps and compass of flamenco are themselves capable of playing the piano. How fast, how ferociously, how close to the piano must one dance before the vibrations of the stage cause the piano's strings to hum in resonance? Galván's improvisation provides a method that unfolds the hidden reserves of his environment onstage, while at the same time integrating them into the creative act.[30]

Improvisation constitutes a significant departure from conventional critical ontogeny;[31] here, production does not emerge from a void or a negation of an existing situation. Unintimidated, it challenges and draws on the potentials of entities within its given situation.[32] Some kind of negentropic mechanism must be acknowledged here. Difference makes a difference, activity gives birth to action in kind. This definition is a pragmatic one (even pragmati*cist*, perhaps) and has obvious parallels in Charles Peirce's concept of "pure rhetoric," in which representation becomes a creative, generative process when signs produce new signs rather than resolving to a simple meaning.[33] Instead, as philosopher Levi Bryant writes,

> It is already misleading to speak of networks or assemblages as this implies fixed and static beings. Rather, we should speak of assembling and networking, where elements brought together

25
As an example, see "ZHA-AKT Vilnius," proposal for Vilnius Guggenheim Hermitage Museum, Vilnius, Lithuania, 2008, accessed March 29, 2012, http://www.youtube.com/watch?v=ywzOruQMW3E&.

26
See Enric Ruiz-Geli and Cloud 9, *Media-ICT Building* (Barcelona: Actar, 2011).

27
Gramazio & Kohler, "Christmas Lights, Bahnhofstrasse, Zurich, 2003–2005," in *Manufacturing Material Effects: Rethinking Design and Making in Architecture*, ed. Branko Kolarevic and Kevin R. Klinger (New York: Routledge, 2008), 103–118, especially 106–108.

28
"Since dance is a showing of the fore-name [*l'avant-nom*], it must deploy itself as the survey of a site. Of a pure site." Badiou, *Handbook of Inaesthetics*, 63.

29
Israel Galván, Ines Bacán, and Sylvie Courvoisier, *La Curva* (*Tabula Rasa*), at Theatre Vidy-Lausanne, Lausanne, December 7–19, 2010.

30
"Deleuze said that any vibrating space curves, bends and folds up. Here in this spatial fold is where Israel Galván now wants to dance." Pedro G. Romero, artistic director, in the production notes and program for *La Curva*, accessed August 1, 2012, http://www.anegro.net/dossiers/Dossier_ISRAEL-CURVA_(11-03-14)_ING.pdf.

31
"In the case of thinkers such as Žižek, it is argued that change can only be thought if we theorize the existence of a subject that is in excess of any and all symbolic structuration, a subject that is a pure void irreducible to any and all of its predicates, and the act of which this subject is capable. In the absence of such a subject and a completely undetermined act, it is held that any actions on the part of the agent would simply reproduce the existing system of relations. A similar line of thought can be discerned in Badiou's account of the void, events, subjects, and truth-procedures." Levi Bryant, "The Ontic Principle," in *The Speculative Turn*, 272. This is the major point of departure from the Badiousian line followed elsewhere in this essay.

32
Peter Eisenman, "Autonomy and the Will to the Critical," in *Written into the Void: Selected Writings, 1990–2004* (New Haven: Yale University, 2007), 95–99.

33
Charles Sanders Peirce, "Division of Signs," in *Collected Papers*, vol. 2, *Elements of Logic*, ed. Charles Hawthorne and Paul Weiss (Cambridge: Harvard University, 1932), §1.229, 135–36.

evoke action in one another, producing unforeseeable results and configurations.[34]

To sustain engagement requires a flexibility to go off-script; the uncertainty of the reconfiguration reinforces the necessity of sounding the environment for resonances.

In lieu of scripts or narratives, then, architecture needs to access procedures, which should be thought of as the incremental or atomistic units of performance rather than the rigid roadblocks they are sometimes considered. In fact, as Bogost has argued, most of the negative connotations associated with procedures result from situations which have too few of them to deploy or are fixed in a sequential linking that prohibits a nimble reassessment of conditions.[35] A positive model of procedure occurs in choreographer William Forsythe's use of "propositions": instructions characterized by indefiniteness about the form a movement might take, though this does not mean they are undirected.[36] "Propositions alter the ground of active relations," writes Erin Manning of Forsythe's approach, and while propositions can often clearly indicate the type of change or positioning they are meant to effect, they also acknowledge that every change is implicated in other relationships and connections.[37] These connections may resist the action of the proposition or they may dissolve and need to be reassembled; the results will vary in every occurrence according to the dancer's instantaneous momentum, balance and flexibility.[38]

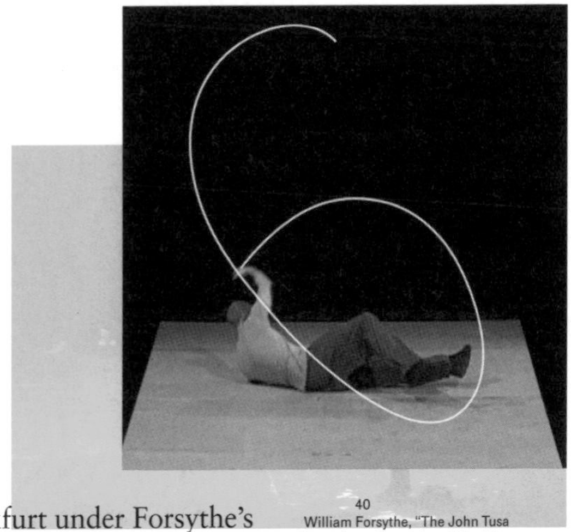

William Forsythe, *Dropping a Curve*, on *Lectures from Improvisation Technologies*, The Forsythe Company and ZKM, 2011

Likewise, the performances of Ballett Frankfurt under Forsythe's direction (1984–2004) have been described by Mark Goulthorpe as "a staging of the very possibility of ballet."[39] They involved working through or over the material of ballet while shedding the identity of the whole and the habits that reinforce that identity. Throughout his career, Forsythe's choreography has asked, "Can ballet, something we know, actually produce something we don't know?"[40] By not

34 Levi Bryant, "Towards a Critique of the Politics of the Void: Notes towards a Politics of Assemblages" (presented at the Rocky Mountain Modern Language Association, Reno, NV, October 9–11, 2008), 9, http://larvalsubjects.files.wordpress.com/2008/11/towards_a_critique_of_the_politics_of_the_void3.pdf.

35 See Bogost, *Persuasive Games*.

36 A number of these propositions were collected in an interactive CD-ROM; see William Forsythe, *Lectures from Improvisational Technologies* (The Forsythe Company and ZKM, 2011).

37 Manning here is also referencing processual philosopher Alfred North Whitehead in her use of "proposition." See Erin Manning, "Propositions for the Verge: William Forsythe's Choreographic Objects," *INFLeXions: A Journal for Research-Creation* 2 (January 2009): n.p.

38 When Alain Badiou writes that dance "finds its essence in what has not taken place, in what has remained either ineffective or restrained within movement itself," he is pointing to conservation of these connections by the dancer. Badiou, *Handbook of Inaesthetics*, 60.

39 Mark Goulthorpe, "Cut Idea: William Forsythe and an Architecture of Disappearance," in *The Possibility of (an) Architecture: Collected Essays by Mark Goulthorpe, dECOi Architects* (New York: Routledge, 2008), 50.

40 William Forsythe, "The John Tusa Interviews: Transcript of the John Tusa Interview with William Forsythe, BBC 3," reprinted in *Ballet.Magazine* (February 2003), http://www.ballet.co.uk/magazines/yr_03/feb03/interview_bbc_forsythe.htm.

41 Bruno Latour, "Reflections on Etienne Souriau's *Les différents modes d'existence*," in *The Speculative Turn*, 309.

dictating the position of the entire body as conventional ballet poses do, Forsythe allows the possibility of unknown, unnamed movements to emerge outside of what is scripted. Forsythe develops this idea further in his installations of "Choreographic Objects" like *Scattered Crowd* (2002–2014), which uses a dense cloud of balloons suspended at different heights to give the audience subtle prompts that alter how they move through the gallery. *Scattered Crowd* evinces the impossibility of a single, perfect interpretation of the choreography; the viewer's movement is always a negotiation between engagement with the installation, an individually desired trajectory and the influence of other bodies.

Similarly, Galván and his collaborating pianist, Sylvie Courvoisier, cast off the traditional form of flamenco, reworking its procedures precisely to explore the potential they contain. Galván's *La Curva* is unique not simply because it involves improvisation in the movements and music, but because both were developed in an ecology of codependence with the equipment and materials of the theatre, set and piano. The mechanical modifications and unconventional playing techniques Courvoisier employs maximize the percussive potential of the piano in the same way that Galván's stage preparation and aggressive auditory (rather than visual) movements enhance the percussive potential of the flamenco and the mutability of the *compás* or rhythmic pattern of the dance. Arguably, the high point of the performance is an intensely visceral, droning buzz that fills the theatre; the footfalls are inseparable from the piano, and one feels that even the catwalks are sounding. It is a moment irreconcilable to any classical definition of flamenco, but assembled out of the excess of potential which *La Curva* discovers within it.

Israel Galván, *La Curva*, Théâtre Vidy-Lausanne, Lausanne, 2010, with Sylvie Courvoisier, piano; Inés Bacán, voice; Bobote, compás

Forsythe's oeuvre suggests ways in which architects might also work free of specificity by opening up or preparing a space for action, working to "set up what comes next without impinging in the least on what is actually said" to create an effect "that is light but also decisive."[41] Architecture is always a trajectory of emergence that outlives its constitutive event. The option of staging re-showings of architecture's same old performances in the face of environmental pressures and diminishing returns requires us to agree to ignore its inherent multiplicity in favor of unambiguous limits, while also reducing the plurality and agency of the public realm. The alternative is to explore architecture's reserve of potential to produce new and unique events that are materially present within the discipline.[42]

Since the state of an architectural object engaged with its environment typically follows a process of differentiation—whether through adaptation, direct response or withdrawal—what is needed is a parallel process that vigorously stirs these components to prevent sedimentation, a procedure which effaces this differentiation. We need an architecture capable of *forgetting*.[43] In other words, we need an architecture composed of generic, mutable procedures (or propositions) that propel architecture to move toward the position of an interface that both acts and is acted upon. As an interface, architecture is capable of steering the directions in which identity and information are shaped, though only indirectly, because an interface directs interaction without defining it while also enabling action.[44] Occupying such a position constitutes a substantial reconstruction of authorship[45] and implies a forgetting of (a singular[46]) desire inasmuch as it requires a commitment from the architecture to the inconstancy of the future.

In my reference to the generic, I do not mean simply the homogeneous, the unconsidered or "all the same."[47] I am suggesting *that we deliberately forget the specifics of formation*: interiorizing and subsuming the details, the knowledge and the definitions that are necessary for the production of architecture. These facts of architecture would continue to structure the responsivity of the discipline in an infrastructural or prepositional mode. Nor is there anything preventing such details from re-exerting themselves, just as one can forget a set of directions and yet reconstruct the way from recognizable landmarks. By avoiding explicit articulations (through processes of indexical trace or didactic physicalization), the architect prevents preexisting definitions from overdetermining the forms which future activity will take. The generic is "a subset that is 'new' insofar as it cannot be discerned"[48] from the situation; that is, while the generic may be identified, its limits are not yet drawn: it cannot be comprehended in its entirety.

Likewise, mutability can refer to a remedial quality that addresses the tendency of architecture to reinforce and stabilize identity by undoing the privileging of the present.[49] Architecture has to shift from being a reaffirmation of itself to being available as a set of procedures that can expand and adapt. This would entail the exacerbation of the many modes of reception to which architecture is subject, that is, the seeking out of disequilibrium, much as the artificial intelligence behind Cedric Price's *Generator* developed patterns of organization to

42
Brian Massumi, "On the Superiority of the Analog," in *Parables for the Virtual: Movement, Affect, Sensation* (Durham: Duke University, 2002), 133–43.43 Maurice Merleau-Ponty, *The Visible and the Invisible*, ed. Claude LeFort, trans. Alphonso Lingis (Evanston: Northwestern University, 1968), 197.

44
"The ontology of prepositions immediately takes us away from the all-too-familiar sorts of inquiry in the philosophies of being. ... The *if* or the *and* has no region. But as its name perfectly suggests, the preposition prepares the position that has to be given to what follows ... their mode of existence." Latour, "Reflections on Etienne Souriau's *Les différents modes d'existence*," 309.

45
Mario Carpo, "Authors, Agents, Agencies, and the Digital Public," in *Visions: Catalogue for the 9th Edition of BEYOND MEDIA*, ed. Marco Brizzi and Paola Giaconia (Firenze: Image, 2009), 71–73.

46
Jean Baudrillard and Jean Nouvel, *Singular Objects of Architecture*, trans. Robert Bononno (Minneapolis: University of Minnesota, 2002), 48ff.

47
Rem Koolhaas and Bruce Mau, *S,M,L,XL*, ed. Jennifer Sigler (New York: Monacelli, 1995), 1248.

48
Oliver Feltham and Justin Clemens, "An Introduction to Alain Badiou's Philosophy," in Alain Badiou, *Infinite Thought: Truth and the Return to Philosophy*, ed. and trans. Oliver Feltham and Justin Clemens (New York: Continuum, 2003), 29–30.

49
See Michael Guggenheim, "Building Memory: Architecture, Networks, and Users," *Memory Studies* 2, no. 1 (January 2009): 39–53.

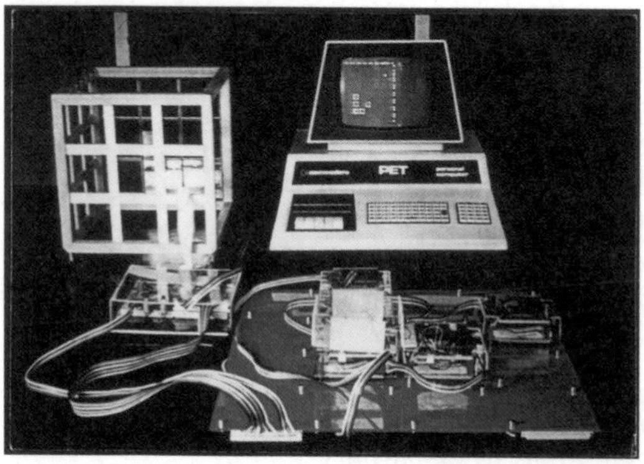

Cedric Price, *Generator Project*, White Oak, Florida, Five Enclosures, Model and Baseboard. 1978–1980

accommodate its occupants, but was programmed to become bored with stasis, even when reconfiguration required unlearning all the patterns it had developed.[50] In the context of architectural representation, this principle is especially opposed to iconicity. Additionally, mutability suggests that current networks ought not to define the type or form of future networks which may be created or to which an object might align. If the generic allows architecture to emerge, mutability prevents it from calcifying in its first configuration. Forgetting allows architecture to remain creative.

Together, these three characteristics of a forgetful architecture—interfaciality, genericity and mutability—would contribute to the establishment of an agonistic architectural environment that would formulate the contested status of its own inherent complexity as a condition to be extended rather than resolved. This is not an easy challenge; the techniques are not yet well defined, and addressing the nonspecific always proceeds less surefootedly.

Ultimately, whether taken individually or as an entire spectrum, the performative still lacks the capacity to produce this uniqueness. It is, at the same time, too little a scenography for projecting desire and too much a capitulation to technological optimization. It has, however, done well in pointing to a space for interpreting architecture's subtraction from the specific. Undoubtedly, many elements of the performative will continue to supply important tactics and provoke further adjustments. Efforts in digital simulation suggest positive steps toward embracing genericity in both design and authorship, but tend toward a hyperspecific and unseverable connection between form and its representation within data-structures.[51] Attempts to de-emphasize representation draw on the variability of the environment and its reception, but too often posit the singular performance as a solution.[52] Both approaches assume that belonging to a set, network or assembly is contingent on or confers similarity.[53] Yet, belonging does not equal becoming, nor does engagement at one stratum erase autonomy at another. Thus far we have not been able to see architecture for its inconsistent multiplicity; thus far we have not seen past the performance.

50
Cedric Price, *Cedric Price: The Square Book* (West Sussex: Wiley, 1984), 92–97.

51
See Neil Leach, "Swarm Urbanism," in "Digital Cities," *Architectural Design* 79, no. 4 (2009): 56–63.

52
See Somol and Whiting, "Notes around the Doppler Effect," 72–77.

53
See R. E. Somol, "The Seduction of the Similar," *Assemblage* 40 (December 1999): 68–79.

A PLAZA IN A CAMP: A PLAY IN FOUR ACTS

SANDI HILAL

Act One

May, 2008. An open space about 500 square meters in area in a crowded neighborhood of the Fawwar Refugee Camp in the West Bank. The ARCHITECT, *who is the head of the United Nations Relief and Works Agency for Palestine Refugees in the Near East* (UNRWA) *Camp Improvement Program in the West Bank, sits on a chair in the center of the space. She is turned to her left to face a group of about twenty women of all ages, who are sitting in chairs or on the ground. They include* HADIYAH, AMEENAH, HALAH, HAJAH SALMA, *and* JAMILAH. *To her right, a group of about the same number of men, also of all ages, but with a large proportion of young men, or* shabab, *sits or stands silently. They include* AHMED, ABU RABIH, *and* ABU RAMI. *A* shader, *or cloth canopy covering, protects everyone from the sun.*

HADIYAH[1]

(*Emphatically*) There is no problem with building a plaza for our neighborhood. But it has to be only for the people of our neighborhood and not for all the people of the camp. Casual passersby cannot use this plaza. Young males who have nothing to do can't just come and hang out in our plaza. Yes for the neighborhood, no for the camp.

The women nod vigorously.

HADIYAH

I will give you a concrete example of what I am speaking about. Yesterday, as soon as the shade (*gestures to the* shader *covering overhead*) and lighting were installed, this plaza was immediately transformed from an invisible plaza for the neighborhood into an attractive hangout for the young people from the entire camp. A bunch of young *shabab* that I had never seen before came and spent the entire day in front of my house. Yesterday evening I wanted to go to my sister's, but when I opened my door to leave, I immediately felt that the plaza was not mine anymore and that it had been taken over by these *shabab*. I felt shy about crossing through them and I had to find a different way to get to my sister's. Do you understand what I mean? This is *my* plaza, this is the plaza of our neighborhood, it is not a plaza for everybody. This plaza must maintain its invisibility.

The women nod and some make eye contact with the ARCHITECT *to signal their complete agreement.*

ARCHITECT

(*Aside*) I tried to understand the difference between a plaza for a neighborhood and a plaza for a camp by asking about the ways these women imagined they might use the space.

(*To the women*) Would you ever come to this plaza and have morning coffee together, out in the sunshine?

1 Names have been changed to respect the identities of the people involved.

2
One of the most important Egyptian newspapers.

AMEENAH (A strong woman with a hard face, dressed in a glamorous purple *jilbab*)
(*Forcefully, but with humor*) What woman would leave her home, her kids, and come to drink coffee in a plaza? It would be a shame for a woman to leave her home without a proper reason. Do you want us all to come here in the plaza and have coffee and tea? Do you want them to write about us in *Al-Ahram*?[2] We already cannot deal with our husbands; never mind us going out and having tea and coffee in the plaza!

The other women laugh and break into amused side conversations. AMEENAH *looks around at them with an air of victory. 1st* FAWWAR WOMAN *comes out of one of the adjoining houses, carrying a coffee pot, and 2nd* FAWWAR WOMAN *exits a different home with cups for everyone. The women begin distributing coffee to everyone in the plaza. The* ARCHITECT *takes the cup offered to her and looks around incredulously. The women settle down with their coffee, still laughing and talking among themselves.*

ARCHITECT
Then why are you doing just that right now? Look at us! We are sitting here happily and enjoying our coffee.

AMEENAH
We are sitting here while our husbands are at work. (*Boldly locking eyes with the* ARCHITECT) Do you think that they know that we are here?

The other women look at each other, at AMEENAH *and the* ARCHITECT, *and many renew their laughter. Some cover their faces shyly, but they are really enjoying what their brave neighbor,* AMEENAH, *is saying. Other women, however, are pensive and a bit sad.*

HALAH (A serious woman dressed in a black *jilbab*)
(*Making eye contact with the* ARCHITECT, *and speaking seriously*) Do you want us to gather and have coffee and tea here together? This is a problem, darling, it is a real problem.

HAJAH SALMA (An older woman in a Palestinian dress with a black headscarf and a walking stick)
(*Breaking in emphatically, and punctuating her words with her walking stick*) *I* will come and sit here by myself. I don't care what anybody says.

ANOTHER HAJAH *nearby, dressed in the same manner, makes a motion to silence her. Undaunted,* HAJAH SALMA *turns to her challengingly.*

Nobody would dare to tell me that I cannot sit here in front of everybody.

ARCHITECT
(*Soothingly*) Is there any activity you could do here?
(*Aside*) Even if the answer is "nothing," this will still be a way to lessen the tension and change the direction of the conversation.

1st FAWWAR WOMAN
Any other cultural activity would be acceptable. We could see a film or come and have a lecture. But not tea and coffee. A cultural activity is OK, but not a leisure activity.

ARCHITECT
(*To the women*) But if you got together, all of you, to prepare tabbouleh, would this be considered a cultural activity or a leisure activity?

HADIYAH
(*Laughing hard, and trying to cover her face*) Darling, tabbouleh is a prohibited activity.

The women redouble their laughter, and HADIYAH *joins in.*

ARCHITECT
But wouldn't you like to get out of the house and get some sun and fresh air?

AMEENAH
(*Sharply*) Of course we would like to, but we are controlled.

HALAH
(*Breaks in sadly*) The women here in Fawwar don't participate in activities anyhow. A few days ago, there was a great activity for the girls—our daughters—at their school, and very few women attended. Even if making tabbouleh together out of doors was considered totally permitted in Fawwar Camp, how could we imagine that these women, who don't even participate in school events, would come?

ARCHITECT
But don't you think that to change this situation will require some time, and that if people in Fawwar begin to see women outside of their homes, they would get used to such a new reality and slowly begin to accept it?

1st FAWWAR WOMAN
(*Shaking her head*) Not in Fawwar, darling.

2nd FAWWAR WOMAN
(*Shaking her head*) Not in Fawwar Camp.

3rd FAWWAR WOMAN
(*Shaking her head*) This might happen in the Dheisheh camp or in the Arroub camp, but not here.

4th FAWWAR WOMAN
(*Shaking her head*) Here everything is prohibited.

AHMED (A young man with black hair and thick eyebrows, wearing a track suit; it's clear that he is as comfortable in this plaza as he is at home)
(*Thrusting himself suddenly into the discussion from the men's side of the plaza*) Don't you think you are complicating the situation, all of you, by exaggerating things?

AMEENAH
(*Furiously*) Shut up. You would be the first one to gossip about these women if you were to see them sitting here. Even if we walk alone in the street, everyone speaks badly about us behind our backs—how much worse would it be if we were to start sitting in the plaza?

AHMED *retreats, crushed.*

ARCHITECT
(*Aside*) It's so clear that Ameenah has complete control of the discussion that it's really hard for me to believe such a strong woman would not be able to challenge the society in the same way, or easily organize a gathering for women to sit and have coffee in the plaza.
(*To the women*) What would you like the plaza to look like?

JAMILAH (An unmarried young women with a black head scarf, living with her brothers and one niece)
(*Pulling on her black scarf, and speaking with emphasis*) We want a *closed* plaza, with walls around it, so that all of us women can come here and finally use it.
(*Beat*) *Maybe* we could finally use the plaza.

AMEENAH
(*To* JAMILAH, *bossily*) What is the meaning of a closed plaza? Did you ever see a closed plaza? Is it a home or a plaza?

JAMILAH
I mean, the plaza should be walled in, and part of it should be for men and the other part for women, and we should prohibit men from coming into the women's section of the plaza. Even if we agree to come to the plaza, our brothers and husbands would not let us go if it's not segregated. They would tell us, "What are you going to do, are you going to sit in a plaza where there is a mix between men and women?"

HALAH

(*Confidently*) The real problem is the women in this camp. Even if you enclose the plaza, they will still not come. They will never leave their work and their homes and come and gather in the plaza.

ARCHITECT

(*Aside*) It was clear to me from what I had heard from the other women that Halah did not want to enclose the plaza because her home was directly in front of it. She was worried about the plaza cutting off sunlight and air to her home.

HALAH

(*Tensely, anxiously*) I would not accept walls around the plaza. No way.

JAMILAH

Well, you might not accept it, but I *might* accept it.

ARCHITECT

Is it that you *might* visit a closed plaza, or are you *sure* you would be able to?

JAMILAH

For myself, I would come as long as this is a very closed place where nobody could see me. I could come here with my niece. While she is playing with the other children, I could get some fresh air, and it would be better for her to play here instead of going to play in the streets with the cars.

ARCHITECT

(*Aside*) Jamilah is clearly unsure that she will be able to use the plaza, but she is trying to come up with a scenario in which this would be possible.

The women fall silent. The ARCHITECT *shifts her chair ninety degrees, so that she is now facing the group of young and old men who had up until now been listening to the conversation.* ABU RABIH *is sitting in the center of the group. He beats the ground with his walking stick to call the meeting to order. Everyone falls silent and listens.*

ABU RABIH (The oldest of the camp's elders, and one of the most important, wearing a black robe over his white *dishdasha*, an ankle-length, long-sleeved robe, with a very white *hattah*, or scarf, on his head. He carries a walking stick.)

If you think that this plaza would be open to anyone, whoever he is, to come and bring his chair and sit, or to have fun or to stay during the night, you are absolutely on the wrong track. This is unacceptable in

Fawwar Camp. Mixing between men and women would be unacceptable, especially mixing between young ladies and young men.

ARCHITECT
What do you think the plaza should look like?

ABU RABIH
This is a good plaza. It has to be taken care of by the neighbors. People should not be allowed to come here and cut firewood in the winter. People have to take care of this plaza as if it were their home. This is the real secret for the success of this plaza.

ABU RABIH *is sitting next to* ABU RAMI, *who now draws himself up, looks around at the group, and begins to speak in clear, classic Arabic as though giving a formal lecture.*

ABU RAMI (Another highly esteemed camp elder, he wears a khaki *dishdasha*, a white *hattah* and also carries a walking stick)
This plaza should be organized. We should have a guard on duty at all times because our kids will not be able to take care of it without supervision. If this plaza were to be open for people to come and go as they pleased, it would never work. People would steal and destroy everything. They would rip up the pavement, they would take the ironwork; nothing would stay put. The plaza needs to be organized and *official*. It has to have a door, it has to have a lock, it has to have a key and it has to have a guard. (*He gavels his stick to signal the end of his speech.*)

ARCHITECT
(*Aside*) Abu Rabih and Abu Rami are considered among the founders of this camp, having already spent sixty years in exile. They are among those who witnessed the tents of Fawwar replaced by masonry homes, and now they are living to see its inhabitants begin to consider the spaces between homes as well. Surely Abu Rami is remembering how difficult the decision was to build concrete walls instead of maintaining the tents. Would this move let the world forget that what they really wanted was to return home to their villages rather than settle permanently in the camps? And now they are not only building homes but also beginning to shape common spaces. Is this another concession—another way of accepting the permanency of the camp and giving up the dream of return? Is the plaza merely a wretched attempt to mitigate the conditions of total subjugation? Or is the plaza the physical indication that the refugees have abandoned their strategy of convincing the whole world of their misery through their architectural misery; that they are instead initiating a new strategy of capitalizing on their strengths as refugees rather than their weakness as victims? Abu Rami's father had been among the main opponents of building

more durable homes. No doubt he remembers his father telling him, "Son of mine, if you ever begin to enjoy your life in the camp, you will forget the land you came from." Would his father have even agreed to be part of the discussion taking place today? Is it historically acceptable to think about the public space of a temporary camp? Of course, what is claimed as "private" in the camp is not really private, because the homes are not registered as private property, and what is claimed as "public" is not really public because neither the host government nor the residents themselves recognize it as such. The UNRWA claims that it does not administer the camps, only its own installations and programs. How does one define "private" and "public" in a camp?

1st SHABAB (Wearing a dark blue jacket and jeans, with a shy manner)

(*Addressing* ABU RABIH *and* ABU RAMI *respectfully, but earnestly*) This plaza will serve this neighborhood very well; here the kids will play, here we will have our important occasions, here we will have our weddings and funerals. It is the only open space in this big neighborhood: how come you think that we will not take care of it? This plaza will be a treasure for all of us.

2nd SHABAB

This is a good plaza. It has to be beautified with some graffiti and some slogans expressing that this plaza belongs to the society of Fawwar. But in my opinion, it has to stay open. It has to be taken care of by its neighbors, who should have responsibility for it.

AHMED

I don't think that the idea of enclosing the plaza is a very good one. I am against keys, I am against locks, I am against doors, I am against the idea that this plaza would open and close at certain hours. How could our kids play here? How would we feel that we own this place? I am not against having a guard to take care of this place, but no keys, no locks, no closing time. Because if we use it this way, we will cancel out any idea of a common plaza and it will function like a private space.

ARCHITECT

(*Sharply*) Ahmed, what were you saying earlier about the women in Fawwar?

AHMED

(*Confidently*) The women in Fawwar used to get out and sit outside their homes in the afternoons, even late in the evening—

ABU RAMI

(*Interrupting*) Old women could do this, but not young ones.

The ARCHITECT *looks from one man to the other doubtfully.*

2nd SHABAB
This plaza should be a plaza for our children, first and last. My young friends and I will not come and play with the kids, so the women—the mothers of these kids—could come and take care of them without being bothered. I believe that at the end of the day, the plaza should be for the kids and their mothers.

ARCHITECT
(*Aside*) He is giving up his right to this space in order to assure everyone that they don't need to worry—that the *shabab* won't take over the plaza.

3rd SHABAB
I believe that children have the right to play near their mothers and that their mothers have the right to be near their sons while they are playing. This would give more confidence to the kids themselves: as the proverb goes, "The child will play with a strong arm."

ABU RAMI *begins to beat the ground with his stick nervously.*

3rd SHABAB
(*Glancing at* ABU RAMI, *swallowing, and continuing*) If his mother is sitting nearby, a child will feel secure and protected from any bad thing that might happen to him.

ABU RAMI *beats the ground more slowly and softly and then lapses.*

ARCHITECT
(*Aside*) All of a sudden, the plaza has become the site for a young generation to negotiate their rights with the older generation: the place to discuss what is right and what is wrong, what is possible and what is not possible. In the past, people haven't had the chance to discuss matters in a common space. All the previous negotiations and conflicts were focused on the problem of how to enlarge individual homes at the expense of shared space. Homes in the camps are very small and crowded—they were built within the original footprints of the tents they replaced—and the main concern of the camp inhabitants until now has been ensuring that there is at least one bed for each child in the family. Until now, the common space and how to use it has been the last thing on their minds.

Act Two

Two years later. Inside the Youth Program Center, the ARCHITECT, ABU TARIQ *(the camp service officer),* ABU SAMI *(the principal of the Boys' School), the* DEPUTY DIRECTOR *of the Youth Program Center, as well as many of the other male members of the community, including many of the camp elders, are waiting. The air is abuzz with simultaneous conversations, most of them referencing a man who is not present,* ABU AHMED. *People keep exiting and entering and monitoring their cell phones to check on* ABU AHMED*'s whereabouts. A table with a plan of the plaza and pens is in the center of the room. The* ARCHITECT *is standing near the table.* ABU AHMED *finally arrives. His manner is aggressive and determined. He turns to the* ARCHITECT.

ABU AHMED (A very tall man, about forty-five years old, wearing khaki military-style fatigues)
You will never be able to continue this plaza if I cannot park directly in front of my home.

ARCHITECT
(*Aside*) The design is already done, and we are in the middle of construction. Abu Ahmed has stopped the work.

(*To* ABU AHMED) But as far as I can tell, your car could be parked only five meters from the entrance to your home. This is a very short distance in any part of this world. To be honest, I can't really understand your problem.

ABU AHMED
(*Nervously*) I want to park my car immediately in front of the door of my home. It's my wife's right to step out of the front door and find the car waiting for her, and I have the right to be able to unload my groceries right in front of my house.

ARCHITECT
(*To* AHMED, *calmly*) What is the real reason behind this demand? The plaza's main purpose is to be a safe play area for kids, and to give the people in the neighborhood a place to sit outside on hot summer nights and get fresh air outside of their tiny homes. This is a plaza for weddings and funerals. This is not a plaza for parking cars.

ABU AHMED
I'm not asking to turn the plaza into a parking lot. I want to be the only one allowed to drive in.

ARCHITECT
(*Incredulously*) What do you mean, the only one? How you would resolve the problem, from your point of view?

ABU AHMED *takes a pen from the table and begins to sketch on the map.*

ABU AHMED

I would suggest that we would put a gate here. I will be the owner of the keys to the gate. I could open and close it only when needed and that's it. I will be the guard of the plaza.

ARCHITECT

(*Surprised*) Who appointed you the boss of the plaza? Did the people in the neighborhood elect you to keep the keys?

ABU AHMED

(*Throwing down his pen and shouting angrily*) Either this or you will not be able to work in the plaza.

The men in the room try to calm ABU AHMED *down.*

ARCHITECT

Who do you think you are, to be able to stop a plaza that is owned by the whole neighborhood? This is not your plaza, it's not your property. It's everyone's.

ABU AHMED

I work in the security services in the Palestinian Authority, and I will absolutely be able to stop this if you will not accept my demand.

ARCHITECT

I will tell you for the thousandth time that this is not a parking lot, it's a plaza. It's not for you and it's not for others; it's for all. I still cannot understand why you can't park your car only five meters away. If every person in the camp demanded to be able to park in front of his entrance, we would be obliged to demolish half of the camp's homes in order to fulfill this request. And don't forget that we only managed to achieve this plaza after we demolished two homes in order to make space for it. What more do you want?

ABU AHMED

(*Glaring angrily at the* ARCHITECT) For me, it's not only the parking.

ARCHITECT

(*To the group*) Here comes the real issue.

ABU AHMED

(*Calming down*) If I want to build a new story on my house, I will save a lot of money if I have staging space for heavy equipment rather than being limited to manual construction, but the design as it stands now makes this impossible.

ABU RABIH

But you are not even sure, ABU AHMED, that you will be adding another story on top of your home.

ABU RAMI

Yes. Why are you creating problems now?

ABU AHMED

Even if the possibility is remote, I want at least to know that I am doing everything I can to ensure a better future for my family.

ARCHITECT

(*Aside*) What would Abu Rami's father say to such a problem? Abu Ahmed is not only planning to have a concrete roof and extended columns for future floors. He is also looking to plan for the very far future.

(*Speaking* to ABU AHMED) We cannot really modify the entire design depending on what you *might* do in the future. This is a plaza for all the inhabitants to use and enjoy today.

ABU AHMED

(*With finality*) Either this or no plaza. I will not permit access to the site. From now on, you will not be able to put a single stone in place.

ARCHITECT

(*Aside*) If this same person who is arguing over a meter here or a meter there were asked about the right of return by a journalist, he would aver without hesitation that he is ready to leave everything he ever built in the camp to return back to his original home and village in Palestine. How can refugees plan for a "possible" future and keep the hope of a return that may be impossible alive without one of these visions betraying the other? How can I blame someone for not taking the public into consideration when all he wants is to ensure a better future for his family after he has lost everything he had?

(*To the group*) This is a plaza for all of you. If you are not able to convince Abu Ahmed to allow the construction to continue, then let's stop the project immediately. I will not solve this problem. This is not my problem, it's a camp problem. If each person imposes his own desires on the others, then the camp is not ready to have a collective space.

The ARCHITECT *exits.*

Act Three

One year later. An unusually large living room, about 30 square meters, in ABU ATA*'s home.* ABU ATA*, his wife, his seven children, the* ARCHITECT*, and the neighborhood women, including* HADIYAH, AMEENAH, HAJAH AMEENAH, JAMILAH, *and* UMM ALI, *and many men from the camp, including* AHMED, *are all sitting on four mattresses that line each wall. The* TODDLER, *the youngest member of* ABU ATA*'s family, wears pink. She is fascinated by the* ARCHITECT*'s red bag, and keeps trying to explore it. She moves from one group of women to another, smiling at everyone. The adjacent plaza, where a number of kids are playing rambunctiously, is visible and audible through several open windows. The guests of* ABU ATA *take no notice of this activity.*

ARCHITECT

(*Aside*) Abu Ata was one of the first and most adamant supporters of the idea of the plaza. He came up with the original proposal to buy the two shelters that were demolished to make the space for it. He was responsible for managing many of the community negotiations that were needed to implement the design, and he was the one who insisted from the beginning that he would be the plaza's caretaker, in order to be an example to the rest of the neighborhood. He has invited all of the women of the neighborhood to come to this meeting at his home to discuss the issues around the plaza.

(*To the group*) What do you think now about the plaza, after all this time?

UMM ALI (An elderly woman dressed in black)

(*Gently moving the* TODDLER, who is standing directly in her line of sight to the ARCHITECT, *to one side, and making eye contact with the* ARCHITECT) This is an *excellent* plaza. But now we can't wait to see it finished. We are tired of living with construction, and we are eager to see the plaza ready.

ARCHITECT

I know how much you are looking forward to it, but now you can finally imagine it: the rest is only finishes.

The TODDLER *plants herself firmly in front of* IMMAM HAMA *as if the older woman is a character on* TV, *blocking the* ARCHITECT*'s view.*

UMM ALI

(*Leaning to either side in a vain attempt to reestablish eye contact with the* ARCHITECT *while the* TODDLER *tracks her movements, and speaking with great authority*) This plaza is open to kids until they reach thirteen years old. If a male older than that comes into the plaza, I will kick him out. I will tell him, "This is not your plaza, you have no work to do here, and it's prohibited for you to remain. We have a lot of girls and women here who want to feel comfortable, who want to be able to get outside and hang the laundry, and I will not permit any stranger to be around our homes or in our plaza."

ARCHITECT
(*To the group*) But are you using the plaza?

ABU ATA'S WIFE
(*Smiling broadly*) Yes, I go out with my husband quite every day and sometimes I also go with my husband's brother and his wife. We prepare coffee, we go out, and we drink it in the plaza.

ARCHITECT
(*Delighted*) Then you are using the plaza! It's not unacceptable anymore to drink coffee and tea in public.

(*Looks at* ABU ATA'S WIFE) Do you remember how you were opposed to the idea of drinking tea and coffee or preparing tabbouleh in the plaza?

ABU ATA'S WIFE *looks stricken as she realizes what she has just admitted.*

ABU ATA'S WIFE
Maybe with time, you know? Sometimes we need time in order to get used to doing things we didn't formerly accept in Fawwar. (*Rallies*) Because now I am often out in the plaza with my kids, running after them and playing together with them, and this is why I believe that everything will come with time.

The WOMEN
(*Speaking to each other*) This is a very good plaza.

1st FAWWAR WOMAN
(*With pride*) My parents live in another camp, and when they came to visit me and they saw this plaza, they told me how lucky my children and I are to have this place to play near our home from now on.

ARCHITECT
What do you think about the final form of the plaza—a kind of home without a roof? What do you feel about the walls surrounding the plaza?

2nd FAWWAR WOMAN
Thank God the wall in front of our home is the highest of them all. It gave my husband and me the chance to create a private terrace in front of our home where we can sit outside without being seen. You didn't just create the plaza, but you also created very small plazas in front of all of the homes that border on it, where we can be outside in the sunshine and still enjoy some privacy. If the wall were not so high, my husband would not have let me come out and get some sun and have

coffee outside while the *shabab* are playing nearby. Also, for me, it's not at all a closed plaza—why are we speaking about closed plazas? It has entrances and exits. We can easily come and go.

HALAH *arrives, greets everyone, and sits down.*

ABU ATA'S WIFE
(*To the* ARCHITECT) Sandi, do you know HALAH?

ARCHITECT
(*To* HALAH) Yes, of course, I remember you. I remember every word of your opinion about the plaza. And now I am very interested to know if your opinion has changed with time.

HALAH
(*Looking around the group, triumphantly*) There were some *shabab* in the plaza a few days ago. I told you this would be a problem.

UMM ALI
(*In a pacifying tone*) Yes, but we kicked them out, and they left without any problem. We have control of the plaza, and there's no chance of it becoming a hangout for *shabab*.

IMAD (A self-confident man in his forties, he represents the new generation in the camp. He is very active in NGOs and other activities, and he has a great deal of credibility.)
If any *shabab* comes and plays in the plaza—

ABU ATA (The father of six daughters and one son, he is a jovial and dynamic figure in the camp)
(*Interrupting*) But listen: I am a *shabab*, and I swear to God that I was also playing in the plaza!

IMAD
Yes! Actually, that's true! Last time I passed through the plaza I saw Abu Ata playing with all the neighborhood kids. (*Looks challengingly at* IMMAM HAMA)

UMM ALI
There is a huge difference between a local *shabab* and the *shabab* off the street. Besides, you are not really a *shabab*—forty-five years old is a young old man. (*Laughing*)

IMAD
(*To* UMM ALI) If I come with my wife to drink tea with you in the plaza, what would you think about that?

1st FAWWAR WOMAN
Of course you would be welcome!

2nd FAWWAR WOMAN
You and your wife are among the best people in Fawwar.

3rd FAWWAR WOMAN
You are welcome any time.

UMM ALI
(*Looking at the* ARCHITECT, *conceding*) You know what, it's okay because his wife is my cousin.

ARCHITECT
So you want the plaza to be only a family plaza?

Everyone laughs.

UMM ALI
No, no no! Even neighbors are absolutely welcome! But not strangers, you know? Not strangers from outside the neighborhood.

A number of simultaneous conversations break out and the noise level increases. ABU ATA *prepares to speak, and everyone falls silent to listen to him.*

ABU ATA
(*To the* ARCHITECT) Sandi, sister of mine, I will tell you one very important thing. This is not a plaza for old people. This is not a plaza for the *shabab*. The *shabab* in this camp have other places where they can congregate. We have a Youth Program Center, we have a very big stadium; they have a lot of other places to go. They are independent enough to spend time in places that are not necessarily near their homes, but the small children still need to be around their mothers and close to where they live. We need to protect our young kids from the main streets and the cars. This plaza helped to preserve the open space we all need. Now we have a different life and a different perspective on the future. Now, when my wife sees me in the plaza, and you know, I am a very open person (*Chuckling*), I tell my wife, "Why don't you bring a cup of coffee or tea, and we will sit together and have it in the plaza?" The first time, she felt a bit shy. The second time she brought the coffee, and the third time she did not feel shy anymore.

ARCHITECT
But if someone from outside the neighborhood wanted to have his wedding in your plaza, how would you react?

1st FAWWAR WOMAN
How could we say no?

2nd FAWWAR WOMAN
This plaza is open for any wedding or funeral from any part of the camp.

3rd FAWWAR WOMAN
Everyone is welcome.

ABU ATA
(*To the* ARCHITECT) We are not just saying this to be polite. I have turned a small room that faces the plaza into a "service room." This room is available for anyone who wants to hold a ceremony in the plaza to use, in order to distribute food or drinks, etc. I also let people use the electricity in my home for whatever they need, like powering lights and stereos for a wedding.

ARCHITECT
But would you expect that a lot of people from other parts of the camp would come and use this space for their weddings and funerals?

1st FAWWAR WOMAN
Of course!

2nd and 3RD FAWWAR WOMEN
Of course they will!

ABU ATA
(*Doubtfully*) You know, many people would prefer to hold their wedding ceremonies nearby their homes, for logistical reasons like food distribution. This is why, as a community, we are beginning to think about how to create similar plazas in other parts of the camp. The enclosure of the plaza was a very important step, I think, and absolutely essential. Imagine if the kids were to play soccer and kick the ball through one of the neighbor's windows. These kinds of accidents used to happen all the time, but now we don't have to worry about this issue anymore. The walls create a special and protected space, because a person who is simply passing through the neighborhood would never find himself in the plaza by chance. (*Triumphantly*) But now, with the new plaza's design, whoever is passing in the street can pass without interruption, and whoever wants to enter the plaza does so at their own risk, which means that the person has to accept the possibility that he might get hit by a soccer ball, which means in turn that if he gets hit by the ball, he will just laugh and be happy to be part of the game. For me, this is what makes this plaza a special one.

The women in the room nod in agreement.

ARCHITECT
What nice news you are giving me! This means that the plaza did not create any problems for you, and all the issues that you were afraid of did not materialize.

(*To* HALAH) You remember how skeptical you were about this plaza?

HALAH
I never was able to picture what this plaza would look like. I never imagined that we would have been able to find a solution that would satisfy everyone. I have to be honest with you: this plaza created a lot of discussion and conflict in the camp.

ABU ATA
Yes. I suffered a lot as a defender of this plaza.

HALAH
Yes, you are right, and I can understand everything that you had to go through.

ABU ATA
(*To the group*) I took the plan of the plaza to the home of every person who was against this project, and I sat with them, reviewed the plan and explained the design. I was so patient with everybody. I discussed each and every centimeter of this plaza with everyone, and now here we are, finally seeing its form, and finally many people are now reconsidering their opinion.

(*To the* ARCHITECT) You have to understand one important thing: neither my wife nor my sister-in-law are architects who can read a plan and understand how it will look.

HALAH
(*With relief*) Yes. You're right. I didn't understand the plaza at first because I am not an architect. I honestly was so afraid that this plaza would block the windows of my home, and that the façade of my house would become the wall of the plaza. This would have created a lot of problems for my family. This is why we were absolutely against the plaza at first. But during construction, when we started to understand it, my husband and I stopped being skeptical, and during the whole period of implementation, my family never created any problems.

ARCHITECT
(*To the group*) How do you plan to clean the plaza?

IMAD
We already have UNRWA cleaning crews that come through and clean the camp—

3 A traditional dish made of lamb cooked in a sauce of fermented dried yogurt and served with rice or bulgur, usually reserved for special occasions like weddings in the camps.

4 An inexpensive, workday meal made with rice and lentils and commonly eaten in the camps.

AMEENAH

(*Interrupting, to the* ARCHITECT) We women will be cleaning the plaza. Of course we will clean the plaza and take care of the plants.

ABU ATA

Yes, but you will not be the only ones. Each time we have a weding or a funeral, this plaza will be cleaned from top to bottom, because the bride and all of her friends will give it a thorough shower. We have only to help our children understand that they are not to pick the plants or cut the flowers. I will take care of this.

ABU ATA'S WIFE

(*Complaining*) Abu Ata has become the caretaker of this plaza. As if he has nothing else to do or think about!

ABU ATA

(*Complacently*) Look, I will give you an example of why this will not be a difficult mission for me. (*Looking around at the group magisterially*) If you serve *mansaf*[3] to someone who is not used to eating meat or rich food, he will stuff himself. If you give the same person *mansaf* for a second day, he will eat, but perhaps a bit less. If you serve the same thing to the same person for a third day in a row, he will again be happy to have it, but he will certainly have a more controlled appetite. If you serve *mansaf* to this person for the fourth day in a row, he might ask you for some *m'jadarah*[4] instead. In the same way, the kids will see the flowers in the plaza for the first time, and they might be tempted to pick them even though I teach them not to. The second day, they may grow a little more used to them, and so on. By the fourth day, they will see the *mansaf* as if it were *m'jadarah*, something that they are used to, and they won't pick the plants. I don't think I will have a very difficult time of it. I am absolutely not worried. People will get used to the plaza even faster than we can imagine.

Side discussions break out anew about how the plaza will be used. The role of the women pops up again in their debates.

UMM ALI

(*Insistently*) I will never let my daughters or my daughters-in-law sit outside in the plaza by themselves and have tea or coffee.

The group shifts and subtly splits into two faintly delineated groups: a smaller cluster of mostly older men and women on UMM ALI*'s side and a much larger contingent of mostly younger men and women on* ABU ATA *and his wife's side. Those closer to* ABU ATA *begin to try to reason with* UMM ALI *and those in her group, telling them that they will change their minds over time.*

HADIYAH

(*To* UMM ALI, *in a confessional tone*) Weeks ago, my neighbors and I went out to the plaza and drank coffee. (*Looks at* ARCHITECT *shyly, as though revealing a secret*) But the first time I have to admit that I felt shy about going, and I was worried that someone would pass by and see me, and say, "What is this woman doing in the street?"

ARCHITECT

But maybe the example that Abu Ata gave us before is applicable here too: you might feel shy the first day, the second day less so, and the third day you will feel totally comfortable—

UMM ALI

(*Interrupting, sarcastically*) Yes, it will then become what we call in Arabic an agency without a door—a place where anything goes!

Everyone laughs.

ARCHITECT

(*Aside*) Yes, but one thing is very clear: what they used to see as a taboo three years ago is not a taboo anymore. They have already begun using the plaza, even though it's not finished, for the exact purposes they were not convinced they would be able to one year ago. Everyone is describing the plaza as though it has become the home of the neighborhood.

(*To the group*) Only one year ago, your manner was totally different.

IMAD

(*Confidently*) A year from now, things will be even more completely changed.

UMM ALI *harrumphs discontentedly. The smaller group that had assembled around her shuffles back into the larger group, so that the assembly is no longer faintly divided into two groups.*

UMM ALI

(*Threatening, but with a comical edge*) I will kick you all out if you insist on using the plaza in this way! All of you! And I will tell all of the women: Shame on you because you are doing things like this!

ABU ATA

(*Looks at* UMM ALI *challengingly, and turns to the* ARCHITECT) Listen, I promise you that I will take a photograph of Umm Ali together with her daughters and her neighbors in the plaza, drinking coffee and pulling *molokhiya* leaves off of their stems.[5]

5 *Molokhiya* is a spinach-like Egyptian plant that is prepared for cooking by removing each leaf by hand from the stems. The work is tedious, much like shelling peas, and so it is usually done in a group setting where women can talk as they work.

The group laughs uproariously. Even the children in the room, who have not been following the discussion, smile and join in the merriment.

HALAH
I can see that this plaza will give us women a way to see each other more. We are neighbors and yet we hardly have the opportunity to meet. This place will give us more of a social life.

1st FAWWAR WOMAN
(*Kicks the* ARCHITECT's *leg lightly*) I promise you that we will not drink coffee at home anymore. We'll have it in the plaza, absolutely. But we'll have our first cup of coffee with Abu Ata so he'll give us legitimacy, and then we'll go out and have coffee alone the next time.

Everyone laughs.

IMAD
(*To the group*) Listen. The habit of sitting out of doors is not new for us in Fawwar. On the contrary, it is an old tradition that all of us used to do when I was a kid: we would sit outside our small homes and have a bit of fresh air. I think that the main reason that this habit faded is the crowdedness of the camp. As people expanded their homes, the streets became narrower and narrower, until they became very tight alleys. If I were to take a chair outside and sit in the alley, I would block the entire street. This is why I think we lost this tradition, and people became unused to taking leisure time and having activities out of doors. For me, the main reason is therefore that we didn't have any adequate space where we could sit without feeling that we are basically sitting in the streets and blocking traffic. I think that the plaza is giving us the possibility to recreate that culture of using outside spaces, especially because, if you look at us as a society, we are a society where the relationships between neighbors are very close.

HALAH
Listen. I will admit one last thing: two nights ago, I had dinner with my husband in the plaza.

Everyone looks at her in astonishment.

EVERYONE
Dinner?

HALAH
(*Sheepishly*) Yes, and actually I have to admit we've had dinner in the plaza *twice*.

Act Four

Six months later. A large, rectangular meeting room on the fourth floor of the Local Committee Building in Fawwar Camp, with a bank of computers along one of the long walls and a large round table in the middle. The UNWRA *has orchestrated a visit to the Fawwar Camp for members of the Talbieh and Hus'n refugee camps in Jordan. A number of men and women from both of these camps are sitting around the table, including camp service officers as well as* ABU RAJA *and* RAMSEY *from Talbieh. From Fawwar,* ABU TARIQ, *the camp service officer, is at the table, as are* ABU RABIH, ABU RAMI, ABU ATA, IMAD, *and* ABU SAMI. *The* ARCHITECT *and members of her team, including* SAMI MURA, *are also present. The mood of the meeting is serious and ceremonial, and everyone speaks very formally. Everyone wears their best clothes or official uniforms, as if it were a Palestinian national occasion.*

ABU TARIQ (The Fawwar Camp service officer, he is well known in the camp, with white hair)

(*Dignified yet emotional*) Welcome to our esteemed guests from Jordan. Let me tell you about the camp of Fawwar. The camp of Fawwar is the camp of resistance. It is located in the south of the West Bank, ten kilometers from Hebron. Now is our glorious moment of welcoming our brothers and our lovers from the refugee camps of the Diaspora. I want to ask if we could first introduce ourselves to each other, as this is surely the most important thing we could gain from this visit.

Everyone begins to introduce themselves to everyone else, identifying themselves as coming from their original villages rather than from the camps where they now reside.

ARCHITECT

(*Aside, in a low tone*) It's rare that any personal meeting takes place between refugees in the camps and refugees in the Diaspora. Often you will find relatives living in different parts of the Diaspora who have never met. For all of the visitors from Jordan, this is their first time to set foot inside what is known as historical Palestine. Even if they will not be able to visit their proper villages and cities, this still feels like a step toward return—a kind of dream fulfilled. And in hosting them, the people of Fawwar feel as if they are sharing in the same moment. This lends an air of unreality to the meeting. I notice that people are behaving as though they were characters in a great novel: the novel of their return. (*Smiling*) They speak self-consciously, as though their words were being broadcast on Al Jazeerah.

(*To the assembly*) I want all of you to give us a moment to discuss the important topic of the plaza, especially because we have the people of Talbieh with us, and they had a similar intervention in their camp. It is very easy to create a gathering space inside an institution because the institution will be the responsible entity. But what we've been trying to do in this case is understand how to create a collective and open space for the society without having to rely on an umbrella organization. I remember when we first broached the idea of the plaza, everyone had a lot of fear about this foreign body that was being introduced into the camp. This is why I propose that while we are all sitting here under the same roof, refugees from both the West Bank and Jordan discuss the lessons we can draw from one of the most difficult questions we have to face: how to intervene in the common space of a camp that is not seeking an image of the public any more than it is seeking permanence, that wants rather to disband and to be erased. How does one give an image of a public space to a camp whose only desired self-image is that of ceasing to be imaginable? I realize I am raising questions we cannot answer right now, but at least I would like to formulate the questions.

ABU TARIQ *sits on the edge of the table with great solemnity.*

ABU TARIQ

(*Importantly*) The Fawwar Refugee Camp originally used to host very small open spaces. As you know, these tiny areas are used for the social occasions of the camp, such as weddings and funerals. When we first began to think about creating the plaza, the open area that we started with was around 200 to 250 meters square. Then, some of the neighbors of the plaza began to think about these two very small homes next to the open space, and began to ask if there was a way to include the area these two shelters took up in a larger plaza. We found a very creative way, working with the local committees, to buy the homes, compensate their former owners, and demolish them in order to enlarge the dimensions of the plaza to 700 square meters.

We decided that we also needed a safe play area for our kids. Fawwar is located at one of the main crossroads of the West Bank, and this busy intersection actually used to be the official playground for our kids because there was no other place where they could play. We were sure that we needed different spaces in the camp, but we were not sure how to create them, who and what would be permitted in them, and who would be responsible for maintaining them. We had a long and intense process of community meetings and discussions, from which it became completely clear that this plaza could work only if its neighbors took primary responsibility for it. We also began to understand how to use the space. We knew that it was to be a place for our kids to play, and that if we installed playground equipment, it would become the most attractive play space ever for all the kids of the camp. But we felt that this would simultaneously create a huge problem: the presence of the kids by themselves would cause tensions with the neighbors and among the children and their families. Actually, we have only to consider the Women's Program Center in Fawwar: they have a small play area for the kids, and after closing time, kids of all ages try to climb the walls in order to get into the play area, which is dangerous for them and damages the equipment. We wanted to avoid anything that would create social problems like this when it came to the plaza.

This is where the community participation became critical. We discussed every single thing, such as the distance between neighboring homes and the walls of the plaza, the height of each wall that would separate the private from the public, and issues that might arise in the future. Still, that did not save us from having a lot of problems even during the implementation. People opposed the project, or weren't happy with parking arrangements, or wanted things changed, and once they began to see the whole thing, everyone came up with fresh demands. We tried to deal with each case in the best way. And now, thank God, we are very near to the end of this project. We already did all of the structural work and now we are just doing the finishes, and we are quite sure that the plaza will be a success. And here it is very important to say that all the other projects we managed to do before this were sponsored by institutions. This is the only project that could be considered a collective project of the camp.

NAIM (The project manager of the Camp Improvement Project in Talbieh Camp, Jordan)

(*Formally*) I would like to reciprocate with some historical background on the case of Talbieh. Yes. We also had a similar experience. But before I begin to explain what we did in Talbieh, I want to pose two questions to the people who are assembled here. The first question is: what is your definition of community participation? And second, did the idea of the plaza come from the people of the camp, and if not, how did it develop? Was the plaza one of the priorities of the residents of Fawwar?

ABU TARIQ

On community participation, we talked about this project intensely for five years. We spent so long discussing it that we started to feel as though the project was imaginary and that nothing would actually come out of so much talk. By the time we began implementation, we were all looking forward to seeing the first tangible results of a project which had until that point been entirely community participation and nothing else!

ARCHITECT

The Fawwar people weren't the only ones tired of endless discussions about the plaza—my team felt the same way! When it came to the plaza, I became the joke of the office. I was never able to deliver, but I was constantly pushing everyone to think with me about what a collective space in a temporary camp might look like.

The ARCHITECT *looks over to her* TEAM MEMBERS *and smiles ruefully. They are laughing quietly. All of the people from Fawwar Camp are smiling as well, imagining the* ARCHITECT*'s office as a kind of microcosm of their own endless site of discussion, the plaza.*

ARCHITECT

I was convinced that even if this took us five or six years to finish, getting this plaza right would allow us to replicate it all over the West Bank. On the other hand, if we failed, it would become the first and last plaza in the West Bank. I also didn't want to create a plaza and then imprison it within barbed wire. This would have simply proved the argument that we hear so often, that Palestine refugees are not ready to manage their own affairs. I have to admit that my fears were reduced each year, and I am now almost convinced that we managed to find a way to translate all of what happened these last few years into an architectural reality that is ready to be part of the whole texture of the camp. (*The group nods in understanding and agreement.*)

ABU RAJA (A visitor from Talbieh Camp in Jordan, he is a man in his mid-forties, wearing a leather jacket with a white dress shirt and tie. He acts as an unofficial spokesman for the whole contingent from Talbieh.)

I want to underline my alliance with what Sandi just mentioned: the importance of having enough time to study all the ramifications of such a public project. And now I want to explain the story of the plaza in Talbieh Camp.

(*Clears his throat*) Talbieh is a camp that lacks any sort of open space. The plaza we managed to create is only twelve meters square.

One person in the group laughs.

ARCHITECT

(*Aside*) It's hard to know if he finds the idea of a twelve-meter-square plaza ridiculous or ridiculously sad.

ABU RAJA

We also used the method of community participation. We discussed the plaza with all of the neighbors, all of them participated in thinking about how the plaza was supposed to function and what it ought to look like, and we reviewed each and every detail of the design. Our kids also participated in the process. We too spent more than two years figuring out how to implement the plaza. Like you (*gesturing to the people from Fawwar*), we also weathered challenges to the design during implementation that required additional meetings and negotiations. The final design featured an elaborate set of playground equipment, and this was what we all agreed would be the best. But when the equipment was finally installed and the plaza was finished, the place was overrun with kids and the neighbors became extremely upset. Older kids started visiting the playground after dark, and who knows what they were up to. Of course, this plaza became *the* place to go for every kid in the camp—exciting equipment, nice pavement, everything perfect—and the neighbors didn't want them there anymore. This was the situation that we faced.

Among the group from Talbieh, many people begin speaking at the same time.

TALBIEH MAN 1
A lot of kids in a very tiny space.

TALBIEH WOMAN 1
But our kids want to play.

TALBIEH WOMAN 2
Many teenagers that were not really kids anymore used to come and play in this space, and of course the age difference created a lot of problems—

ABU RAJA
(*Interrupting*) Because of this, we finally decided that the best way to use the plaza was to surround it with barbed wire to institute hours of operation. We installed a gate and a lock, we gave the keys to the neighbors, and we arranged for schools to use the plaza for certain hours of the day. We absolutely thought that the only way we could use it was to institute a very precise program under the supervision of the schools and neighbors.

RAMSEY (A very young man, a social worker from Talbieh Camp in Jordan, he is very involved and open to discussing and understanding social problems)
What I think the people of Fawwar have benefited from is the first kids' park that they created inside the Women's Program Center. This gave them insight into many of the problems that they might face in the plaza. For us in Talbieh Camp, our plaza was our first ever experience of this kind ... (*Smiling wistfully*) all those colors, all those colors! (*Sighs*) The plaza that we created in Talbieh was so amazing that it became an object of contention.

4th FAWWAR WOMAN
(*Breaking in curiously*) Could you please describe the place for me? What is it like?

RAMSEY

(*Emotionally*) It's a huge playground! It has a lot of places for kids to climb and jump, a lot of ways to get in and get out—it's really nice! It introduces new colors in the middle of the camp. Everybody was looking forward to such a thing ... (*sighs again*) and this in my opinion was the reason the plaza was finally closed. (*Pauses, then brightens a bit*) But now we have another example of a plaza in the camp, which is a much simpler layout, more like your plaza (*gestures to the people of Fawwar Camp*); it is merely a paved space with some greenery. Neighbors totally refused to have anything else in this plaza, and the only thing we did was to improve the conditions that were already in place a little. The high visibility of the first plaza created a lot of trouble, so we made our next plaza invisible. We also planted a garden for the kids on the edge of the camp, and now they go there instead of crowding the old plaza, but the neighbors still feel very unhappy about it. The plaza became a kind of catalyst for opposition and a pretext for conflict.

ABU SAMI (The principal of the Fawwar Camp Boys' School and an Arabic teacher, very elegantly attired in a suit and tie, he speaks in flawless classical Arabic in public settings)

(*A bit testily*) I don't think that you can consider the Women's Program Center experience a test case for the plaza. The Women's Program Center is a private institution that happens to contain a play space for their kindergarten. A public plaza where the entire camp is theoretically welcome is radically different.

The people of Fawwar Camp nod in agreement.

SAMI MURA (The urban planner for the UNRWA Camp Improvement Program of the West Bank, and a member of the ARCHITECT's team)

I want to give my perspective as part of the design team for the Fawwar plaza. I don't think that this plaza was an architectural project. It's not enough to design a nice plaza and implement it in order to ensure that it will be a success. For me, the most important thing was how long it took to implement this plaza. We had different phases. Buying the two shelters, demolishing them, clearing away the rubble—all of this took time, and it gave people a chance to come to grips with the change. I think the main difference between the Fawwar experience and the Talbieh experience is that in spite of the fact that you (*gesturing toward the visitors from Talbieh*) had a lot of community participation during the design phase, the implementation happened very abruptly. Most of the project was finished within a month.

The visitors from Talbieh nod in agreement.

SAMI MURA

(*Continues*) Giving people the time to imagine and reflect is a very important thing. We spent more than one year building the basic form of the plaza—work that could have been done in three months. And, of course, we often had to stop work and allow for additional negotiations. But I think this gave people the time to shape the vision of what we were doing. We could have finished the plaza design in less than a month. We could have even arrived at the same design solution. But I doubt that people would have been as happy with the results. Without all the efforts of Abu Ata, for instance, this plaza would have been impossible.

The people of Fawwar Camp nod in agreement.

ABU TARIQ

(*Smiles at* ABU ATA) It's true! Without Abu Ata we wouldn't have the plaza.

ABU ATA

(*Laughing*) Now I feel ready to be an architect, specializing in plazas. (*Looking at the* ARCHITECT *and her team*) Would you hire me to be on your team?

End

M. Monachus, Feral Urbanist

Jonathan Tate

Detested or beloved, the monk parakeet (*Myiopsitta monachus*) in New Orleans is unmistakable. High-decibel screeches between small clusters of the birds as they aerially interact can be heard throughout the year. On the rare occasion when one alights within eyeshot, it is just as visually arresting as it is aurally powerful: seductive, gorgeously iridescent green with a pale gray crown and chest. Unlike other parrots, the monk chooses to build elaborate, multi-chambered communal nests, often on power poles, adjacent to the warmth of an electrical transformer, or in the upper reaches of an isolated radio tower. The scale and complexity of such infrastructural appropriations are extraordinary in their own right, with intricate agglomerations of sticks and twigs recalling the work of Andy Goldsworthy, only wilder.

As in many cities around the United States, the monk was first noticed in New Orleans sometime in the early 1970s. Legend has it that a pet store caught flames and released some monks along with a bevy of other nonnative species. Whether this is true or not, the bird has taken hold. Exact numbers remain unknown, but today it is estimated that there are over 250 of the parrots living in the city, with nests scattered throughout the metro area. Known for their resilience in the face of habitat loss in their native area of central South America, monks have adapted well to urban environments in general, capitalizing on limited ecological resistance, accommodating structural armatures for nests and—with the increased presence of tropical seed- and berry-producing plants—abundant food sources. The monk's existence in New Orleans is just one example of the ever complex interweaving between characteristically adaptive and fundamentally exploitive natural systems and our urban fabric.

The monk's nest-building patterns serve as intriguing examples of potentially novel forms of engagement with the city. As an uncontrolled form of invasive urbanism, they take advantage of the city's material detritus and infrastructural space to develop ordered and organized interventions that eschew traditional relationships between the man-made and the natural. The parrots seek out and opportunistically exploit these unconventional vacancies and hidden resources. Both artifacts and evidence of these underutilized urban assets, their nests model a challenge to normative urban design and planning discourse.

The monk collectively exploits objects with established functions that are otherwise physically vacant. Working and vital communication and power infrastructures such as radio towers and power poles are augmented with their nests, thus creating an enmeshed and additive condition that eschews the notion that openness and clearing are prerequisites for development. In other words, monk settlements reject traditional spatial requirements for finding vacancies in already-functioning systems with the capacity to support additional density, by engaging in a sophisticated form of coupling or piggybacking. Their habitats express both the masked opportunities of the site and their own capacity to engage these conditions. They obviously do this with no regard for existing legal and political boundaries. The invisible structures in place that often impede human development (property lines, zoning ordinances) offer no resistance to the monks, who remain essentially free to facilitate their objectives using instinctive, extralegal tactics.

For these reasons, the monk's peculiarities are instructive not just for New Orleans, but for other cities forced to rethink the efficacy of heroic-scale development strategies. Be it Detroit—the model shrinking city—or other, more modestly divested Rust Belt cities and post-boom depopulating Sun Belt cities, these specific urban challenges urgently require ideas for creating a viable new fabric. The monk represents an opportunistic approach that reminds us, above all, that development can be reimagined as something we achieve rather than something that happens to us, and that the psyche of these cities, damaged as a result of loss and change, can be revived through collective action.

What follows is a demonstration of how some typically underused urban spaces in New Orleans might be creatively developed.

CANALS

In addition to its massive, intricate and predominantly hidden drainage network, New Orleans possesses four major outflow canals which contain and remove all precipitation that accumulates in the topographic bowl of the city. These storm water canals contribute to

the city's notoriously underutilized waterfront in myriad ways. The protected nature of their design and their position in the city render them incongruent with egalitarian public use. The multi-jurisdictional oversight that resists the erection of permanent buildings within certain distances so as not to interfere with their operation has also impeded their evolution. One waterway in particular acts as a separation barrier between two parishes: Jefferson and Orleans, rich and poor. No place would be better for a public beach. Using the sedimentary potential of the entire city, jetties could be introduced to capture the debris and aggregate washed particles from the streets during a rainfall. Their accumulation would provide the base for a proper sandy beach. Walkways that affix to the floodwalls could be moved about to connect developed or desirable areas and demarcate the hidden amenity.

TRACKS

In contrast to today's system of a few heavily traveled lines, the streetcars in New Orleans were once routed via a thick network that navigated almost every neighborhood in the city. Remnants of the abandoned streetcar tracks can be found everywhere, surfacing on side streets and during municipal excavation. This disused infrastructure could be reactivated as a connective apparatus for the distribution of services. The remaining and otherwise visible tracks could be adapted with a supportive apparatus to expand the otherwise limited reach of the ubiquitous French Quarter food cart, giving it easy mobility. The humble cart could be dispatched about the city, offering Lucky Dogs and Snow Balls to the masses. The immutable pull of our economic hub could, as a consequence, offer a more democratic dispersion of the resources enjoyed by the visiting few while adding a bit of comic relief: the sight of a hotdog vendor gliding along with the streetcar.

900
KIEFER

OAKS

A common fixture in the city, the live oak tree (*Quercus virginiana*) is a point of pride in New Orleans. Its low, wide crown provides a continuous canopy along most streets and acts as the armature for parasitic plants like ferns, Spanish moss and air plants. The underside of the canopy in its current state offers an ample informal protective zone from sun and rain. Building from this canopy, the formalization of the space for more structured activities—play, events—could be easily accomplished though the collection of the natural detritus from the tree: sticks, leaves and clumps of fallen moss could be piled in a series of simple gabions that would provide spatial separation while also functioning in the longer term as compost depots.

FLOODWALLS

Often inaccurately referred to as "the levee," a massive concrete floodwall constitutes the linear protective and support structure that encircles New Orleans, the city's first and last defense for approaching floodwaters caused by rising rivers or storms. It is a menacing yet sinuous edifice whose height marks a theoretical datum of assumed maximum event protection, be it the 100-year flood or whatever category storm. Since it is consistently the highest ground in the city, the structure could provide a continuous support platform for critical services or materials. A network of evacuation spaces and storage areas for public use could be banded along the top of the wall, which could be widened into a usable platform utilizing the same structural systems found in the neighboring decayed port facilities.

MEDIANS

Roadway medians have become a distinct feature of New Orleans. Once the location of above-ground drainage routes, they presently mark the locations of main trunks of subsurface storm water drains. But perhaps more significantly, these otherwise forgettable linear tracts of land once served an important social and political function. Marking the boundaries between different neighborhoods, this land in-between was deemed "neutral" in an attempt to alleviate ethnic tension. Over time, the medians have evolved into informal neighborhood gathering grounds, evinced by the chairs and coolers chained to trees and signposts every evening in anticipation of the next day's social. Coupling these social and infrastructural uses, these "neutral grounds" would make opportune locations for both urban agricultural production and market space. By putting the resource of buried water to use, the grounds could be developed for local, water-intensive agriculture—to produce rice, crawfish, fish farms—and bookended by open structures for the sale of the yields. During off-market times, they could resume their role as shaded neighborhood gathering spaces.

A Taxonomy for Architects

dpr–Barcelona
and
Francesco Vedovato

Architecture is not over, only mutating.

In biology, a mutation is an inheritable alteration in the genetic information (genotype) of a living being that occurs suddenly and spontaneously. In multicellular beings, mutations can be inherited only when they affect the reproductive cells. In creative tasks like those of the architect, these nodes of reproducibility could be located at the level of ideas.

Although in the short term mutations may seem harmful, in the long term they are essential to the continued existence of any given species. No mutation would mean no evolution, and species that fail to adapt become the first casualties of an ever-changing environment. Like all human creations, whether technical or cultural, architecture is also subject to evolutionary pressures within the ecosystem of ideas.

Keeping this in mind, we propose a nomenclature capable of registering the fecundity and longevity of various architects' ideas. This taxonomy would also attempt to demonstrate that the main accomplishments in architecture are not the product of isolated genius, but the result of an evolutionary process in constant interaction with other species. Under this regime, an architect's scientific classification would place him or her within a genealogy of ancestors and begin to sketch the future options available for any offspring. Adopting a primitive scheme in the manner of Linnaeus, this classification system is deliberately incomplete: it aims not to represent the whole history of architectural thinking in itself, but rather to present an alternative process of analysis capable of outlining a new understanding of the discipline from kingdom to order, genus and species.

Kingdoms
Architecturalia, Engineerisciurus, Populi, Artistaeum

Orders
Teoricus, Architecturae, Designerium, Artem

Genus
Functionalimus, Futurismus, Expressionalicus, Organicus, Rationalis, Constructivicus, Modernus, Brutalicum, Structuralismus, Metabolicum, Functionalismus, Postmodernus, Deconstructivicus, Regionalismus, Utopicus, Interactivus, Parametricus, Sustainabilicum, Thermodynamicus, Entropicus

Species
If a particular species disappears, this nomenclatural system would be able to trace its ancestry and present the context for causal surmises about its extinction; conversely, species that have not yet emerged can be projected into certain viable environmental settings based on likely lineages. The species in the *Architecturalia* kingdom face existential constraints stemming from their parasitic codependence on the market, clients, colleagues and society. They are also challenged by competitive developments in production and construction technologies that threaten to relegate them to the overpopulated ranks of assemblers of new materials and systems in preset spatial configurations. Given these conditions, what are the characteristics that will determine which individual species survive and which disappear? Using the comparative anatomical techniques made available through dissection, we will venture to describe the mutational conditions of architects to come.

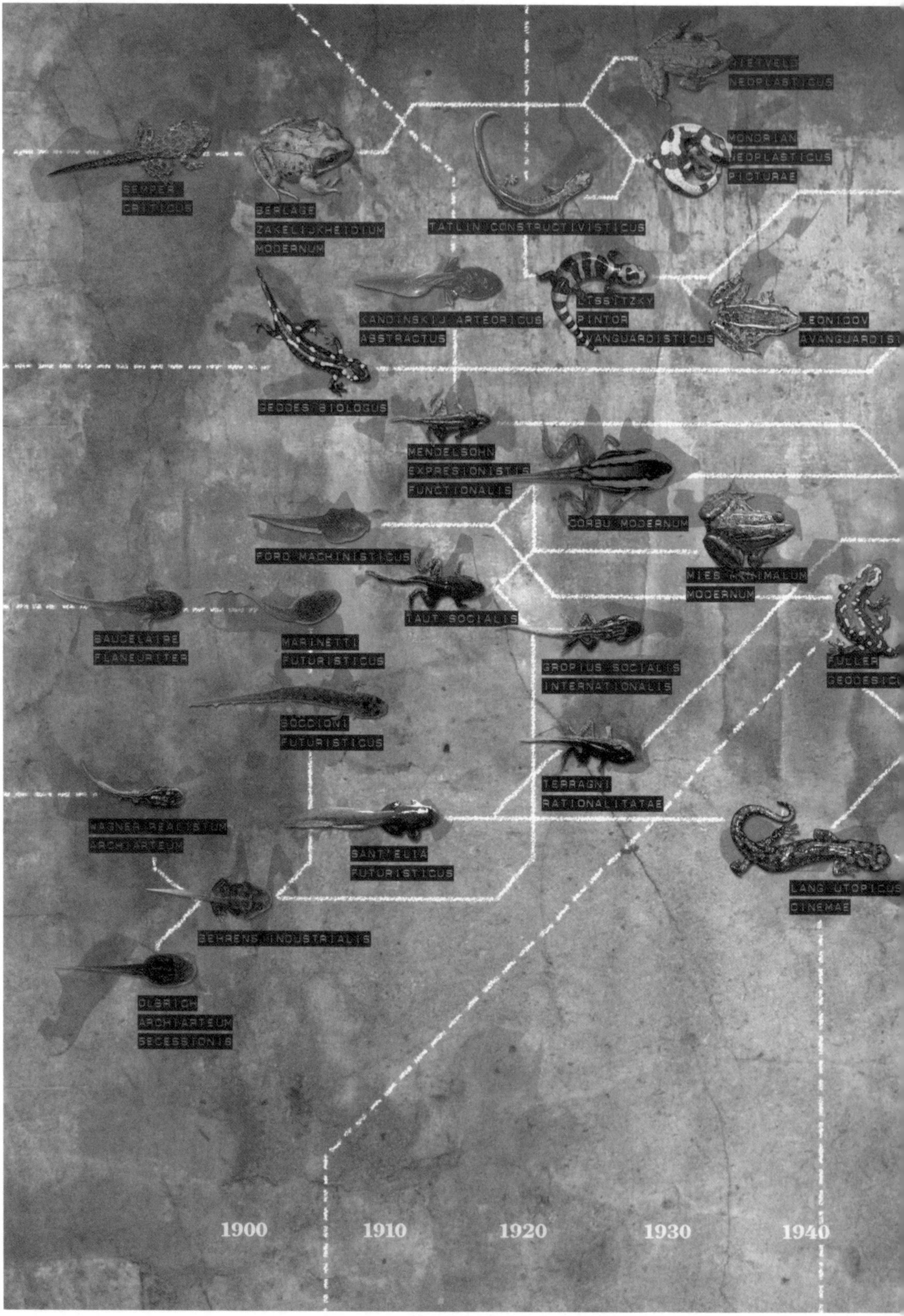
NEOPLASTICUS
MONDRIAN
NEOPLASTICUS
PICTURAE
SEMPER
CRITICUS
BERLAGE
ZAKELIJKHEIDIUM
MODERNUM
TATLIN CONSTRUCTIVISTICUS
LISSITZKY
PINTOR
AVANGUARDISTICUS
KANDINSKIJ ARTEORICUS
ABSTRACTUS
LEONIDOV
AVANGUARDIST
GEDDES BIOLOGUS
MENDELSOHN
EXPRESIONISTIS
FUNCTIONALIS
CORBU MODERNUM
FORD MACHINISTICUS
MIES
MODERNUM
TAUT SOCIALIS
BAUDELAIRE
FLANEURITER
MARINETTI
FUTURISTICUS
GROPIUS SOCIALIS
INTERNATIONALIS
FULLER
GEODESIC
BOCCIONI
FUTURISTICUS
TERRAGNI
RATIONALITATAE
WAGNER REALISTUM
ARCHIARTEUM
SANT'ELIA
FUTURISTICUS
LANG UTOPICUS
CINEMAE
BEHRENS INDUSTRIALIS
OLBRICH
ARCHIARTEUM
SECESSIONIS
1900
1910
1920
1930
1940

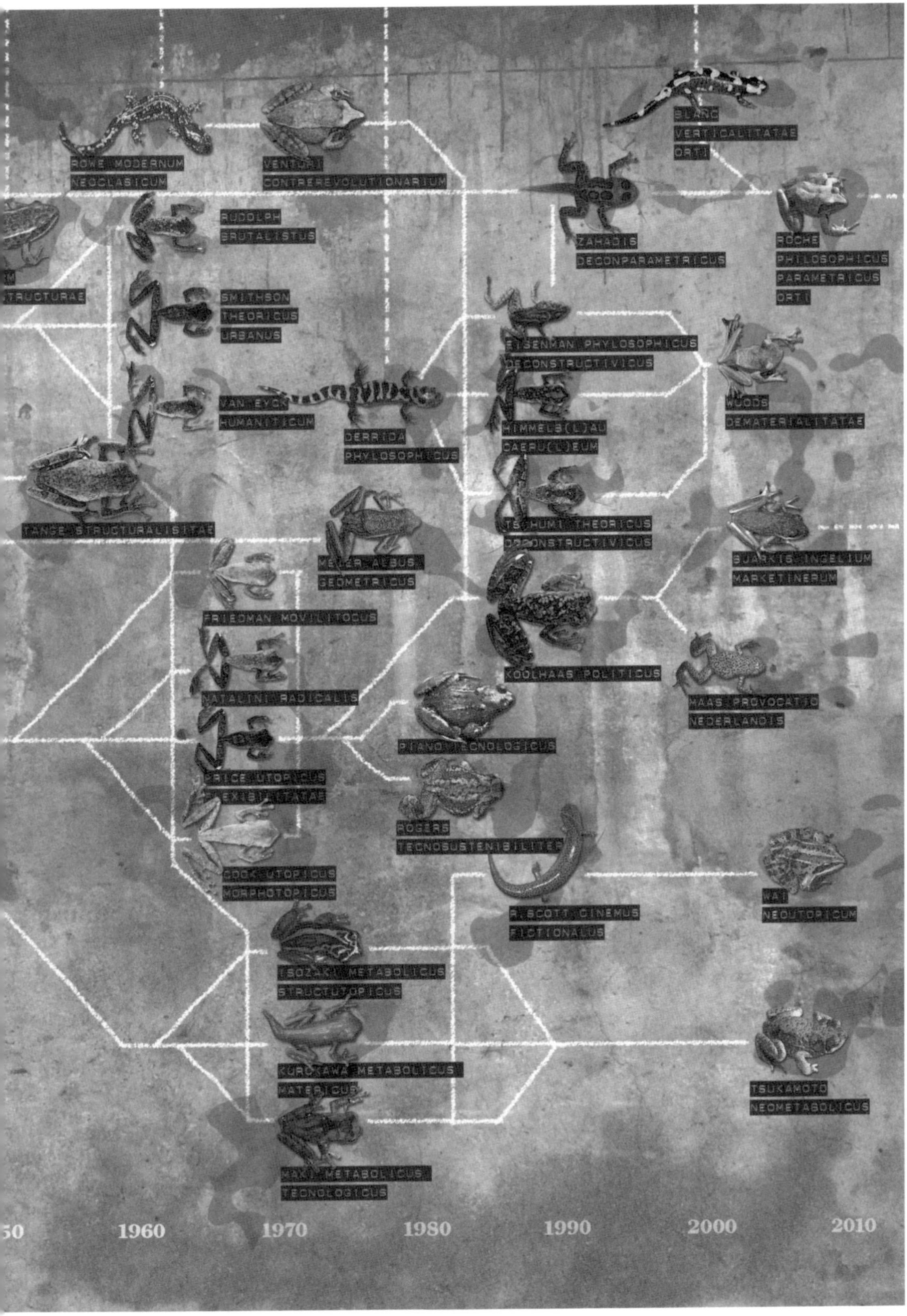
ROWE MODERNUM
NEOCLASICUM
VENTURI
CONTREREVOLUTIONARIUM
BLANC
VERTICALITATAE
ORTI
ZAHADIS
DECONPARAMETRICUS
ROCHE
PHILOSOPHICUS
PARAMETRICUS
ORTI
RUDOLPH
BRUTALISTUS
SMITHSON
THEORICUS
URBANUS
EISENMAN PHYLOSOPHICUS
DECONSTRUCTIVICUS
WOODS
DEMATERIALITATAE
VAN EYCK
HUMANITICUM
DERRIDA
PHYLOSOPHICUS
HIMMELB(L)AU
CAERU(L)EUM
TANGE STRUCTURALISITAE
TSCHUMI THEORICUS
DECONSTRUCTIVICUS
MEIER ALBUS
GEOMETRICUS
BJARKIS INGELIUM
MARKETINERUM
FRIEDMAN MOVILITOCUS
KOOLHAAS POLITICUS
NATALINI RADICALIS
MAAS PROVOCATIO
NEDERLANDIS
PIANO TECNOLOGICUS
PRICE UTOPICUS
ROGERS
TECNOSUSTENIBILITER
COOK UTOPICUS
MORPHOTOPICUS
R.SCOTT CINEMUS
FICTIONALUS
ITO
NEOUTOPICUM
ISOZAKI METABOLICUS
STRUCTUTOPICUS
KUROKAWA METABOLICUS
MATERICUS
TSUKAMOTO
NEOMETABOLICUS
MAKI METABOLICUS
TECNOLOGICUS
1960
1970
1980
1990
2000
2010

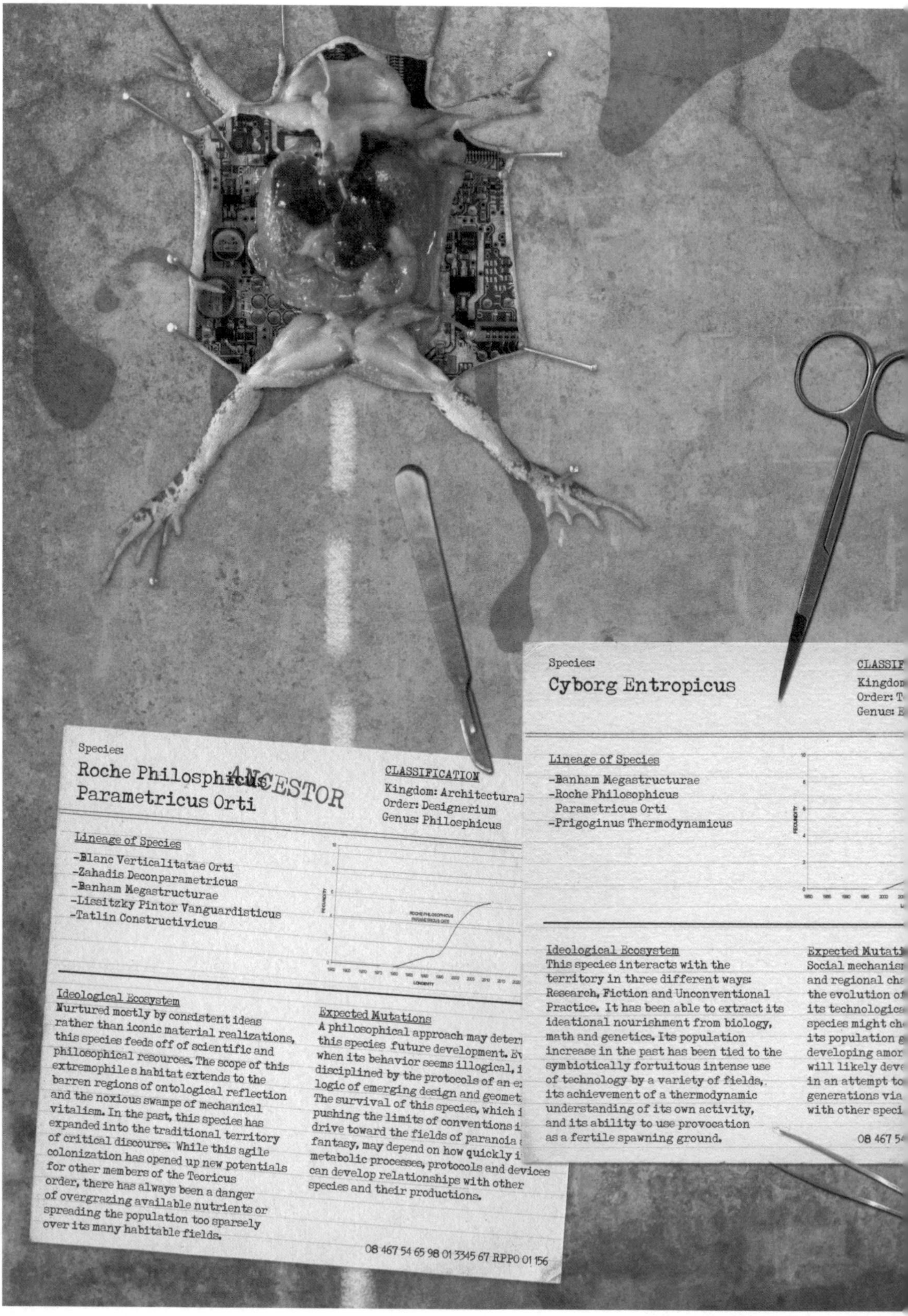
Species:
Cyborg Entropicus
CLASSIF
Kingdom
Order: T
Genus: E
Lineage of Species
-Banham Megastructurae
-Roche Philosophicus Parametricus Orti
-Prigoginus Thermodynamicus
Ideological Ecosystem
This species interacts with the territory in three different ways: Research, Fiction and Unconventional Practice. It has been able to extract its ideational nourishment from biology, math and genetics. Its population increase in the past has been tied to the symbiotically fortuitous intense use of technology by a variety of fields, its achievement of a thermodynamic understanding of its own activity, and its ability to use provocation as a fertile spawning ground.
Expected Mutati
Social mechanis
and regional ch
the evolution o
its technologic
species might ch
its population g
developing amo
will likely dev
in an attempt to
generations via
with other speci
Species:
Roche Philosphicus Parametricus Orti
ANCESTOR
CLASSIFICATION
Kingdom: Architectural
Order: Designerium
Genus: Philosphicus
Lineage of Species
-Blanc Verticalitatae Orti
-Zahadis Deconparametricus
-Banham Megastructurae
-Lissitzky Pintor Vanguardisticus
-Tatlin Constructivicus
Ideological Ecosystem
Nurtured mostly by consistent ideas rather than iconic material realizations, this species feeds off of scientific and philosophical resources. The scope of this extremophile's habitat extends to the barren regions of ontological reflection and the noxious swamps of mechanical vitalism. In the past, this species has expanded into the traditional territory of critical discourse. While this agile colonization has opened up new potentials for other members of the Teoricus order, there has always been a danger of overgrazing available nutrients or spreading the population too sparsely over its many habitable fields.
Expected Mutations
A philosophical approach may deter this species future development. Ev when its behavior seems illogical, i disciplined by the protocols of an e logic of emerging design and geomet The survival of this species, which i pushing the limits of conventions i drive toward the fields of paranoia fantasy, may depend on how quickly i metabolic processes, protocols and devices can develop relationships with other species and their productions.
08 467 54 65 98 01 3345 67 RPPO 01 156

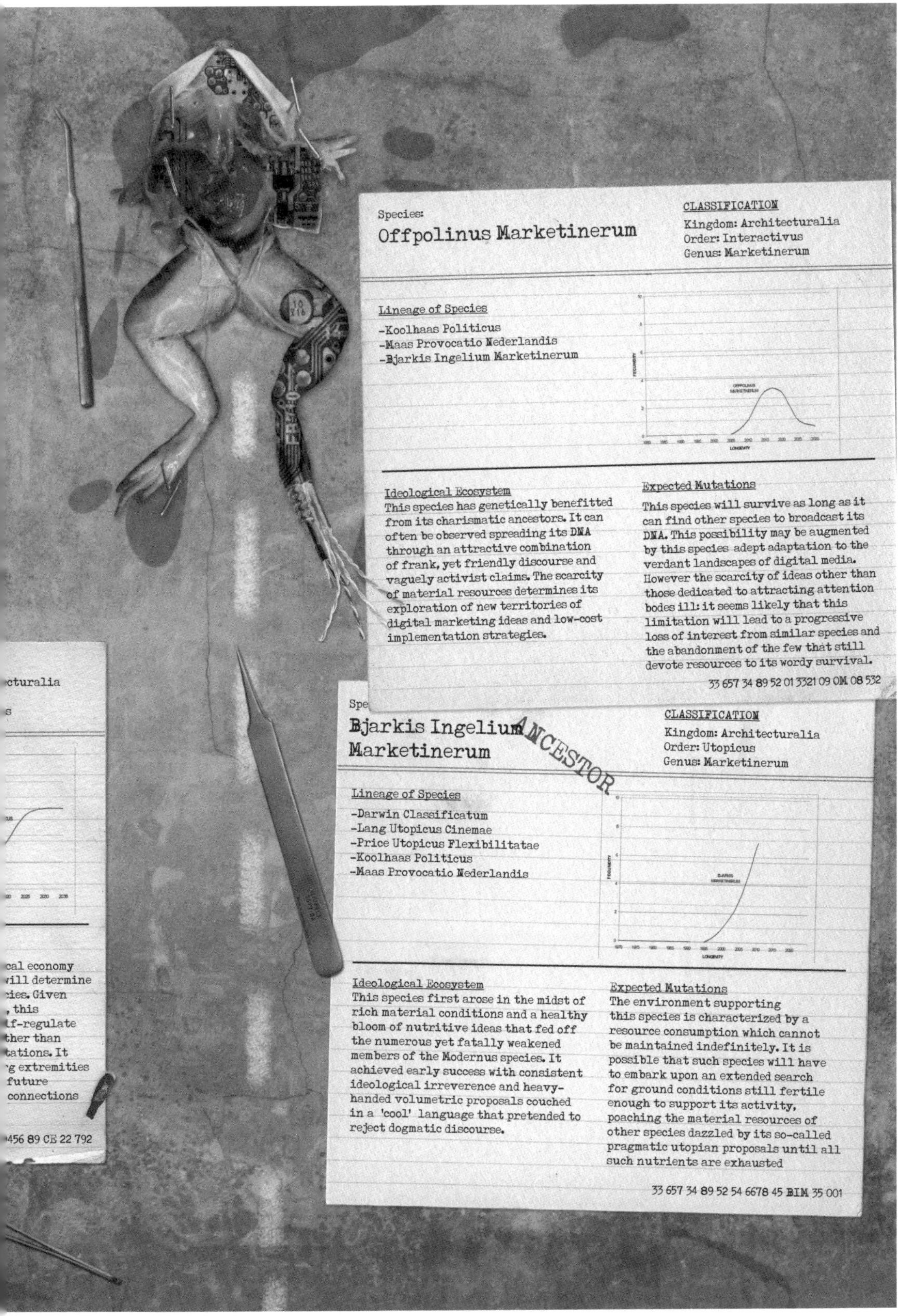
Species:
Offpolinus Marketinerum
CLASSIFICATION
Kingdom: Architecturalia
Order: Interactivus
Genus: Marketinerum
Lineage of Species
-Koolhaas Politicus
-Maas Provocatio Nederlandis
-Bjarkis Ingelium Marketinerum
Ideological Ecosystem
This species has genetically benefitted from its charismatic ancestors. It can often be observed spreading its DNA through an attractive combination of frank, yet friendly discourse and vaguely activist claims. The scarcity of material resources determines its exploration of new territories of digital marketing ideas and low-cost implementation strategies.
Expected Mutations
This species will survive as long as it can find other species to broadcast its DNA. This possibility may be augmented by this species adept adaptation to the verdant landscapes of digital media. However the scarcity of ideas other than those dedicated to attracting attention bodes ill: it seems likely that this limitation will lead to a progressive loss of interest from similar species and the abandonment of the few that still devote resources to its wordy survival.
33 657 34 89 52 01 3321 09 OM 08 532
Bjarkis Ingelium Marketinerum
ANCESTOR
CLASSIFICATION
Kingdom: Architecturalia
Order: Utopicus
Genus: Marketinerum
Lineage of Species
-Darwin Classificatum
-Lang Utopicus Cinemae
-Price Utopicus Flexibilitatae
-Koolhaas Politicus
-Maas Provocatio Nederlandis
Ideological Ecosystem
This species first arose in the midst of rich material conditions and a healthy bloom of nutritive ideas that fed off the numerous yet fatally weakened members of the Modernus species. It achieved early success with consistent ideological irreverence and heavy-handed volumetric proposals couched in a 'cool' language that pretended to reject dogmatic discourse.
Expected Mutations
The environment supporting this species is characterized by a resource consumption which cannot be maintained indefinitely. It is possible that such species will have to embark upon an extended search for ground conditions still fertile enough to support its activity, poaching the material resources of other species dazzled by its so-called pragmatic utopian proposals until all such nutrients are exhausted
33 657 34 89 52 54 6678 45 BIM 35 001
cturalia
cal economy
will determine
cies. Given
, this
lf-regulate
ther than
tations. It
g extremities
future
connections
456 89 CE 22 792

LANDSCAPING FOR CHIMERAS

JILL H. CASID

LANDSCAPING FOR CHIMERAS

JILL H. CASID

During Augusto Pinochet's dictatorship, Chilean poet Raúl Zurita began to imagine writing poems not as graffiti on the walls of the city, but rather in the sky, on the faces of cliffs, and in the desert[1] as a topography of protest, a writing in and of the place against the architectures of the state apparatus.[1] Looking down now from the satellite extension of the bird's-eye view through the screen of Google Earth, one may still read Zurita's declaration of the powers of what Eve Sedgwick theorized as periperformative negation, a defiant *ni pena ni miedo* (translated variously as "neither shame nor fear" and "neither sorrow nor fear") bulldozed into the shifting sands of the Atacama Desert and sustained, according to legend, by the children of the local village sent out every Sunday to maintain the inscription.[2] The hot and moving, convergent and divergent form of the desert of Atacama is both figure and ground for Zurita's negative poetics of ephemeral and yet sustaining resistance, the ground of inscription for "neither shame nor fear" and figure as well as ground for the cycle of poems in his book *Purgatory*. For "The Desert of Atacama VI," the landscape of the desert, like that of the nation of Chile, is neither outside politics or history nor the passive terrain on which brutal politics and the traumas of history are enacted.

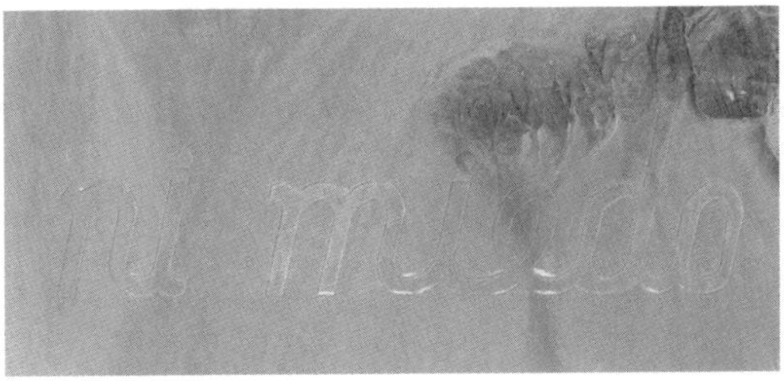

Raúl Zurita, "ni pena ni miedo," Atacama Desert, Chile, bulldozed letters in sand, 1 kilometer × 3 kilometers, aerial view from Google Earth

The poem opens with a declaration: "Arid plains do not dream / No one has ever managed to see / Those chimerical pampas."[3] By the very force of this negation of dried-up fields that cannot dream and the fertile plains posed as "chimerical" because no one has managed to see them, the chimerical landscape of Chile in and of these plains of hell emerges as the socio-political agent of a negative hybridity, one neither dreamed nor seen, and yet, through this imagery and action of negation, both seen and felt as matter and as a dream that matters—painfully and powerfully. The chimera is not merely a hybrid, monster body—whether human, animal, vegetable or some crossing. It is neither stably above ground nor firmly beneath our feet (or hooves or paws).[4] Landscaping for chimeras is not to safely house or stably contain hybrid bodies. Nor is landscaping for chimeras a separate subset of landscape—a special species with the classification "chimerical landscape." Rather, it offers a shift in perspective and practice that reframes the problematic of "architecture is all over" as not merely a matter of dispersion and ubiquity or the crisis of endgames

1
Forrest Gander and Kent Johnson, "Ni Pena ni Miedo: A Sentimental Education in Chile," *Jacket* 30 (2006), http://jacketmagazine.com/30/chile.html.

2
On Zurita's desert sand poem, see Harris Feinsod, "World Poetry Grindhouse," *Arcade*, October 13, 2001, http://arcade.stanford.edu/blogs/world-poetry-grindhouse, and this posting of the sighting via Google Earth: http://googlesightseeing.com/2009/01/ni-pena-ni-miedo-no-shame-nor-fear. For more on the periperformative, see Eve Kosofsky Sedgwick, "Around the Performative: Periperformative Vicinities in Nineteenth-Century Narrative," *Touching Feeling: Affect, Pedagogy, Performativity* (Durham: Duke University Press, 2003), 67–91. On my extension of Sedgwick's concept of the periperformative to theorize landscape as verb, see Jill H. Casid, "Epilogue: Landscape in, around, and under the Performative," *Women & Performance: a journal of feminist theory* 21, no. 1 (2011): 97–116.

3
Raúl Zurita, "The Desert of Atacama VI," in *Purgatory*, trans. Anna Deeny (Berkeley: University of California Press, 2009).

4
Jill H. Casid, "Chimerical Figurations at the Monstrous Edges of Species," *Environmental Criticism for the Twenty-first Century*, ed. Ken Hiltner, Stephanie Lemenager and Theresa Shewry (London: Routledge Press, 2011), 61–83.

and declarations of "architecture is dead" and "long live landscape." Across the six propositions that follow, landscaping for chimeras explores terrains not made *for* but made *from* the possibilities, powers, sensations and affects of these pathetic animal-human-plant hybrids that might otherwise seem orphaned or like matter necessarily without place. Ultimately, we might understand the chimera as an actively shaping potential, as matter that matters, and as the complex ecologies within which what landscape *is* cannot be distinguished from what it *does*.

I

Landscaping for chimeras offers a form of worlding beyond globalization and the human-centered terms of cosmopolitanism or cosmopolite consciousness.

The unearthed letters of Zurita's poem in the sand might seem to posit the alternative to the violence of military dictatorships as a vantage: namely, that which can be seen, read and felt from above and beyond the terrain of the nation. And such an alternative view might seem the terrain of the cosmopolitan, the realm of a kind of cosmopolite or planetary consciousness. One might assert that cosmopolitanism is, as Immanuel Kant suggests, a "chimera." In Kant's 1795 treatise, "Perpetual Peace: A Philosophical Sketch," we find a precariously swinging sign: the "perpetual peace" of Kant's title inscribed on the painted sign of a Dutch innkeeper that invites weary travelers to enter under the depiction of a burial ground that satirically pokes fun at the idea that a state of truly resting in peace could happen anywhere but in one's grave.[5] And, yet, avoiding a certain kind of death and destruction—that of war—is the aim of Kant's construction of a version of universal right, that of the guest who can sojourn unmolested anywhere because of their world citizenship, their cosmopolitanism. And though Kant takes the sign to point not just at humans generally, or at the war-planning rulers of states in particular, but also at the philosopher whose dream of perpetual peace the sign's landscape of graves threatens to puncture, laying out the terms of such a right of visitation (or right of passage) is not a "chimera."

This is no arbitrary metaphor. The related terms "cosmopolitan" and "cosmopolite" are most commonly understood to refer to persons, acquired human qualities or tastes (e.g., the ability to make oneself at home outside of one's culture of origin or the appreciation of differences), philosophical principles or ideologies (such as the tolerance of other beliefs) or rights (such as the dream of a universal right of world citizenship). Less commonly, "cosmopolitan" and "cosmopolite" refer to things or places often characterized by intermingling and mixture as the vehicles or sites of contact from ships to cities to the commodities that travel between them. Even more rarely

5
Immanuel Kant, *Perpetual Peace: A Philosophical Essay*, trans. Mary Campbell (New York: Cosimo Books, 2011), 28. Among the many writers on cosmopolitanism, I have been especially influenced by Kwame Anthony Appiah, *Cosmopolitanism: Ethics in a World of Strangers* (New York: W. W. Norton, 2006); Walter D. Mignolo, *The Darker Side of Western Modernity: Global Futures, Decolonial Options* (Durham: Duke University Press, 2011); Mary Louise Pratt, "Science, Planetary Consciousness, Interiors," in *Imperial Eyes: Travel Writing and Transculturation* (New York: Routledge, 1996), 15–37; and Gayatri Spivak, *A Critique of Postcolonial Reason: Toward a History of the Vanishing Present* (Cambridge: Harvard University Press, 1999).

brought into the conversation is the significance of these concepts within the discourses of botany and natural history—namely, "cosmopolitan" or "cosmopolite" as the term for plants or biological entities that can be found in more than one climate, having been successfully transplanted between climatological zones.[6] The question of the relation between climate and biology—and particularly the shaping force of environment on biological entities—cuts to the core of the ethical and political problematics about race, gender species, property, rights and citizenship we have inherited from the Enlightenment. It is no accident or idiosyncrasy that Kant's central metaphor for the state is that of a tree with its own roots, an image of independence that raises the attendant problem for Kant as to whether such trees—and the nations and cultures for which they stand— can be grafted and transplanted without losing their integrity.

6
See, for example, the use of "cosmopolite" to refer to those plants that can be most widely dispersed in Joseph Dalton Hooker, "The Botany of the Antarctic Voyage: of H. M. Discovery Ships Erebus and Terror in the Years 1839–1843 under the Command of Captain Sir James Clark Ross," *Flora Novae-Zelandiae*, volumes 1–2 (London: Reeve, 1853).

The political task of imagining cosmopolitanism as the vehicle and horizon of a kind of promised peace is necessarily enmeshed with tough considerations regarding the relations between humans, animals, plants, machines and the extent to which their characters (including moral character) and potentials (social, political, economic) depend on the climates and environments from which they are extracted, into which they are introduced and within which they grow. Grounding cosmopolitanism—taking it from the shifty signs of dreams and nightmares to the topography of materialization and the diagram for the built environment—makes the terrain of the global a chimera in the other, far more challenging sense of the inextricable entanglement of political fantasies and ideals with the urgent viabilities and forms of life across "nativist" and human-centered bounds. What would it yield to practice cosmopolitism/cosmopolitanism or a vision of the global beyond the bounds of species, and specifically beyond the human? Landscaping for chimeras as a practice of planetary consciousness or cosmopolitism promises no less than a response to precarity and crisis (economic, environmental, ethical, physical) that works within the conditions of negentropy and contamination.

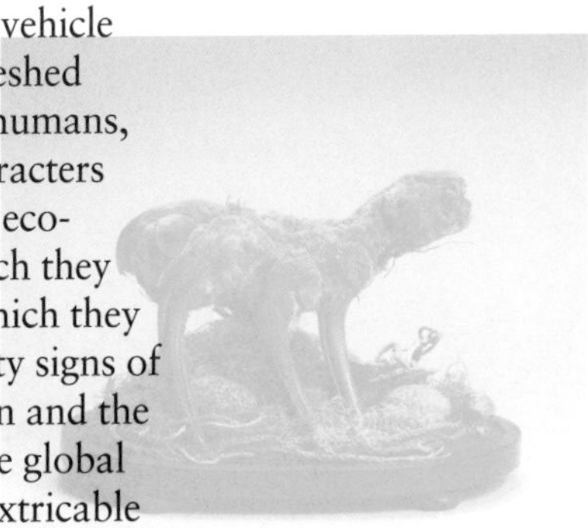

2
Landscaping for chimeras demonstrates the extent to which we are all chimeras.

To return to the giant but also, importantly, lowercase cursive letters of "ni pena ni miedo" (if their arcs do point beyond the nation, to something like a cosmopolitan or planetary consciousness), what is challenging and exciting—even igniting—about Zurita's negative exhortation is the extent to which it is furrowed beneath the promised pampas and the hard actualities of the shifting desert sands of nation and ongoingly so by the disenfranchised and the minor, the anonymous children of a tiny local village, and written not just out

7
Donna Haraway, "A Cyborg Manifesto: Science, Technology, and Socialist-Feminism in the Late Twentieth Century," in *Simians, Cyborgs and Women: The Reinvention of Nature* (New York; Routledge, 1991), 149–81.

8
Hans Sloane, "A Further Account of the Contents of the China Cabinet Mentioned Last Transaction, p. 390," *Philosophical Transactions* 20 (1698): 461–62; John Evelyn, *Silva: or, A Discourse of Forest-Trees, and the Propagation of Timber in His Majesty's Dominions .... With Notes, by A. Hunter, M.D. F.R.S.L. & E. The third edition, revised, corrected and considerably enlarged. To which is added The Terra: A Philosophical Discourse of Earth* (York: T. Wilson and R. Spence, 1801), 2:55.

of but also with the lettering and littering agencies of wind and sand. This giant earthwork land art poem of both the logics of neither/nor and both/and (neither shame nor fear, neither dream nor seen, both dreaming and matter) is not just about landscape or on the landscape but enacts the ways in which the chimerical, agential, sentient, mattering and dreaming landscape in which we live, on which we depend, and with which we speak and act is us. To rephrase Donna Haraway's "A Cyborg Manifesto," we might say that "we are all chimeras."[7] But to say that we are all chimeras is not to make us any less singular. It is precisely to insist on the human as not exceptional or distinct in scaping and shaping the land. To challenge our practice with the rallying cry that we are all chimeras is rather to think of life as inseparable from the environments or niches that sustain its variant forms—both within and without.

Scythian Lamb, preserved specimen under glass

9
Dr. Young Ho Kim of the Chungnam National University in Daejeon, Korea, reported in the *Journal of Natural Products* that compounds isolated from the plant known as the Vegetable Lamb of Tartary inhibit the formation of osteoclasts. See Young Ho Kim et al., "Inhibitors of Osteoclast Formation from Rhizomes of *Cibotium barometz*," *Journal of Natural Products* 72, no. 9 (2009), http://pubs.acs.org/stoken/presspac/presspac/full/10.1021/np9004097.

The Bodleian Library holds the coat and London's Garden Museum holds the preserved artifact of samples of the exotic lamb plant known as the Vegetable Lamb of Tartary that, until a 1698 essay by Hans Sloane, was thought to be not merely a cross between an animal and a vegetable but also a plant that generated a lamb as its offspring. The plant's "fruit" was understood to develop by consuming the surrounding vegetation until the lamb grew large enough to detach itself from the umbilicus of the plant and range freely. This particular print from Elizabeth Blackwell's *A Curious Herbal* (1739) was adapted for an 1801 edition of John Evelyn's 1676 *Terra: A Philosophical Discourse of Earth* and praised for its relative lack of "fancy." Yet even here we find vestiges of the myth as characteristic of a class of plants that "destroy the vegetable virtue where they grow."[8] One of many dusty oddities in the wonder cabinets of a bygone era of perverse marvels, the lamb plant or *Cibotium barometz* is also now at the forefront of experimental research in the treatment of osteoporosis.[9] That is, this zoophyte that kills other plants that grow around it also may have the potential to destroy or "eat" osteocytes, and thus might help correct imbalances between those cells that build up bone and those that break it down. Whether a mythical or actual crossing between animal and plant, the exotic vegetable lamb, when transplanted or transfused, is both destructive and curative or corrective, pointing to the extent to which the chimera is also a kind of pharmakon in the Derridean sense, troubling any easy distinction in both natural and moral order—that is, between good and evil, generative and destructive.[10] Thus, it is no surprise that the three generations of Tradescants known for their botanical collections, now housed in part at the Garden Museum, are buried in a tomb that is invoked as among the rarities they collected. The epitaph analogizes their tomb to the "world of wonders" they gathered into a "closet shut," and imagines their bodies, not unlike the vegetable wonders which they collected and planted, as not just interred or "closeted" but as active relandscaping agents that convert earth to heaven:

> Transplanted now themselves, sleep here, and when
> Angels shall with their trumpets waken men
> And fire shall purge the world, these hence shall rise
> And change this garden for a Paradise.

The chimera is, we could say, not just between earth, heaven and hell but also a switch-point or converter, promising heaven while unearthing our ears in monstrous forms.

10 Jacques Derrida, "Plato's Pharmacy," in *Dissemination*, trans. Barbara Johnson (Chicago: University of Chicago Press, 1981), 63–171.

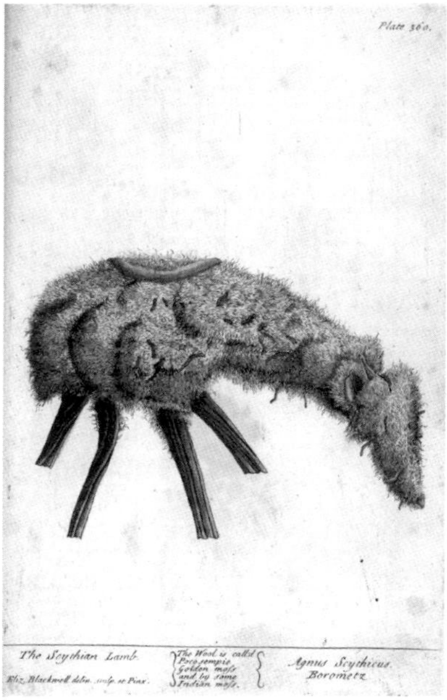

Elizabeth Blackwell, "The Scythian Lamb," engraving, in *Elizabeth Blackwell, A curious herbal : containing five hundred cuts, of the most useful plants, which are now used in the practice of physick : engraved on folio copper plates, after drawings taken from the life / by Elizabeth Blackwell: to which is added a short description of ye plants and their common uses in physick* (London: Printed for S. Harding, 1737–1739), volume 2, Plate 360

11
Critical Art Ensemble, *Molecular Invasion* (Brooklyn: Autonomedia, 2002). See the free digital edition at http://www.critical-art.net/books.html.

12
Arthur Rimbaud, "Les voyelles," *Poésies, Une saison en enfer, Illuminations*, ed. Louis Forestier (Paris: Gallimard, 1999). This translation is my own.

3
Landscaping for chimeras unfounds, confounds and refounds figure and ground, body and niche, language and land, matter and dream.

Thinking, doing, performing with the chimera is to exploit the materializing and scaping powers of language. The chimera transgresses borders and not least those hedges between what might seem the simple muck and mattering ground of landscape, and its framing and transforming discourses and fantasies. At once the scientific term for a biological entity with more than one set of genetic information and the hybrid she-beast, the fire-breathing, multiheaded lion-goat-serpent of Greco-Roman mythology, the chimera gives monstrous, materializing figural form to the crossings of the bounds between species, genres and genders while also functioning as the vivid descriptor for the radical powers of poetics and imagination. As the monster bodies of transgenic hybrids from the geep and the oncomouse to genetically modified "Frankenfood," the chimera often appears without ground in the sense of precedent; it is radically decontextualized as a being without belonging, or as antagonistic or even destructive counter to the environmental as a spoiling, antinatural, artificial and impure incarnation. Thus, the chimera might seem antithetical to landscape. Further, applying the adjectival form of the chimera or the "chimerical" to landscape might seem to create not only a special class, sub-species or sub-genre of landscape, but one that either takes up the sense of the fantastically imaginary and even impossible to designate (a kind of scaping that remains unrealizable, unrepresentable and utopian in the sense of having no place) or that demarcates a particular restricted terrain for what the art collaborative Critical Art Ensemble call the "Fourth Domain," the domain of the Transgeneae and the technologies of genetic mixing.[11]

But far more provocatively and radically, the chimera brings out the mixed, hybrid, protean and auto-generating powers already lurking within landscaping or landscape understood as active verb and as sensorially resounding vowels. In French poet Arthur Rimbaud's "Vowels" or "Les voyelles" (also known as "L'alchimie des voyelles") from *A Season in Hell*, alchemical crossings and synaesthetic mixings (including the matching of each vowel with a corresponding color) provide a way to sing the mutual suffusions of language and an anti-natural or transformed, counter-normative nature. Land and sea, peace and tempest, planting and writing, seeds, humans and animals crisscross in waves and wrinkles that reference, for example, the "U" of viridian seas, the "U" of the "peace of fields sown with animals," and the "U" of "the peace of furrows which alchemy imprints on studious foreheads" into chimerical landscapes, seascapes and thoughtscapes in rippled motion.[12] But one might also say not that vowels sing in the language that is landscape but rather that they growl with the long vowel sound of the painful "ow." Rimbaud's soundings are also the exquisitely beautiful and grotesque vowels of "buzzing flies" and "cruel smells," "spat blood," "beautiful lips" laughing in anger or penitent drunkenness, and strident noises ("strideurs"). The affective energies of the intransitive form of the verb "to be growled," meaning to be terrified or frightened, may bring up the nightmares and fears that the chimera's monstrosity negotiates. Related to latent births ("naissances latentes"), Rimbaud's vowels that growl in and through the language of landscape carry a complex temporality, linking something of the echoed archaic and the ostensibly surpassed to the future of the as yet.

Rimbaud's alchemical, metamorphic genealogical tree—"A black, E White, I red, U Green, O blue: vowels, I shall tell one day of your mysterious origins"—is echoed in Italian sculptor Giuseppe Penone's *Tree of Vowels* (L'arbre des voyelles). This work turns a dead tree, felled in the storm of 1999 (in the Jardin des Tuileries, Paris), into, at a stroke, a bronzed fossil and an arboreal sign system in which the vowels of "love" and "death" are not just the semiotic or linguistic carved into the bark of trees but emerge as the beneath or before of the uprooted roots of vocality or the voice from which the vowel and the word are traced. In a new twist on the question of animal and vegetable souls that so vexed the Enlightenment, the *Tree of Vowels* might also be understood to vibrate the upended tree whose below-ground roots now function as branches with the refused animism of linguistic systems that would turn consonants and semi-vowels into bodies or skeletons animated, made to quiver, sense and feel by the "soul of vowels."[13] Landscaping for chimeras, we could also say, gets us to the heart of the matter of the knotted nots of minimal life and animate death with echoes of the souls that scintillate and sound even through the voweled hollows of dead matter.

13 R. L. Tafel, "Investigations into the Laws of English Orthography and Pronunciation," *Proceedings of the American Philosophical Society*, vol. 8 (Philadelphia, 1861), 290.

Giuseppe Penone, *L'Arbre des voyelles*, 1999, oak cast in bronze, 30 meters long, installed in the Jardin des Tuileries, Paris

4

Landscaping for chimeras radically ambiguates forms of life and challenges binary conceptions of landscape premised on oppositions such as city/country, natural/cultural, paradise/pollution and free/colonized.

Landscaping in the long wake of colonization is a chimera productive of queerly monstrous conjoinings and protean interspecies encounters, the outcomes of which are still uncertain.[14] Perhaps the most famous figuration of the fabled, fire-breathing, monstrous animal hybrid of ancient Greek mythology with a lion's head, animal body (often a goat) and serpent's tail is the Etruscan bronze known as the *Chimera of Arezzo*, unearthed in 1553, placed prominently in the Palazzo Vecchio by the Medici dukes, and now preserved in the archaeological museum in Florence. In its bronze casting, the chimera would seem to appear not just as a singularity but also as radically deracinated, unhomely and permanently unearthed, a figure necessarily without grounding. Recast in the midst of battle, *Bellerophon Fighting the Chimaera* (1821), by Vienna-based sculptor Johann Nepomuk Schaller, pits man against monstrous beast. While this hot entanglement and erotically enmeshed figuration in unifying white marble may derive its energy from the extent to which man and monster are nearly indistinguishably locked, *Bellerophon Fighting the Chimaera* might nonetheless seem to share with the *Chimera of Arezzo* an abstraction of the menacing figure of the chimera and its implied or depicted action from any foundation. But the chimera is always both figuration and (re)grounding. The latent action of these gestures necessarily implies a landscaped and de-landscaped terrain of menace and conflict, an agonistic field within which the entangled figures pose and which they also remake by the arc of their gestural lines. The monstrosity and the threat of the chimera (from Homer through Hesiod to Ovid's *Metamorphoses*) lies not merely in its body but in the body's charged relation to the landscape it ravages and incorporates. The second-century writer Pseudo-Apollodorus, for example, positions the chimera in and as a rogue transformer of relandscaping energies:

> He [Iobates] ordered Bellerophon to slay the Khimaira, assuming that he would instead be destroyed himself by the beast, since not even a quantity of men could subdue it with ease, let alone one. For it was a single being that had the force of three beasts, the front part of a lion, the tail of a drakon, and the third (middle) head was that of a goat, through which it breathed out fire. It despoiled the countryside and ravaged the herds.[15]

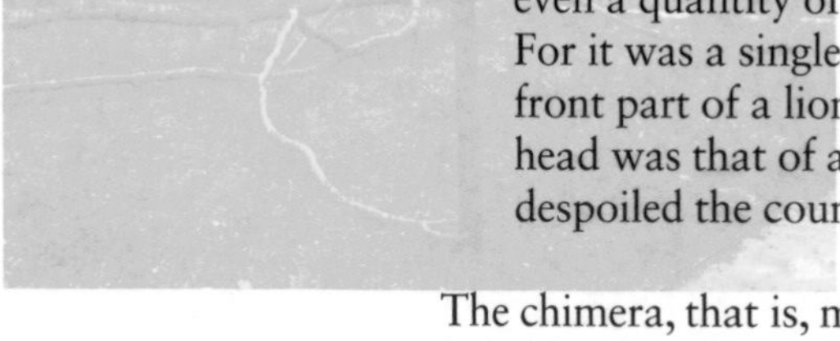

The chimera, that is, manifests as a threat not just in its monstrous hybridity but also as an agent of destruction, ravaging the land of

14
See especially Donna Haraway, *When Species Meet* (Minneapolis: University of Minnesota Press, 2008).

15
Pseudo-Apollodorus, *Bibliotheca* 2.31–32, trans. Keith Aldrich.

Chimera of Arezzo, c. 400 B.C., bronze, Museo Archeologico Nazionale, Florence

Johann Nepomuk Schaller, *Bellerophon Fighting the Chimaera*, 1821, marble, 201 cm high

Lycia, killing cattle and setting fires. As a monstrous product of nature, a figure without prior ground and a figure set against ground, the chimera intrudes as an active menace to nature and its acculturated forms—to agriculture and the breeding of livestock. And this version of myth with its apparently stock lesson repeats. Yves-Marie Allain and Guy Prouveur's recent book on "monstrosities and chimeras of the vegetable world" frames concerns over genetic manipulation in terms of the long history of botanical marvels, grafts and transplants, relating the fears and ferocities of current debate over genomic experimentation to the monstrous nightmare forms of the "plantimals" (plant-animals) and "animans" (animal-humans) of genetic manipulation. Their clarion call answer? Enter the new Bellerophon who arrives on his flying horse to eliminate the monstrous chimeras of fear and return peace and reason to our planet.[16]

Such a reanimation of the imperial fantasy myth of a sovereign human agency that can reassert control over roiling, chimerical nature and rescue the good hybrids from the shadow of the monstrous chimeras of unfounded superstition is not a solution but a symptomatic rearticulation of the very problematics it promises to do battle to resolve. If the chimera within and not just without bears a promise, it does so not on the fantasy wings of reason unfettered by madness, not under the sign of a peace that comes from the violent suppression of the din of debate or from the denial of fear and shame, but by taking us into the unsettling and uneasy mire of the residuum of colonial histories from below and between—not just from above. In Odilon Redon's haunting charcoal drawing (1881) variously titled "Plante Grasse" (succulent plant) and "Cactus-Man," a blackened totemic

16
The rhetorical question they ask is articulated thus: "Qui sera et d'où sortira le future Bellérephon pour évacuer la peur et ramener sérénité et raison sur notre planète?" See Yves-Marie Allain and Guy Prouveur, *Monstruosités et chimères du monde vegetal* (Paris: Ellipses, 2009), 134.

head sprouting thorns rises on a long, thick trunk of a neck from the potted soil of an isolated planter emblazoned with a scene of an Amazon warrior. The charcoal's ghosting repetition of the many slave heads of the imperial archive rehearses the colonial tropics of violence, fetishism and animism displaced onto the primitivized periphery, and works through the post-Darwinian imaginary of race in terms of both human and plant bodies.[17] Through its colonial re-do of the myth of warriors sown from seed, the poignant barbs of regrowth also serve to dramatize, even if as nightmare, the latencies and potentialities of the as yet unfinished or as that which may return, giving us a version of the kind of tropicopolitan insurgency theorized by Srinivas Aravamudan as an uncanny agency that works through the unsettled field of the very colonial tropology to which we are also subjected.[18]

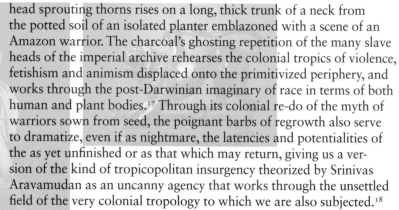

17 On practices of destruction and death as contested forms of colonial biopower or "mortuary politics," see also Vincent Brown, *The Reaper's Garden: Death and Power in the World of Atlantic Slavery* (Cambridge: Harvard University Press, 2008). For a reading of Odilon Redon's plant-human hybrids, see Barbara Larson, "Evolution and Degeneration in the Early Work of Odilon Redon," *Nineteenth-Century Art Worldwide: A Journal of Nineteenth-Century Visual Culture* 2, no. 2 (2003), http://www.19thc-artworldwide.org/index.php/spring03/220-excavating-greece-classicism-between-empire-and-nation-in-nineteenth-century-europe.

18 Srinivas Aravamudan, *Tropicopolitans* (Durham: Duke University Press, 1999), 6.

Odilon Redon, *Cactus-Man*, 1881, charcoal, 49 × 32.5 cm

5
Landscaping for chimeras inextricably intermeshes the mattering of bodies and environments, reorganizes kinship, and upends the sequential relations of descent.

The chimera is a matter of soil but also of blood. The first use of the nomenclature "chimera" for a transplanted organism produced from the engrafting of distinct species refers not to humans or animals, but to plants. Hans Winkler, the early twentieth-century German botanist who created the neologism "genome," poached the term "chimera" in 1907 from ancient myth to apply it to transgenic hybrids—in this case, a tomato spliced with nightshade (*Solanum nigrum*).[19] One of the first applications of the term "chimera" to humans was employed to characterize individuals with mixed or doubled blood type in a published paper by Dr. Robert Race, director of the Medical Research Council Blood Group Unit in London, who, in 1951, appropriated the term from experimental botany and embryology to characterize a "Mrs. McK" who was found to have both her own blood type (O) and that of her dead fraternal twin brother (A).[20] In an article on "incongruous juxtapositions" in not just blood but also nomenclature,

19 Hans Winkler, "Über Pfropfbastarde und pflanzliche Chimären," *Berichte der Deutschen Botanischen Gesellschaft* 25 (1907): 568–576.

20 Cited in Aryn Martin, "'Incongruous juxtapositions': The Chimaera and Mrs. McK," *Endeavor* 31, no. 3 (2007): 99–103.

the sociologist of science Aryn Martin concludes that Race's act of naming such naturally occurring mixtures of blood type with the term "chimera" deceptively and problematically renders Mrs. McK the kin of such "monsters" as experimentally created interspecies mixtures of plants and animals, infertile cattle twins, the geep and "innumerable other laboratory creations": "Although there is little to connect this healthy blood donor with these creatures, the process of naming has nevertheless driven them together into one family."[21] The problem with the chimera, Martin argues, is its lack of definitional clarity and the incongruous taxonomic uses to which it is put.[22]

The promiscuous kinship of the very name "chimera" and its mating of different types of hybridity produced by different processes and productive of different outcomes attests even more poignantly to the power of the chimera as not a static thing but a dynamic, living entity of both destructive and generative potential. The chimera is more than a taxonomic classification and hybrid form of being; it is a force that severs ties assumed to bind—turning, for example, the "normal" into the "monstrous"—and that forges alternate bonds of kinship across the divides of difference and the ruptures of death (e.g., between a dead and a live twin). As a vital force, the chimera traverses the imagined distance between being and doing, while altering and even pulling up the ground behind it and casting new terrains ahead. And it does so through its powers of materializing figuration—its potential to give active, viable material form to that which would seem to be without ground because it is taken to be out of order in the senses of sequence or chronology (the dead or past that resurfaces unexpectedly), nature (that which appears unnatural not merely because it is artificially or technologically produced but also because it is prodigious, in the sense of lacking precedent), logic (the leap from imagined to real), and/or hierarchy (the overturning of priority, value and positions of dominance and submission).

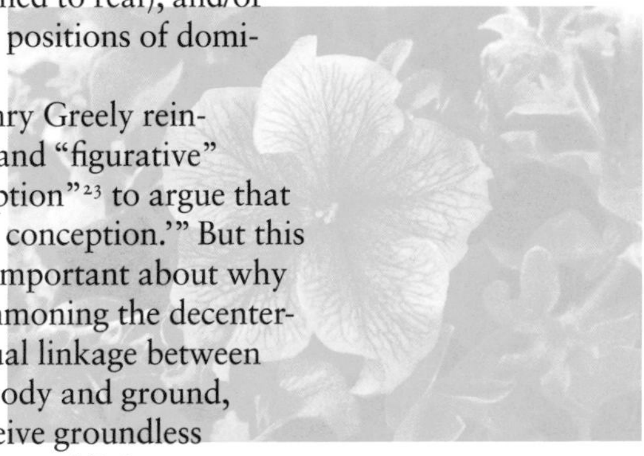

In his article on the chimera, bioethicist Henry Greely reintroduces the *Oxford English Dictionary's* third and "figurative" definition of a chimera as "an unfounded conception"[23] to argue that "chimerism per se might itself be an 'unfounded conception.'" But this "figurative" usage also tells us something quite important about why the chimera should trouble at all, namely in summoning the decentering, degrounding potential of an active conceptual linkage between idea and matter that overturns the relations of body and ground, before and after, in its power to potently reconceive groundless abstract, speculative and fantastic ideas in the form of living matter that landscapes its own grounds and futures. Thus, understanding landscape in terms of the chimera promises to bring out the vital and constitutive relations between landscaping as roving, materializing, generative and destructive force, and landscaping as fantasy projection

21
Ibid., 103.

22
In his essay on the definitional problem of the chimera, Greely calls for a parsing of ontological and ethical questions, asserting that ethical issues are raised not by whether something is a chimera but by the question of its "humanity," "naturalness" and "its proposed uses." See Henry T. Greely, "Defining Chimeras ... and Chimeric Concerns," *The American Journal of Bioethics* 3, no. 3 (2003): 17–20. For an effort to distinguish different types of chimeras, see Jason Scott Robert and Françoise Baylis, "Crossing Species Boundaries," *The American Journal of Bioethics* 3, no. 3 (2003): 1–13.

23
Greely, "Defining Chimeras," 12–13.

or as unfounded conception, procreation and ideation that casts its own ground.

The genealogical tree gives way to the promiscuous poetics and new reproductive technologies for queer generation. As if in answer to some deadly serious but no less funny or gorgeous joke about what happens when you cross a new version of Nietzsche's *The Gay Science* with the old gay stereotype of the closeted pansy, meet Edunia, the genetically engineered offspring at the center of contemporary bio-artist Eduardo Kac's *Natural History of the Enigma* (developed from 2003 to 2008 and first exhibited at the Weisman Art Museum in Minneapolis in 2009).[24] Edunia is a genetically engineered strain of the petunia whose pink petals manifest veins of red as if in a living allegory of the gene isolated and sequenced from Kac's blood and now expressed as a visible protein pigment in the "veins" of the plantimal offspring of Kac's mating with the particular plant he calls Petunia with a capital P. Kac relates his florid adventures in queer technologies for kinship and reproduction to Julien Offray de La Mettrie's *L'homme plante* [Man a Plant] (1748) and to La Mettrie's contention that "the singular analogy between the plant and animal kingdoms has led me to the discovery that the principal parts of men and plants are the same."[25] Yet, what is arguably most challenging about project Edunia is not the ground of similarity between humans and plants but the possibility latent in the limited-edition set of seed packets that forecast a future in which "Edunias can be distributed socially and planted everywhere." By extension, the future unfurls in and as an unruly garden not just of proliferation but also of forms of desire and potentials for generation that cross the furrowed possibilities of kin well beyond the mating of Ken and Ken and our ken.

Eduardo Kac, *Plantimal I–VI*, lambda prints on diasec, from the Natural History of the Enigma series, 16.5" × 16.5" each

24
See Eduardo Kac, *The Natural History of an Enigma*, http://www.ekac.org/nat.hist.enig.html. On the longer arc of Kac's practice with transgenic mutation, see also Eduardo Kac, "Life Transformation—Art Mutation," in *Signs of Life: Bio Art and Beyond*, ed. Eduardo Kac (Cambridge: MIT Press, 2007), 163–184.

25
Julien Offray de La Mettrie, *L'Homme-Plante* (1748) (Paris: Le Corridor Bleu, 2003) and Julien Offray de La Mettrie, *Man a Machine and Man a Plant*, trans. Richard A. Watson and Maya Rybalka (Indianapolis/Cambridge: Hackett, 1994).

6

Landscaping for chimeras releases the volatile and destructive but also auto-generating and transformative powers within landscape that turns landscape into a mattering not just of space but also of time, processes with histories that, as radical trajectories of becoming, forging new collectivities, assemblages and creative swarms, are uncertain in their outcomes.

To think, feel, imagine and practice landscaping for chimeras is to reimagine the interior of the body and the bodies of human, animal and plant as open systems, as branched bodyscapes perhaps not unlike queer artist Robert Flack's *Anatomical Garden* (1990). The exposed skeleton, circulatory and nervous systems of the anatomical diagrams in the Enlightenment *Encyclopédie* now, in the face of AIDS, turn not defensively inward but, in an expressive alternative to what Ed Cohen powerfully theorizes as the lethal biopolitical model of "immunity-as-defense," tranformatively sprout a bouquet of flowers where the head would be.[26] The chimerical bodyscape opens into and onto a social and interdependent body with healing and generating properties, an auto-generating enmeshment that does not disavow disease or shame or fear but offers a responsiveness besides the defensive or offensive boundaries that, rather than deny our interdependencies, animates the nervous system latent in the lifeless, dissected skeleton of anatomical tradition and makes a garden of the bones that are no longer barricades.

26 Ed Cohen, *A Body Worth Defending: Immunity, Biopolitics, and the Apotheosis of the Modern Body* (Durham: Duke University Press, 2009).

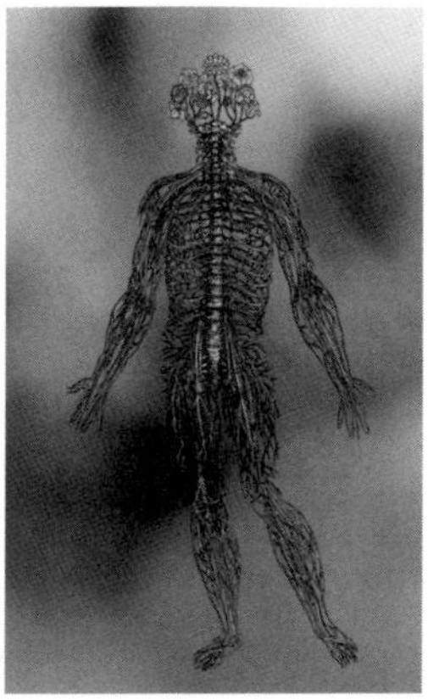

Robert Flack, *Anatomical Garden*, 1990, c-print, 40" × 30"

Thinking critically with the unfinished excess of colonial histories of landscaping also means practicing creatively at the edges of contact, contamination and transformation between animal, plant and environment or niche, unfurling an imaginary of transformation that revalues the impure and the monstrous potentials and powers in the landscapes with and in which we already live. The embrace of future becomings may seem absurdly and even dangerously utopian in the face of climate shift, the capitalization of transgenic hybrids and prospects of uncontrolled and uncontrollable volatility—but strict lines between human, animal and plant, the dangerous purities of conservation and preservation, and hard-and-fast distinctions between natural and unnatural cannot serve an anti-racist, anti-colonial, or queer-feminist vision for landscaping.[27]

While the chimera is us and is marked by its singularity, the chimera is also not one. Via its complex agencies and potentials—both destructive and creative—landscaping for chimeras forges assemblages and shifting collectivities. Landscaping for chimeras is landscaping of and for the multitude, for what Michel de Certeau characterized as the "creative swarm," for the myriad ways in which chimerical landscape is not the static, given, and originary lost or refound garden of Eden but rather gives way to what de Certeau imagines as the creative force of the seemingly stagnant backwater that, nonetheless, "bubble[s] out of swamps and bogs," that swarms, scintillates and throbs its way through everyday waste.[28] Whether we privilege passages and movements (the flights of signs that refuse arrest, the birds that will not be converted into stone) or ephemeral crystallization into the collectivities and momentary contracts that emerge through the ways in which works work or landscapes landscape, such possibilities and potentialities of hybrid, mixed and motley collectivities and assemblages—the multifarious ways in which the chimerical landscape swarms destructively and creatively, despite our intentions and fears—may be sensed in the figurations through which I have presented these propositions.

We have something to hope from and even inhabit in the protean ontological possibilities of the chimeras we are and may yet become. The protean plasticities of matter that the chimera's viability demonstrates expose not just the chimerical "nature" of our bodies and our environment but also the chimerical directionalities of historical time—from political and environmental histories of bodies and land, to the old and new narrative possibilities embedded already in the genomes of human, animal and plant bodies as the expressed, the not yet and the creative chimeric swarms we may yet assemble. Take the guerilla gardening tactics of the seed balls rolling out of the proliferating sites of the offshoots of Occupy Wall Street and the queer technologies of radiant, recombinant recycling set loose in Shu Lea Cheang's science fiction film *Fresh Kill* (1994), in which the Fresh Kills landfill on Staten Island becomes the migratory metaphor and literal streaming conduit for activist channel surfing, global exchange of toxic waste, lesbian parenting, and raw fish lips that talk back to slow the stream and even transform another sense and kind or species of "kill," the slow death of occupations and preservations that stake the killing high grounds of impossible purities or insist on the clear blue O of brave new worlds.[29] Landscaping for chimeras. Now. But on and out of the contaminated grounds of then.

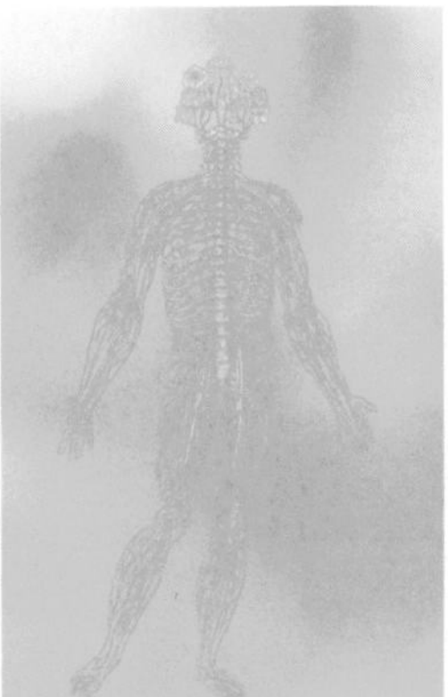

27
On "becomings," see Gilles Deleuze and Félix Guattari, *L'Anti-'dipe:Capitalisme et schizophrénie* (Paris: Les éditions de Minuit, 1972) and *Mille Plateaux: Capitalisme et schizophrénie* (Paris: Les éditions de Minuit, 1980).

28
Michel de Certeau, *Culture in the Plural*, trans. Tom Conley (Minneapolis: University of Minnesota Press, 1997), 139–143.

29
On guerrilla gardening in the United States and Britain, see "Planting Change: Guerrilla Gardening and the Occupy Movement," November 8, 2011, http://occupywallst.org/article/planting-real-seeds-change-guerrilla-gardening-and as well as http://www.guerrillagardening.org. On Cheang's cybernoiac queer science-fiction film, see the interview with Lawrence Chua, "Shu Lea Cheang," *Bomb* 54 (Winter 1996), http://bombsite.com/articles/1915.

Students from Sterling College in Vermont on the site of Occupy Wall Street, demonstrating "guerrilla gardening" techniques and, in particular, how to make seed balls, November 2011

Shu Lea Cheang, *Fresh Kill*, 1994, film

This essay is for Susan Casid Miller. A favorite etymological branch relates "thinking" to "thanks." My thoughts owe their thankful expression to sustaining conversation with Anna Campbell, Florence Hsia, Chele Isaac, Michael Jay McClure, P. A. Skantze and Matthew Fink, to the support of my extraordinary project assistants Jessica Cooley and River Bullock, and the inspiring collaborations of thinking with the brave example of Esther Choi and Marrikka Trotter.

ACKNOWLEDGMENTS

A book like this one, that takes a Janus-faced theme as its gambit and embraces a trans-disciplinary approach to a discipline-specific problematic, requires an adventurous array of contributors. It requires a patient group, too: *Architecture is All Over* has taken seven years to reach publication since its initial conception in 2010. We thank the writers and designers involved in this project for their generous spirit, endurance, and unwavering encouragement. We are honored to have conducted this thought experiment with you.

Architecture Is All Over first took the form of a symposium held at the TIFF Bell Lightbox in Toronto, Ontario, in 2010. The event was co-sponsored by The Office of the President, OCAD University, and the John H. Daniels School of Architecture, Landscape and Design at the University of Toronto, with generous assistance from Bohart and the Social Sciences Humanities Research Council of Canada. We wish to thank President Sara Diamond, Dean Richard Sommer, Dean Vladimir Spicanovic, Brian Boigon and the participants at the event for their support.

We are grateful to the Graham Foundation for Advanced Studies in the Fine Arts for the generous grant that made it possible to take *Architecture is All Over* from an experimental event to an experimental publication. James Graham and Jesse Connuck at Columbia Books on Architecture and the City, as well as Neil Donnelly and Ben Fehrman-Lee, designers extraordinaire, recognized the value of this intellectual undertaking and helped us to maintain its intrepid spirit through its design and production—a rare feat in the increasingly overdetermined and cautious world of print publishing.

Our thanks go to Marissa Neave, for her efficient and rapid transcription; our student assistants Kelsea Knowles, Angie Snyder, and Nathan Storring for their help at the symposium; Melissa Vaughn, for her expert and kind advice, and Paula Wooley, the copyeditor to whom we will always return, for keeping us on our toes. Caleb Trotter offered critical legal guidance. We are grateful to Beatriz Colomina, K. Michael Hays, Sanford Kwinter, Antoine Picon, and Hilary Sample for their encouragement and support—we are fortunate to have mentors like these. Finally, to Jill Casid, thank you for being our superwoman.

On a personal level, this book is dedicated to Miriam and Harry Choi, Philip Choi, Joan and David Trotter, and Jonathan and Imogen Santos. Thanks for making this, and all our other endeavors, possible.

CONTRIBUTORS

Matthew Allen is a PhD candidate at Harvard University whose work investigates cognitive prosthetics in architecture and science. He holds an MArch from Harvard University and previously taught at the University of Toronto.

Caitlin Berrigan works across performance, video, sculpture, text and participatory public interventions to engage with the intimate social dimensions of power and politics. Berrigan has created special commissions for the Whitney Museum, Harvard's Carpenter Center and the deCordova Museum. Her work has shown at Storefront for Art & Architecture, the Hammer Museum, Gallery 400 Chicago, Anthology Film Archives, Los Angeles County Museum of Art, Lugar a Dudas in Colombia, 0047 Gallery in Oslo and the Grimm Museum in Berlin, among other venues. She is the recipient of a Chancellor Fellowship from the Humboldt Foundation, a sculpture fellowship from the Massachusetts Cultural Council and the Agnes Gund Fellowship from the Skowhegan School of Painting and Sculpture. Berrigan attended Skowhegan, and holds an MA in visual art from the Massachusetts Institute of Technology and a BA from Hampshire College.

Adrian Blackwell is an artist, designer and urban theorist examining the relation between physical spaces and political economic forces. His work has been exhibited at artist-run centers and public institutions in Canada, the UK, the US, and China. Blackwell's research examines the imbrication of public space and private property; his recent sculpture and broadsheet *Furnishing Positions* explores six paradoxes of public space, while his writing on Shenzhen delineates the polarized topologies of neoliberal urbanization. He is an assistant professor at the University of Waterloo School of Architecture and an editor of the journal *Scapegoat: Architecture/ Landscape / Political Economy.*

Keith Bresnahan is Associate Professor of Design History and Theory at OCAD University, Toronto. His work focuses on the intersections of architecture and graphic design with philosophical and political developments in the modern era. He is currently completing a book on architecture and experience in Enlightenment France.

D. Graham Burnett is Professor of History and the History of Science at Princeton University and an editor at *Cabinet Magazine*, based in Brooklyn. He is the author of several books, including *The Sounding of the Whale* (University of Chicago Press, 2012). A 2013-2014 Guggenheim fellow, he works at the intersection of research-based artistic practices and experimental scholarship in the humanities. Recent collaborative projects include "The Work of Art under Conditions of Intermittent Accessibility" (Paris, Palais de Tokyo), "Niblach III: The Unrepresented" (Istanbul, sponsored by the Kamel Lazaar Foundation), and "When Experience Becomes Form" (New York, Guggenheim Museum).

An artist, theorist and historian, **Jill H. Casid** is Professor of Visual Studies at the University of Wisconsin–Madison. Her books include *Sowing Empire: Landscape and Colonization* (2005) and *Scenes of Projection: Recasting the Enlightenment Subject* (2014)—both with the University of Minnesota Press. She also co-edited *Art History in the Wake of the Global Turn* with Aruna D'Souza for the Clark Studies in the Visual Arts series (Yale University Press, 2014). Recent articles have appeared in the TDR special issue on precarity and the special issues of *Women & Performance* dedicated to feminist landscapes and to aging. The essay for this volume is part of a larger book project tentatively titled *Forms-of-Life: Bioethics and Aesthetics.*

Esther Choi is a PhD candidate at the Princeton University School of Architecture, where her dissertation examines the intersection between architecture and the life sciences in the nineteenth and twentieth centuries. She has taught at the Irwin S. Chanin School of Architecture at The Cooper Union and OCAD University, Toronto. Her writing has appeared in publications such as *Artforum, Architectural Review* and *Hippie Modernism: The Struggle for Utopia* (Walker Art Center, 2015). She is the co-editor of *Architecture at the Edge of Everything Else* (MIT Press, 2010).

dpr-barcelona is an architectural research practice based in Barcelona, dealing with three main lines: publishing, criticism and curating. Their work explores how architecture as a discipline reacts when it intersects with politics, technology, economy and social issues. Their publications, both digital and print, aim to transcend the bounds of conventional publications to consider how architecture might operate in the future.

David Gissen is Associate Professor of Architecture at the California College of the Arts, San Francisco. His work focuses on developing alternative historical practices primarily through explorations of nature and landscape in the history of architecture and urbanism. He is the author and creator of books, essays, historic landscape reconstructions, and historical environment and landscape visualizations. His works include the monographic books *Subnature: Architecture's Other Environment* (2009) and *Manhattan Atmospheres: Architecture, the Interior Environment and Urban Crisis* (2014) and the projects *The Mound of Vendome* (2014) and *Pittsburgh Reconstruction* (2006–2010).

John Harwood is Associate Professor of Architecture at the Daniels Faculty of Architecture, Landscape and Design at the University of Toronto. He is the author of *The Interface: IBM and the Transformation of Corporate Design, 1945–1976* (University of Minnesota Press, 2011), and is working on a book on the architecture of mass media. He is an editor of *Grey Room*, a journal of art, architecture, media and politics published by MIT Press.

K. Michael Hays is Eliot Noyes Professor of Architectural Theory at the Harvard University Graduate School of Design. He has played a central role in the development of architectural theory. His research and scholarship have focused on architectural modernism and critical theory as well as on theoretical issues in contemporary architectural practice. His publications include *Modernism and the Posthumanist Subject* (MIT Press, 1995), *Architecture Theory since 1968* (MIT Press, 2000) and *Architecture's Desire* (MIT Press, 2009).

Patty Heyda is Assistant Professor of Urban Design at Washington University in St. Louis. Her research explores emergent urbanisms: the novel formal, aesthetic and social particularities of development in city-regions impacted by the global political economy. Heyda's publications include a forthcoming book with D. Gamble illuminating processes of American urban redevelopment (Routledge, 2015) and contributions to *Conditions* (2010) and *Monu / Magazine On Urbanism* (2011), among other journals. Heyda studied under Rem Koolhaas at the Harvard University Graduate School of Design, and worked professionally on large-scale urban architecture and framework projects throughout Europe and the United States for architect Jean Nouvel in Paris and Chan Krieger Associates (NBBJ) in Boston.

Sandi Hilal is an architect and researcher, and headed the United Nations Relief and Works Agency for Palestine Refugees in the Near East (UNRWA) Camp Improvement Program in the West Bank from 2008 to 2014. She is founding member of DAAR, an architectural office and artistic residency program that combines conceptual speculations and architectural interventions. Alongside research and practice, Hilal is engaged in critical pedagogy. She is a founding member of *Campus in Camps*, an experimental educational program by Al Quds University in partnership with Bard College hosted by the Phoenix Center in the Dheisheh refugee camp in Bethlehem. Hilal is co-author of the book *Architecture after Revolution* (Sternberg, 2014), an invitation to rethink today's struggles for justice and equality not only from the historical perspective of revolution, but also from that of a continued struggle for decolonization. She has co-curated research projects on the contemporary urban condition such as *Border Devices* with Multiplicity (2002–2007) and *Stateless Nation* with Alessandro Petti (2002–2007).

John J. May is partner, with Zeina Koreitem, in MILLIØNS, a Los Angeles–based design practice with projects in California, New York and Beirut. He is currently Design Critic in Architecture and Co-Director of the Master in Design Studies Program at the Harvard University Graduate School of Design. He has previously served as a visiting professor at the Massachusetts Institute of Technology, the University of California–Los Angeles, the Southern California Institute of Architecture, and Rice University. May is also a founding co-director (with Zeynep Çelik Alexander) of The Instruments Project, an independent, multiyear research collaborative that explores the historical and philosophical dimensions of contemporary design technologies.

Marta Guerra-Pastrián is a licensed architect with a degree from ETSAMadrid, where she was awarded the Alejandro de la Sota Award for the best project in 2005. She obtained her master's in architecture and urban design and her advanced architectural research degree from Columbia University as a Fundación Caja Madrid fellow in 2010. Guerra-Pastrián has practiced as an architect and urban designer at Navarro Baldeweg and Associates in Madrid, and at NADAAA Inc. and Sasaki Associates in Cambridge, Massachusetts. Her independent work has won awards in several architecture and urban design competitions. She has been design guest critic at Columbia University, the Parsons School of Design and Northeastern University, and has been studio instructor in advanced architecture at the Boston Architectural College.

Trevor Patt is an Assistant Professor at Singapore University of Technology and Design. He holds a Ph.D. from the École Polytechnique Fédérale de Lausanne. His dissertation, *Assemblage Form: An Ontology of the Urban Generic With Regard To Architecture, Computation, and Design* argues for a reevaluation of urban design and masterplanning, following the framework first outlined in the essay published here.

Cyrus Peñarroyo is a designer based in Brooklyn. He has worked for LTL Architects and OMA in New York, Bureau Spectacular in Chicago, and was project lead on *Cities Without Ground: A Hong Kong Guidebook*. His work has been exhibited in New York, Boston, Sao Paulo, Rotterdam and Venice as well as in publications including *Pidgin* and *CLOG*. He has taught at Princeton University and the Columbia University Graduate School of Architecture, Planning and Preservation. He holds a MArch from Princeton University and a BS in architectural studies from the University of Illinois at Chicago.

Pablo Pérez-Ramos is a licensed architect, and a graduate of ETSAMadrid and the master's in landscape architecture program at Harvard University Graduate School of Design (GSD). He is currently a doctoral candidate at Harvard GSD, where his dissertation focuses on the influence of ecological theory in contemporary landscape design. His research has been supported by the GSD Dean's Merit scholarship, the Fundación Caja Madrid, the Fundación La Caixa and the Harvard Real Colegio Computense. He has taught at the Boston Architectural College, and has had teaching fellowships in landscape architecture and urban design at the GSD and at the ETSAM's Laboratorio de Técnicas y Paisajes Contemporáneos. His recent work includes contributions to *A Line in the Andes* (Harvard GSD, 2012), *MONU* #20 (2014), and the forthcoming *Urban Landscape* (Routledge, 2015).

Troy Schaum and **Rosalyne Shieh** are architects and founders of SCHAUM/SHIEH, a practice based in Houston, Texas, and New York City. SCHAUM/SHIEH has projects at a variety of scales in Detroit, Texas, New York City, and Taiwan. Their work has also been exhibited in both the 2012 and 2014 Venice Biennales. Both Schaum and Shieh are actively engaged in teaching and research. Schaum is assistant professor at Rice University and studied at Princeton University and Virginia Tech. Shieh has taught at the University of Michigan, Yale University, Syracuse University and Cooper Union, and has degrees from Princeton, Berkeley and the Bartlett School of Architecture.

Jonathan Tate is principal of Office of Jonathan Tate (OJT), an architecture practice in New Orleans, and a professor at Tulane School of Architecture. His research includes investigations into opportunistic urban developments—informal settlements, ecological anomalies, etc.—and their spatial and cultural implications in cities. His work with OJT and previous offices includes a wide variety of project and program types, both rural and urban, which have been published nationally and internationally. Tate is a graduate of Auburn University, where he was a participant in the Rural Studio, and the Harvard University Graduate School of Design.

Olga Touloumi is an architectural historian researching constructions of globality in mid-twentieth-century architectural production. She has published articles on cybernetics, media technologies and sound in the built environment. Touloumi was co-curator of the exhibitions *A Media Archaeology* of Boston at the Carpenter Center at Harvard University and *Made in Greece Plus* at the Boston Museum of Science. Her book-in-progress situates the emergence of a "global space" within the framework of postwar debates on the institutional reorganization of the world. Touloumi holds a PhD from Harvard University, an MS from the Massachusetts Institute of Technology (MIT), and a BArch from Aristotle University of Thessaloniki. She is currently Visiting Assistant Professor at Bard College, and has taught at MIT and Harvard.

Marrikka Trotter is a PhD candidate at Harvard University, where her work investigates the intersections between British architecture and geology in the eighteenth and nineteenth centuries. With a background in architectural practice and site-responsive art, Trotter has taught at Harvard University and Boston Architectural College and is a guest critic at Northeastern University, the Massachusetts College of Art and Design, Wentworth Institute of Technology and the Massachusetts Institute of Technology. Her writing has appeared in publications such as *AA Files*, *Harvard Design Magazine*, *Log* and *Big Red & Shiny*. She is the co-editor of *Architecture at the Edge of Everything Else* (MIT Press, 2010).

Francesco Vedovato is founder of the design practice A Spectacular Machine and a designer and communication strategist who works in corporate environments as well as on cultural and editorial projects. He is committed to delivering clarity and strategy to his projects, even if it means acting provocatively. He believes proper research is the starting point for developing critically different work.

Andrew Witt is a designer whose work explores the interrelationship between perception and topology, as well as the relationship of architecture to the deductive and convergent methods encapsulated in digital processes. His recent book *Light Harmonies: The Rhythmic Photographs of Heinrich Heidersberger* (Hatje Cantz, 2014) examines the reciprocity between perception and mechanism. He is currently research advisor at Gehry Technologies (GT) and Assistant Professor in Practice in Architecture at Harvard University, where he teaches on geometry and digital design. His work and research have been published in *AD, Log, Surface, Space, Linear Algebra and Its Applications* and *Linear and Multilinear Algebra*, and his work has been shown at Storefront for Art and Architecture. He has lectured globally, including at Yale, Princeton, and Stanford universities; the Bartlett School of Architecture; the Massachusetts Institute of Technology; ETH Zurich; École polytechnique fédérale de Lausanne and the University of Applied Arts, Vienna. He received an MArch (with distinction, AIA medal) and an MDes in history and theory (with distinction) from the Harvard University Graduate School of Design.

IMAGE CREDITS

The editors and publisher gratefully acknowledge the permission granted to reproduce images in this publication. This academic volume includes images that have been reprinted under the copyright principle of fair use. The publisher encourages notice of incorrect attributions for any images used and will attempt to modify inaccurate attributions in future editions of the book.

p. 7
Photograph provided by Corbis Bettmann Archives
© Bettmann/Corbis

p. 8
Photograph by Annie Jacques
© RMN-Grand Palais/Art Resource, NY

p. 9
Reproduced by permission from Hans Hollein, "Alles Ist Architektur," *Bau: Schrift für Architektur und Städtebau* 23, no. 1/2 (1968), 20–21. Courtesy of Hans Hollein & Partner ZT-GmbH

p. 10
Photograph by Nigel Henderson
© Tate, London 2014

Reproduced by permission from Denise Scott Brown, "Learning from Pop," *Casabella* 359/360 (1971), 14-15. Courtesy of *Casabella*

p. 12
Bernard Rudofsky, *Architecture Without Architects*, 1964

p. 14
Courtesy of the architects
© Ying Xiao and Shengchen Yang

p. 19–27
Courtesy of the artist
© Caitlin Berrigan

p. 32
Artwork in the public domain

p. 35
Courtesy of Bruce Mau Design Inc.
© Bruce Mau Design Inc., OMA and Inside Outside

p. 45–53
Courtesy of the artist
© Cyrus Peñarroyo

p. 58
Photograph by Rob't Hart, courtesy of MVRDV, Rotterdam

p. 59
Photograph by Claus & Kaan Architecten/Luuk Kramerl, courtesy of Claus & Kaan Architecten

p. 60
Courtesy of Experimental Jetset

p. 63
Artwork in the public domain; photograph provided by the Digital Image Archive, Pitts Theology Library, Candler School of Theology, Emory University

p. 67
Courtesy of the author
© Patty Heyda

p. 68
Aerial view from Google Earth

p. 69
Courtesy of the artist
© Jami Desy Schoenewies

p. 71
Photograph by the author
© Patty Heyda

p. 74
Reproduced from Ebenezer Howard, *Garden Cities of To-Morrow* (Paternoster Square: Swan Sonnenschein & Co.), 1902

p. 75
Reproduced from Ebenezer Howard, *Garden Cities of To-Morrow* (Paternoster Square: Swan Sonnenschein & Co.), 1902

p. 75–76
Images and photographs courtesy of the author © Patty Heyda

p. 83
Photograph by Michael Carapetian, courtesy of Architectural Press Archive/ RIBA Library Photographs Collection

Photograph by Leonardo Benevolo. Reproduced by permission from Leonardo Benevolo, *History of Modern Architecture* vol.2 (Cambridge: MIT Press, 1971), 428. Courtesy of Editori Laterza

p. 93
Reproduced from Cesare Brandi, "L'Istituto Centrale di Restauro in Roma e la Ricostituzione degli Affreschi," *Phoebus* 1, no. 3/4 (1946): 170-171

p. 98–117
Courtesy of the architects
© Marta Guerra-Pastrián and Pablo Pérez-Ramos

p. 123
After an illustration in Henri Bergson, *Matter and Memory*, trans. N. M. Paul and W. S. Palmer (New York: Zone Books, 1988), 162. Courtesy of the author © Adrian Blackwell

p. 127
Photograph by Guenter Richard Wett, courtesy of Hannes Steifel

p. 129
Courtesy of Alessandro Petti
© DAAR/Situ Studio

p. 130
Courtesy of the architects
© Lacaton & Vassal

p. 132
Courtesy of the architects
© Atelier d'architecture autogérée

p. 138
Photograph by Catie Newell, courtesy of the architects

p. 139
Photograph by Catie Newell, courtesy of the architects

p. 139
Aerial view from Google Earth

p. 142–157
Images and photographs courtesy of the architects © Schaum/Shieh

p. 161
Reproduced by permission from Martin Pawley, "Architecture Versus the Movies or Form Versus Content," *Architectural Design*, vol. 40 (1970). Courtesy of John Wiley & Sons, Inc.

p. 170
Courtesy of Collection Famille Xenakis

p. 171
© Stockhausen-Stiftung für Musik, Kürten, Germany

p. 172
© Stockhausen-Stiftung für Musik, Kürten, Germany

p. 173
Images courtesy of Collection Famille Xenakis

p. 181
Image in the public domain

p. 183
Reproduced from Tecton, Planned *A.R.P. Based on the Investigation of Structural Protection Against Air Attack in the Metropolitan Borough of Finsbury*. (Westminster [London]: The Architectural Press, 1939), folding plate, facing p.122

p. 195
Courtesy of the author
© Andrew Witt

p. 196
Reprinted from Georges-Louis Le Rouge, *Plan de Lille, de la Citadelle Et de ses Environs*, 1740. Artwork in the public domain; photograph provided by Bibliothèque Nationale de France

p. 198
Triangulation survey of India: "1904 Index Chart To Great Trigonometrical Survey of India." Image in the public domain

p. 199
Reproduced by permission from H.S.M Coxeter, *Regular Complex Polytopes* (Cambridge: Cambridge University Press, 1974, 1991), figure 4.7 C

p. 200
Image in the public domain
Photograph by Iacopo Guidi
© Iacopo Guidi/Shutterstock.com

p. 205
Courtesy of the author
© Trevor Patt

p. 206
Courtesy of the architect
© Jose Ahedo

p. 207
Photograph by Amit Geron, courtesy of Tel Aviv Museum of Art.
Photograph by Michel Legendre, courtesy of Philippe Rahm Architectes

p. 211
Photograph provided by The Forsythe Company

p. 221
Photograph by Félix Vázquez

p. 214
© The Museum of Modern Art/ Licensed by SCALA/Art Resource, NY

p. 248–256
Courtesy of the author
© Jonathan Tate

p. 262–265
Courtesy of the authors
© dpr-barcelona and Francesco Vedovato

p. 269
Aerial view from Google Earth

p. 272
Artwork in the public domain; photograph provided by The Garden Museum, London, UK

p. 273
Reproduced from Elizabeth Blackwell, *A curious herbal : containing five hundred cuts, of the most useful plants, which are now used in the practice of physick : engraved on folio copper plates, after drawings taken from the life / by Elizabeth Blackwell : to which is added a short description of ye plants and their common uses in physick* (London: Printed for S. Harding, 1737-1739), Volume 2, Plate 360. The Lloyd Library and Museum, Cincinnati, OH. Artwork in the public domain; photograph provided by the Lloyd Library and Museum

p. 275
Artwork © Archivo Penone; photograph provided by the Marian Goodman Gallery, NY

p. 277
Artwork in the public domain; photograph provided by De Agostini Picture Library, G. Nimatallah, Bridgeman Images

Artwork in the public domain; photograph provided by Österreichische Galerie, Belvedere

p. 278
Private Collection

p. 280
Artwork © Eduardo Kac; photograph © Rik Sferra

p. 281
Artwork © Estate of Robert Flack; photography provided by Paul Petro Contemporary Art, Toronto

p. 283
Photograph posted on November 8, 2011 by OccupyWallSt, OccupyWallSt.org.

Courtesy the artist © Shu Lea Cheang

INDEX